HIGHER MODERN STU

International Issues

Frank Cooney, Paul Creaney
Pauline Elliott & Graeme Pont

HODDER
GIBSON
AN HACHETTE UK COMPANY

The Publishers would like to thank the following for permission to reproduce copyright material:

Photo credits
p.1 © Björn Kindler / iStockphoto; p.2 © Photodisc / Photolibrary Group Ltd; p.3 © Florian Franke / Corbis; p.9 © Sandy Huffaker / Corbis; p.10 © King / Keystone USA / Rex Features; p.15 © Ron Chapple / Corbis; p.16 © Glow Images / photolibrary.com; p.17 © Ron Chapple / Corbis; p.19 © Washington Post / Getty Images; p.20 © Rex Features; p.24 (t) © Democrat Party (United States), (b) © Republican Party (United States); p.25 (t) © Sipa Press / Rex Features, (b) © Matt Campbell / epa / Corbis; p.31 © STR / epa / Corbis; p.33 (t) © CHARLES SYKES / Rex Features, (b) © Bill Auth / LANDOV / Press Association Images; p.35 (t) © SCOTT AUDETTE / Reuters / Corbis, (b) © JIM LO SCALZO / epa / Corbis; p.41 © Yellow Dog Productions / Getty Images; p.52 (l) © Christopher Pillitz / Getty Images, (r) © GIPhotoStock Z / Alamy; p.61 (t) © ayzek / iStockphoto, (b) © Ulrich Doering / Alamy; p.68 © Gallo Images/Eric Miller / Alamy; p.70 © AFP / Getty Images; p.72 (t) © African National Congress, (c) © New National Party of South Africa, (b) © Inkatha Freedom Party; p.74 © Facundo Arrizabalaga / Rex Features; p.78 © OBED ZILWA / AP / Press Association Images; p.80 © Africa Media Online / Alamy; p.85 (t) © Imagestate Media Partners Limited – Impact Photos / Alamy, (b) © Eco Images / Universal Images Group; p.91 © Supernova / Getty Images; p.94 © Reuters / CORBIS; p.105 © Stock Connection Blue / Alamy; p.107 © Andy Hall / Getty Images; p.109 (t) © Gideon Mendel / CORBIS, (b) © SIPHIWE SIBEKO / Reuters / Corbis; p.110 © NIC BOTHMA / epa / Corbis; p.114 © SIPHIWE SIBEKO / Reuters / Corbis; p.116 © LUCAS DOLEGA / epa / Corbis; p.117 © Getty Images; p.120 © Getty Images; p.123 © NASA Jet Propulsion Laboratory (NASA-JPL); p.125 (l) Courtesy of Wikipedia, (r) © Joe Gough – Fotolia.com; p.128 (t) © Photodisc / Getty Images, (b) © Simon Rawles / Alamy; p.131 (tl) © Ismail Warsameh / Xinhua Press / Corbis, (br) © GRANT NEUENBERG / Reuters / Corbis; p.132 © Getty Images; p.137 © imagebroker / Alamy; p.138 © Eddie Gerald / Alamy; p.140 (tl) © Imagestate Media, (tr) © David Pearson / Alamy, (bl) © Christian Aid, (br) © Save the Children; p.141 (t) © OMAR FARUK / Reuters / Corbis, (b) © Action Aid; p.143 © African Union / Courtesy of Wikipedia; p.146 © Nils Jorgensen / Rex Features; p.148 © Greenshoots Communications / Alamy; p.150 © Unicef; p.152 © Food and Agricultural Organisation; p.154 © World Food Programme; p.155 © KPA / Zuma / Rex Features; p.157 © imagebroker / Alamy; p.162 © Christian Aid; p.163 © PHILIMON BULAWAYO / Reuters / Corbis; p.164 © Save the Children; p.171 © Björn Kindler / iStockphoto; p.173 © Patrick G. – Fotolia.com; p.183 (l) © Imaginechina / Corbis, (r) © Getty Images; p.187 © Lou Linwei/Rex Features; p.188 © AP / Press Association Images; p.191 © Quirky China News / Rex Features; p.194 © Philip Date – Fotolia.com; p.195 © Grace / Keystone USA / Rex Features; p.199 © Xiaoyang Liu / Corbis; p.202 © Fan Rujun / XinHua / Xinhua Press / Corbis; p.205 © Getty Images; p.208 © Sipa Press / Rex Features; p.210 © AFP / Getty Images; p.212 © AFP / Getty Images; p.215 © SALVATORE DI NOLFI / AP / Press Association Images; p.217 © Gordon Wiltsie / National Geographic Society / Corbis; p.219 (l) © Vincent Yu / AP / Press Association Images, (r) © Ryan Pyle / Corbis.

Every effort has been made to trace all copyright holders, but if any have been inadvertently overlooked the Publishers will be pleased to make the necessary arrangements at the first opportunity.

Although every effort has been made to ensure that website addresses are correct at time of going to press, Hodder Gibson cannot be held responsible for the content of any website mentioned in this book. It is sometimes possible to find a relocated web page by typing in the address of the home page for a website in the URL window of your browser.

Hachette UK's policy is to use papers that are natural, renewable and recyclable products and made from wood grown in sustainable forests. The logging and manufacturing processes are expected to conform to the environmental regulations of the country of origin.

Orders: please contact Bookpoint Ltd, 130 Milton Park, Abingdon, Oxon OX14 4SB. Telephone: (44) 01235 827720. Fax: (44) 01235 400454. Lines are open 9.00–5.00, Monday to Saturday, with a 24-hour message answering service. Visit our website at www.hoddereducation.co.uk. Hodder Gibson can be contacted direct on: Tel: 0141 848 1609; Fax: 0141 889 6315; email: hoddergibson@hodder.co.uk

© Frank Cooney, Paul Creaney, Pauline Elliott and Graeme Pont 2011
First published in 2011 by
Hodder Gibson, an imprint of Hodder Education,
An Hachette UK Company
2a Christie Street
Paisley PA1 1NB

Impression number 5 4 3
Year 2013

Cover photo (top) © Kim Ludbrook/epa/Corbis, (centre) © Photodisc/Getty Images, (bottom) © Diego Martin/awl-images
Illustrations by Fakenham Prepress Solutions and Jeff Edwards
Typeset in Minion Pro 12pt by Fakenham Prepress Solutions, Fakenham, Norfolk NR21 8NN
Printed in Dubai

A catalogue record for this title is available from the British Library

ISBN: 978 0340 991961

Contents

1
The United States of America

Background

The United States of America is the fourth largest country in the world, in terms of land mass, after Russia, Canada and the People's Republic of China. It covers an area of 9,826,675 km^2, making it about half the size of Russia and a little smaller than Canada. It is about twice the size of the whole European Union. It has land borders with two other countries: Canada and Mexico.

The sheer size and diversity of America's landscape and terrain has, in many respects, influenced its development and power in the twenty-first century. It is spread over 3000 miles from east to west between the Atlantic and Pacific Oceans. The USA also experiences a variety of climates because its spread-out landmass covers six time zones: the four main time zones of Eastern Time, Central Time, Mountain Time and Pacific Time along with the two separate time zones of Hawaii and Alaska.

Figure 1.1 The states of the USA →

Alaska and Hawaii are not to scale

1 VERMONT
2 NEW HAMPSHIRE
3 MASSACHUSETTS
4 RHODE ISLAND
5 CONNECTICUT
6 NEW JERSEY
7 DELAWARE
8 MARYLAND

American people

Just who can call themselves an American?

The Statue of Liberty was given by the people of France to the people of the USA in 1886 in recognition of their friendship during the American Revolution. Today, the statue symbolises freedom and democracy as well as this international friendship, a colossal symbol of freedom to millions around the world. Its inscription reads:

'Give me your tired, your poor,
Your huddled masses yearning to breathe free,
The wretched refuse of your teeming shore.
Send these, the homeless, tempest-tost to me.
I lift my lamp beside the golden door!'

These words, written by Emma Lazarus in 1883, have come to portray the statue's universal message of hope and freedom for immigrants coming to America and people seeking freedom around the world.

American society has often been described as a melting pot but in recent years, it has also attracted other definitions such as 'salad bowl'.

Figure 1.2 The Statue of Liberty →

For centuries the USA has attracted people in search of a share of 'the American dream' from all corners of the world. In fact, US history is one of immigration. From the Pilgrim Fathers who sailed to America on *The Mayflower* in 1620 to the French, German, Chinese, Irish, Italian and Polish immigrants in the eighteenth, nineteenth and twentieth centuries.

Throughout the twentieth century, the government expanded its immigration control policies introducing a national origins quota system in 1921 whereby the immigrant's country of birth was the prime factor in determining entry. At that time, the three favoured countries were the UK, Ireland and Germany.

By 1965 these restrictions were removed resulting in mass immigration, especially from Mexico and Latin America. The following years also saw an increase in illegal immigration, forcing Congress to pass legislation in 1996 that widened the list of crimes for which immigrants could be deported. Today, there is a raging debate between opponents of illegal immigration who are calling for even tougher laws and pro-immigrant campaign groups who argue that America's economy needs them and that the country was built by immigrants and will collapse without them (see pages 8–14).

Ethnic composition of America

Figure 1.3 The USA is a melting pot of different cultures →

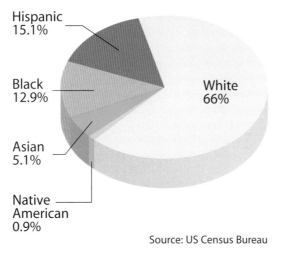

Figure 1.4 Ethnic groups in the USA, 2008 →

Hispanic 15.1%

Black 12.9%

Asian 5.1%

Native American 0.9%

White 66%

Source: US Census Bureau

The population of the USA is made up of five main ethnic groups (see Figure 1.4). The population in 2009 was 307,212,123 and it is rising by about one per cent a year. If this continues, then by 2050 the population will have risen to around 440 million and it is estimated that around 80% of this increase will be due to new immigrants and their future USA-born children.

Fact File

- It is expected that about 20% of Americans, or one in five, will be immigrants by 2050, compared with 12% in 2008.

- The Hispanic population is currently the country's largest ethnic minority group and is expected to triple in size by 2050, accounting for most of the nation's population growth from 2010 to 2050. Hispanics will make up 29% of the USA population in 2050, compared with 15.1% in 2008.

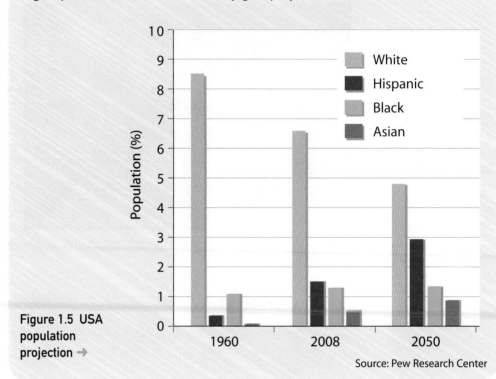

● The white population is expected to increase more slowly than other ethnic groups and will become a minority group by 2050 at 47%.

Figure 1.5 USA population projection →

Source: Pew Research Center

Hispanics

There are estimated to be almost 50 million Hispanics currently living in the USA, making up 15.1% of the population. Hispanic is the largest ethnic minority group, having overtaken black Americans in number in 2001. The growth of the Hispanic population since then has been mainly down to births in the USA, not immigration from abroad.

Around two-thirds (64%) of Hispanics in the USA are of Mexican origin. The other third of the Hispanic population comprises nine of the other ten Hispanic origin groups of: Puerto Rican, Cuban, Salvadoran, Dominican, Guatemalan, Colombian, Honduran, Ecuadorian and Peruvian. These ten Hispanic groups differ in terms of numbers who are foreign-born, numbers who are US citizens by birth, and their proficiency in English. There are also differences in terms of their education levels, homeownership rates, income and poverty rates.

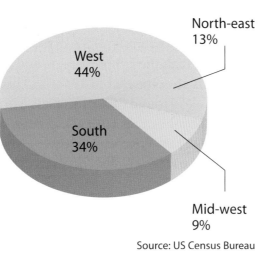

North-east
13%

West
44%

South
34%

Mid-west
9%

Source: US Census Bureau

Figure 1.6 Hispanic percentage of population by USA region of residence, 2008 →

Hispanics of Mexican origin

Hispanics of Mexican origin account for 64% of the US Hispanic population, around 30 million people. Mexicans tend to be younger than other Hispanic groups and the US population as a whole. The median age of Mexicans is 25 compared to 27 for all Hispanics and 36 for the US population as a whole. Most Mexicans live in California (38%) and Texas (25%).

Mexicans tend to be less well educated than the other Hispanic groups. Only nine per cent of Mexicans aged 25 and above have obtained a bachelor's degree compared to 12.6% of the others. As far as income levels and poverty rates are concerned the numbers are similar for all Hispanic groups but lower than those for the US population as a whole. The median annual income for Mexicans aged 16 and above in 2007 was $20,238 and for all US Hispanics was $21,048. The number of Mexicans living in poverty in 2007 was 20.8%, which is roughly the same as the other Hispanic groups at 19.5% but higher than that of the US population as a whole at 11.9%.

Hispanics of Puerto Rican origin

There are currently 4.1 million Hispanics of Puerto Rican origin living in the USA, which is more than the population of Puerto Rico itself at 3.9 million. Around two-thirds of the Puerto Rican population were born in the USA and one-third was born in Puerto Rico itself. Anyone who is born in Puerto Rico is considered to be an American citizen by birth.

Puerto Ricans are the second largest population of Hispanic origin living in the USA after Mexicans and made up nine per cent of the Hispanic population of the USA in 2008. They are generally less well educated and are more likely to be unemployed than Hispanics or the US population as a whole. Similarly, as a rule they achieve lower incomes than the US population as a whole and are less likely to own their own homes.

Hispanics of Cuban origin

Hispanics of Cuban origin account for 3.5% of the US Hispanic population. Cubans tend to be older than the US population and Hispanics overall. The median age of Cubans is 40 compared to 27 for all Hispanics and 36 for the US population as a whole. Around 70% of Cubans live in Florida. Cubans tend to be better educated than the other Hispanic groups, with 25% of those aged 25 and above having obtained a bachelor's degree compared to nine per cent of Mexicans. However, the rate of Cuban homeownership is 61.1%, which is higher than the rate for all Hispanics at 49.9% but lower than the 67.2% rate for the US population as a whole.

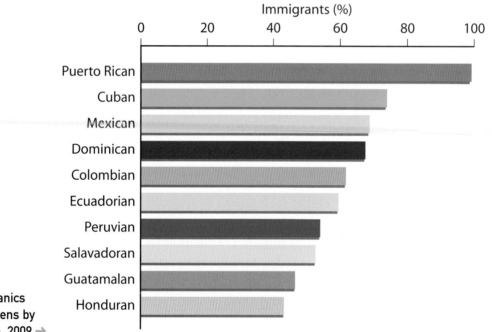

Figure 1.7 Hispanics who are US citizens by country of origin, 2009 →

Source: Pew Hispanic Center

As far as income levels and poverty rates are concerned, the numbers are higher than for all other Hispanic groups but lower than for the US population as a whole. The median annual income for Cubans aged 16 and above in 2007 was $26,310 and for all US Hispanics was $21,048. The number of Cubans living in poverty in 2007 was 12.3%, which is lower than the other Hispanic groups at 19.5% but slightly higher than the US population as a whole at 11.9%.

Asian and Pacific Islanders (APIs)

Asian and Pacific Islanders account for 5.1% of the US population and are the third largest ethnic minority group in the USA. They are a diverse ethnic group who have come from countries in Asia such as Korea and China or the Pacific Islands. APIs are generally well educated and have the highest educational attainment levels and median annual income of all the ethnic minority groups. As a result they also have one of the lowest poverty rates.

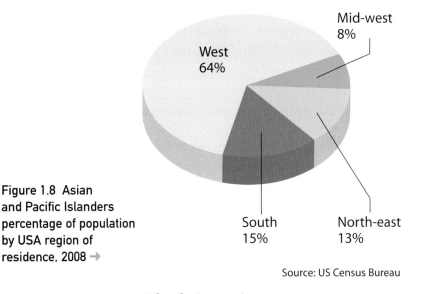

Figure 1.8 Asian and Pacific Islanders percentage of population by USA region of residence, 2008 →

West 64%

Mid-west 8%

South 15%

North-east 13%

Source: US Census Bureau

Black Americans

The 40 million black Americans are descendants of African slaves brought over to the USA from Africa to work on the plantations of the southern states in the seventeenth and eighteenth centuries. Slightly more than half of this group are concentrated in the states of the south and south-east and the rest are to be found in the industrial cities of the north-east, and in central and Pacific Coast states.

After the Civil War (1861–65) slavery was abolished but black Americans still faced massive political, social and economic inequality, especially in the south. The civil rights movement of the 1960s and subsequent civil rights acts finally gave them full equality. Blacks account for 12.9% of the US population and are the second largest ethnic minority group in the USA.

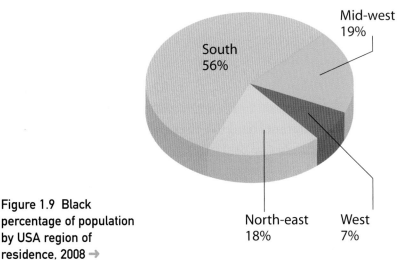

Figure 1.9 Black percentage of population by USA region of residence, 2008 →

South 56%

Mid-west 19%

North-east 18%

West 7%

Source: US Census Bureau

It is expected that all ethnic groups will see a dramatic rise in their populations by 2050 with the Hispanic and Asian and Pacific Islanders groups tripling in number. In addition, by 2030 the whole country's population is expected to become older with 20% of people, one in five, being over the age of 65.

Case Study: California

If you consider the USA to be a melting pot of different people, then California is an ethnic microcosm. Year on year it receives the most immigrants, more than 200,000 per year, and its racial mix is America's most diverse. The percentage of white and black Americans is lower than the national average while the number of Asian Americans is more than three times the national average. Most noticeable is the fact that more than 25% of Californians are Hispanic. This ethnic salad bowl is clearly visible in large cities such as San Diego, Los Angeles and San Francisco.

The increase in the total population in recent decades has upset the rural and urban mix. Over the last 50 years arable land has been reduced to make way for housing and farming has declined in favour of new and expanding employment areas in the service industry and in Silicon Valley.

Immigration

Those classified as illegal immigrants either enter the USA without any documentation or arrive legally but overstay the number of days permitted on their visa. Most immigrants enter the USA in search of a better life for themselves and their children; children of illegal immigrants automatically gain US citizenship. Many are escaping political persecution, leaving family and possessions behind.

Some Caribbean immigrants cross the Atlantic Ocean to reach the USA in homemade boats or even tubes. Those from South America may fly into Mexico and seek the help of a 'coyote' (smuggler) to help them get across the border. Some even hide in trucks or ships to get across the border. In areas with already high immigrant populations, cultural enclaves can be found that offer support to new immigrants. As an example, Little Havana in Miami in Florida is a cultural enclave that formed as a result of the high rate of immigration from Cuba.

Once in the USA, illegal immigrants tend to gain employment in 'low-skilled jobs' that may be labour-intensive and don't attract many American employees. For example, the landscaping and construction sectors are popular with immigrants as there is generally no requirement to be fluent in the English language. Other employment sectors that attract illegal immigrants include restaurants, hospitality, prostitution, agriculture and domestic service. One view of illegal immigrants is that they take the jobs that residents refuse, while another is that they take away jobs in general.

Despite the law prohibiting employers from hiring illegal immigrants, many do and some even exploit the worker. Employers often pay low wages and may allow an employee to work in unsafe conditions. Often employers get away with this because they know the illegal immigrant cannot report their employer out of fear of deportation.

Immigration debate

Immigration, both legal and illegal, is a hot topic in the USA today. Former president George W. Bush found it difficult to reform immigration law and get both a Republican- and then a Democrat-controlled Congress to pass legislation. Now President Obama has seen reform efforts checked by pro-immigration groups while those who oppose immigration call for tougher controls. Here is an outline of the great immigration debate taking place in the USA today.

Just what is the problem?

The problem is that 40 million people in the USA are immigrants, with illegal immigrants accounting for around 12 million. In addition, around 1.5 million more immigrants enter the country each year, mainly through the 2000-mile-long Mexican border. For many more, however, entry is blocked.

Figure 1.10 The border between the USA and Mexico →

Many immigrants lack any formal education and therefore seek work as unskilled labourers. They often take the sort of jobs that most native-born Americans refuse to do for the wages offered. For example, a lot of California's agricultural sector is dependent on the thousands of immigrant labourers.

Why is the issue so tense?

The situation has caused tension between those who are opposed to the increase in immigration and who want increased border controls and the supportive employers who want cheap migrant workers. Immigrants themselves have also entered the debate, claiming that restrictions only block their 'right to citizenship'.

Politicians are aware of the growing immigrant electorate and so are reluctant to annoy and put off potential voters. The Republican Party faces confrontation from its social conservatives and the business lobby because of the view from some that a harder line is required and illegal immigrants should be criminalised.

Similarly, the Democratic Party is trying to avoid conflict with trade unions who claim that the Guest Worker Programs only drive down wages and cause unemployment for American employees.

Groups opposed to illegal immigration have formed Minutemen groups. These comprise residents who patrol the US borders and seek out illegal workers in cities.

What are the key issues?

The key issues are focused around controlling illegal entry. In the aftermath of 11 September 2001, the influx of illegal immigrants may pose a threat to national security. The US business sector claims that immigrants are a necessary workforce for the economy and so supports changes in the law to control entry and to clear up issues surrounding those already in the country illegally. The business sector would like to see illegal immigrants being allowed to remain in the country legally and wants the Guest Worker Program extended.

Others want tougher enforcement of the land borders and existing laws on immigration. For example, some want to extend the fencing that already exists along a part of the US–Mexican border and introduce tougher penalties for businesses caught employing illegal migrants. Despite objections from the Mexican government, this fence has been extended by 700 miles and is now patrolled by several thousand reserve soldiers of the USA National Guard.

Figure 1.11 A
Minutemen group →

Case Study: Immigration

Congressman Tom Tancredo has campaigned throughout the USA in support of tighter border controls and immigration reduction.

Case Study: Continued

'Americans are rightly outraged by our broken immigration system: there are roughly 12 to 15 million illegal aliens in the US, and hundreds of thousands sneak across our borders each year. Our porous borders pose a major national security threat because not all of the illegal aliens are coming to "do the job that no American will do". For example, the US Border Patrol has apprehended many Iranians, Syrians and Iraqis who tried to cross our southern border illegally.

Why are Iranians, Syrians or Iraqis trying to get into the US, travelling a great distance and at a great cost? Certainly, it's not to work at minimum-wage jobs.

Illegal immigration also has a negative effect on the US's economic security. It doesn't take a degree in economics to realise that a massive flow of low-skilled labour puts downward pressure on the wages of native-born Americans. These low-wage workers – who are largely paid off the books and without benefits – meanwhile cost the American taxpayer in terms of social services. Illegal aliens rarely pay taxes, yet they send their children to our schools free of charge, they receive welfare benefits and they get free medical treatment.

The best solution to our illegal immigration problem is to begin enforcing our laws. That means the federal government needs to get serious about prosecuting employers who lure illegal aliens into the US with jobs. The threat of hefty fines and possible jail time will chasten employers' desire to hire cheap, illegal workers. We also need to recommit to guarding our borders with more personnel and increasing physical barriers like fencing. And, we need to enable local police departments to aid the federal government in finding and deporting illegal aliens.

Over time, as it becomes more difficult to come here illegally, fewer will try. And, as it becomes harder to stay illegally, more will leave over time. That's a workable solution to our broken borders.

Nativo Lopez is national president of the Mexican–American Political Association, which campaigns for the Latino community.

'With a wink and a nod, the United States government essentially allowed millions of people into the country to be employed in vital strategic industries. These workers produce value and that value is appropriated by business owners. The worker is never remunerated fairly for the value he creates and the immigrant worker creates a value far and above what a native worker creates because he works for a lower wage, does not have paid holidays, a pension plan or sick pay. They make an incredible economic contribution to the economy. A fair exchange would be a streamlined procedure allowing them to legalise their status.'

Felipe Aguirre is deputy mayor of Maywood, California. The town, which is 97% Hispanic, is a self-declared sanctuary for 'undocumented' immigrants.

'We believe that no human being can be described as illegal. These are people who work hard, pay taxes, buy houses and keep on the right side of the law for fear of being deported – they are part of the fabric of America. Many have families and have been contributing members of the community for years. But the debate is now affecting family units. Many people who do not have the right documents have children who are US citizens. These families need to stay united. That is why we have seen so many young people taking part in the demonstrations, fighting for the rights of their parents. These people pay their taxes through the payroll system, but do not qualify to receive any

Case Study: Continued

benefits at the end of the working week. And, while they pay sales taxes and property taxes, they do not qualify for any of the benefits that are associated with this, such as health care.

There is a tremendous amount of hypocrisy surrounding the debate. So many businesses are doing well on the back of undocumented workers – from the oranges that are picked in Florida to the tomatoes harvested in Illinois. Yet, their basic rights, such as the right to a safe workplace and fair treatment, are not protected. Undocumented workers never file complaints for injuries sustained at work for fear of being sacked. Rich families in Los Angeles employ undocumented nannies to look after their children. They also employ undocumented housekeepers, cleaners and gardeners – many of whom have keys to their houses. How can we be called criminals when we hold the keys to the houses of some of the richest people in the state?'

Source: adapted from the BBC

Possible legislation

President Obama gave a firm commitment to reforming immigration in his first term of office. While some Americans are anxious about being beaten to jobs by immigrants, many also say that immigrants generally take jobs American workers don't want (59%), rather than taking jobs away from Americans (30%). See Figure 1.12.

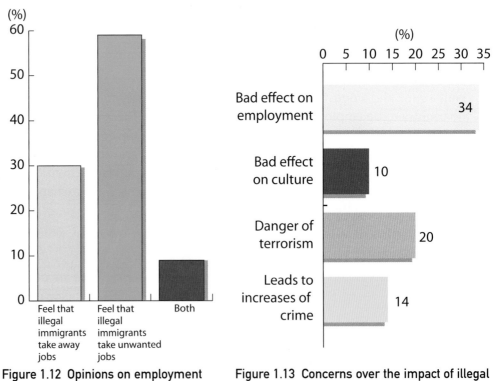

Figure 1.12 Opinions on employment and illegal immigrants

Source: *New York Times*

Figure 1.13 Concerns over the impact of illegal immigration ↑

Source: *New York Times*

The Department of Homeland Security is proposing a 'no-match' regulation. This electronic system would alert employers if they inadvertently hired someone who provided an inaccurate Social Security number. In addition, an ID card for legal foreign workers would show their legal status so that employers could easily identify them.

A temporary Guest Worker Program would allow employers legally to hire the workers they need. American workers would be given priority for positions, and only after positions remained unfilled would the jobs be made available to temporary workers. The number of temporary guest workers would be determined by the market.

Another area in need of legislation is the issue of the undocumented immigrants already residing in the USA. There are numerous illegal immigrants who have lived in the USA for many years and despite having no legal documentation are hardworking, trustworthy and are considered to be 'good citizens'. It has been suggested that these illegal immigrants should be given the opportunity of a 'path towards citizenship'.

Arizona's immigration crackdown

Arizona's new state law, signed in April 2010, enables police to check the immigration status of people who cause 'reasonable suspicion' and to arrest them if they lack the proper documents. This new law has been compared to the notorious Pass Laws of white South Africa during the apartheid years, which led to population segregation and limited the free movement of the black South Africans. This has caused a Hispanic backlash, with demonstrators protesting in cities such as San Francisco and wearing t-shirts that proclaim *Todos somos Arizona*, We are all Arizona. A Federal Court has blocked this Arizona law, claiming it is a federal and not a state responsibility.

Arizona is witnessing a dramatic change in its ethnic composition. While 83% of Arizona's older people are white, only 43% of its children are white. Older white voters resent paying local taxes to enable illegal immigrants to go to school or be treated in hospital.

This new law has mobilised Hispanic voter registration. The South-west Voter Registration Education Project (SVREP) with its slogan *Su voto es su voz,* Your vote is your voice, stated that this new law 'has done more to organise our (latino) community than we could have done'.

Activities

1   Describe the five main ethnic groups that make up the population of the USA.

2   What are the distinct groups into which the Hispanics can be subdivided?

3 Why is immigration a 'hot topic' in the USA?

Essay question

'Immigration is an issue over which public opinion in the USA is divided.'
Discuss. (15)

The political system in the USA

Alastair Cooke, the British journalist, wrote that the American Constitution was founded upon three great principles: compromise, compromise and compromise.

The US system of government was written by the founding fathers, after the thirteen colonies gained their independence from Britain in 1783. The then thirteen states agreed to devise a new form of government – a federal state. Here power would be divided between the national (federal) government and the respective states. A second compromise was to have a Congress made up of two Houses: the Senate and the House of Representatives. In the Senate there would be equal representation for all states. In contrast, in the House of Representatives there would be representation proportional to the population of each state. Another compromise was to have the President elected indirectly by the people. The citizens would elect the Electoral College and the latter would choose the President. A Bill of Rights would protect the rights of all citizens.

All these compromises and more helped to create the written Constitution of the USA, based on federalism, separation of powers and checks and balances. The Constitution is a set of rules by government establishing how it should be run. The Constitution was ratified in 1788, just a year after it was written.

The Constitution is the supreme law of the USA, and it defines the relationship and allocation of powers between the Executive, Legislature and Judiciary. This separation of powers or doctrine ensures that no one branch of government can dominate and thus protects the fundamental rights of US citizens.

The founding fathers had clear ideas of what they hoped the Constitution would achieve:

The preamble

'We the People of the United States, in Order to form a more perfect Union, establish Justice, insure domestic Tranquillity, provide for the common defence, promote the general Welfare, and secure the Blessings of Liberty to ourselves and our Prosperity, do ordain and establish this Constitution for the United States of America.'

Figure 1.14 Congress →

The federal government

The federal government deals with matters concerning collective state issues and also foreign affairs. All powers not allocated to the federal government are retained by the respective states. The 50 states have the right to make their own laws on internal matters. At present the state of Arizona is in conflict with the federal government over immigration (see page 13).

Fact File

The federal government has authority over:

- armed forces
- the post office
- currency of the USA
- disputes between states
- foreign relations, for example declaring war.

The separation of powers

The American political scientist, Neustadt, wrote that 'the Constitution had created a government of separated institutions sharing powers' and Professor Finer described the Legislature and Executive as being 'like two halves of a bank note – each useless without the other'. This separation of powers or doctrine of shared powers ensures that no one branch of government can become dominant.

The legislative branch makes laws

Established by Article 1 of the Constitution, the USA Congress comprises two chambers: the Senate and the House of Representatives. Congress is the legislative (law-making) and oversight (government policy review) body of the national government. For a law to be made, it has to be passed by both chambers and finally signed by the President. Under the Constitution, each state is entitled to be represented by two senators (each serving a six-year term) and at least one representative (serving a two-year term).

The House of Representatives has several powers exclusively assigned to it, such as the impeachment of federal officials.

The Senate has the sole power to ratify treaties.

The Executive branch carries out laws

The chief executive of the USA is the President. The President is responsible for implementing and enforcing the laws written by Congress. The President appoints the heads of federal agencies, including the Cabinet. Each Secretary (Cabinet member) is in charge of a Department of State, which employs thousands of people to do the day-to-day work. The President is elected to a four-year term, and may only be elected to serve two terms.

Figure 1.15 The White House is the President's official residence →

The Constitution lists only three qualifications for the presidency. The President must:

- be at least 35 years of age
- be a natural born citizen
- have lived in the USA for at least 14 years.

The Judicial branch interprets these laws

Article 111 of the Constitution establishes the Judicial branch. The Supreme Court is the highest court of the USA and the only one specifically created by the Constitution. Members of the Supreme Court are appointed by the President and confirmed by the Senate. The Supreme Court consists of nine Justices who are appointed for life and are replaced when a previous Justice dies or retires. In 2009 President Obama appointed Sonia Sotomayor, with the approval of Congress, to fill a vacancy in the Supreme Court. Federal Courts hold the sole power to interpret the laws. The judges determine whether a law that has been passed is constitutional or not. The Judicial branch determines whether Legislative or Executive acts conform to the Constitution. In 2006, the Supreme Court declared that the military commissions set up by the Bush administration to try suspected members of al-Qaeda held at Guantanamo Bay in Cuba were unconstitutional.

Figure 1.16 The Supreme Court →

Checks and balances

The USA Constitution includes a series of checks and balances to reinforce the separation of powers. These checks create a balance of power, where no one branch of government has too much authority.

Congress can check the power of the President and the Supreme Court can check the power of Congress. It is important to note that the system of checks and balances was designed to ensure that no one branch became too powerful.

'The three branches of government should not be so far separated as to have no constitutional control over each other.'

James Madison, fourth President of the USA 1809–17

Table 1.1 **The three branches of the US government**

Legislative branch	Executive branch	Judicial branch
Checks on the Executive	Checks on the Legislator	'Guardians of the Constitution'
Power to declare war	Vice President is President of the Senate	Checks on the Legislator
May override presidential vetoes	Power to use veto	Judicial review – ability to declare a law 'unconstitutional'
Senate approves departmental appointments	Commander-in-chief of the military	Checks on the Executive
Senate approves treaties and ambassadors	Emergency calling into session of one or both chambers of Congress	Judicial review: check decisions made by the President follow the rules laid down by the Constitution
Checks on the Judiciary	Checks on the Judiciary	
Senate approves federal judges	Power to appoint judges	
Power to initiate constitutional amendments	Pardon power	
Power to alter the size of the Supreme Court	*Obama appointed 2 in 2010 – Elena Kagan*	
Power to set jurisdiction of courts		

The Constitution of the USA allows for overlap between the three branches to ensure the people's interests are upheld. For example, the President can propose changes in the law but cannot introduce a new bill directly. It is the role of Congress to pass these changes and introduce new laws on behalf of the President.

However, the President must sign new laws. If the President refuses and uses his or her veto, this could prove extremely difficult for members of Congress to pass a new law.

Having said this, if a law is passed by Congress and signed by the President, the Supreme Court can still deem it unconstitutional and prevent it from being upheld in the USA.

The powers of the President

Article 11 of the Constitution sets out the powers of the President. They are both defined and limited by the Constitution.

The constitutional powers can be divided into three categories:

1 legislative powers
2 head of state powers
3 executive powers.

Chief legislator

As chief legislator, the President is expected to suggest proposals on laws to Congress. The President can refuse to sign a bill that he or she does not feel is in the best interest of the American people. Article 1 of the Constitution lays down the President's veto power:

'Every bill ... shall, before it becomes a law, be presented to the President of the United States; if he approves he shall sign it, but if not he shall return it, with his objections, to that house from which it shall be originated.'

However, Congress has the power to override the veto with a two-thirds majority in both houses.

The President uses the annual State of the Union address to expand the legislative role of the presidency. At the start of each session in Congress, the President outlines important issues that have affected the country. The President discusses the Executive's actions in the past year and the intended actions of the next 12 months in office. At this stage Congress may pass proposed legislation on behalf of the President. In his second State of the Union address, President Obama reiterated his determination to complete his health reforms in 2010 (see page 20).

The President can also submit an annual budget to Congress with great fanfare – perhaps at a ceremony in the White House. All Presidents, even if their party controls Congress, must try to work in a bipartisan way. George W. Bush achieved his education reforms – No Child Left Behind – in 2002 because he

Figure 1.17 President Obama's State of the Union address in 2010 →

worked with leading Democrats such as the late Edward Kennedy to enable the bill to be passed.

Head of state

The President is the chief public representative of the USA, embodying a sense of national pride. The presidential role combines the duties that would be carried out in the UK by a monarch and a Prime Minister. The President and Vice President are the only elected members of the government. A President carries out the following duties:

- meets with leaders of other countries
- makes treaties
- appoints ambassadors.

Passing of legislation in the USA: Obama's Health Bill 2009–10

Presidents can outline their legislative goals in their State of the Union address. However, it can be very difficult, as stated, to get their policies through – even when their party has a majority in Congress. President Clinton only enjoyed two years of a Democratic-controlled Congress. At the first mid-term elections the Republicans gained control and for the remaining six years of his presidency, the Republicans controlled Congress. It was therefore no surprise that Clinton's health reforms were never implemented.

In contrast, President Obama seemed to be in a perfect position to push his health reforms through a Congress controlled by the Democrats. By late December 2009, Obama seemed to have achieved success in his health reforms. Both the House of Representatives and the Senate had passed their respective Health Bill versions. All that was required in January 2010 was for the two bills to be combined and a joint version passed by each chamber. The Republicans would not be able to use the filibuster (this enables a senator to block almost any measure just by keeping on talking), as under Senate rules the assent of three-fifths of senators can prevent a filibuster.

The Democrats, with 60 of the 100 senators, would ensure passage of the Health Bill. Unfortunately for President Obama, the vacant seat created by the death of Teddy Kennedy was lost by the Democrats and Scott Brown became the 41st Republican senator – the Democrats had lost their super majority. The Democrats' strategy was for the House of Representatives to pass the bill and to add a reconciliation clause which would mean that a simple majority vote in the Senate

Figure 1.18 President Obama signing the Health Bill ↑

would pass the bill. In March 2010 the House of Representatives passed the bill by 219 votes to 212. On 23 March 2010, President Obama signed the health care reform bill into law. Obama had achieved his health reforms.

Commander-in-chief of the armed forces

The President is the head of national security. He or she is the highest military officer in the USA, with control of the entire military establishment. This power is derived from Article IV, which stipulates that the President has the power to protect every state 'against Invasion ... and against domestic Violence.'

The President can order the use of troops overseas. The President is also responsible for the internal security of the USA. However, only Congress has the power to declare war and Congress controls the appropriation of finance for the armed forces.

Chief executive

As chief executive, the President is responsible for the implementation of laws and policy: 'he shall take care that the laws be faithfully executed.'

The President has a duty to uphold the decisions of the Supreme Court.

Executive Order – the President can use this in certain emergency circumstances. This has the power of law but does not need Congress to pass it.

Power of 'patronage' – the President controls the civil service, meaning that he or she can fill government offices. Therefore, the President appoints the top four layers of departments:

- Cabinet
- officials of the Executive office
- heads of independent Executive agencies
- independent regulatory commissions.

Control of Congress

In the USA, where the Executive and Legislature are elected separately, there is no guarantee that the President's party will be in majority in either house of Congress. Nor is it guaranteed that the President will have any control over his or her party in the Legislature.

- **President Clinton** was more of a 'defensive President' as he faced a hostile Congress dominated by Republicans. He failed to get his Health Bill through and used the veto 36 times. The Republican Congress tried to impeach Clinton. The House of Representatives passed two articles of impeachment by simple majority. The Senate conducted the trial and failed to obtain a two-thirds majority that would have removed Clinton from office. (President Nixon resigned rather than face certain impeachment.) Therefore Congress can remove the President but the President cannot remove Congress.
- **President George W. Bush** was more of an 'imperial President'. In his first six years he was allowed to expand the office of presidency, partly due to the fact

that his own party controlled both chambers and partly due to the crisis created by 9/11. This all changed when the Democrats regained control of Congress in December 2006. Bush had not used his veto in his first six years; in his last two he used the veto eleven times. Congress overrode four of his regular vetoes, including his veto of the 2008 Food Conservation and Energy Bill.

- **President Obama** faces a predominately Democratic Congress and this enabled him to appoint a Latino liberal judge to the Supreme Court. This would have been difficult to achieve had the Republicans controlled Congress, as they would have blocked this appointment.

Presidential powers

The creation of the Department of Homeland Security in 2002 enabled the President's office to increase its power. As a consequence, the government can now monitor the lives of US citizens on the pretext of the war on terrorism.

In 2001 an Executive Order, the USA Patriot Act, gave the Attorney General (a presidential appointment) the power to overrule the courts if they ordered the release of any person deemed to be a terrorist or linked with terrorism. It could be argued that the growth of presidential powers is linked to 9/11. After 9/11 the President had the support of the American public; this in turn promoted a positive public image of the President and could have helped the powers of persuasion with members of Congress.

In January 2009, newly appointed President Obama issued an Executive Order on the review and disposition of individuals detained at Guantanamo Bay Naval Base and the closure of its detention facilities. This detention centre was previously set up by the Bush administration.

Congressional Committees

In the USA, no Executive staff are members of Congress and there is no equivalent of **Question Time** in the House of Commons in which members of the government are grilled by the opposition parties. As a former President once wrote: 'Congress in session is Congress on public exhibition, whilst Congress in its committee rooms is Congress at work'. Congressional Committees in the USA are far more independent and powerful than their UK counterparts. Overall, there are 199 committees and subcommittees in Congress.

Standing Committees

Congressional Standing Committees are permanent policy specialist institutions which play a strategic role both in legislation and in overseeing the Executive branch. In 2008, members of President Bush's Cabinet made 68 appearances in front of Standing Committees.

They are permanent legislative panels established by the House of Representatives and the Senate rules. Standing Committees consider bills and issues and recommend measures for consideration by their respective chambers.

Select Committees

Congress can also set up Select Committees to investigate Executive action. In 2005, the House of Representatives set up a Select Committee to investigate the preparation and response to Hurricane Katrina which devastated New Orleans. The Committee reported in 2006 and heavily criticised the Bush Administration.

Conference Committees

These ad hoc (short-term) committees are set up towards the end of the legislative process. Bills tend to have a House version and a Senate version and members from each chamber try to create an agreed form of the bill. If agreement is reached, the full Congress votes to accept or reject – no amendments can be made.

Activities

1 Describe how power is separated between the three branches of government.

2 Outline the powers of the President.

3 Explain the constraints placed on the President's powers.

Essay question

To what extent can Congress and the Supreme Court limit the powers of the President? (15)

Political parties in the USA

Political parties in the USA are different from those in the UK. They are more state-based than national and, in elections, the candidates matter more than the party. Political parties in the USA are decentralised. They do have a national party organisation, but its role is mostly limited to the choice of presidential candidate at their respective National Conventions, held every four years.

The USA is often described as a 'two-party system'. This refers to the fact that the Democrat and Republican parties dominate politics. Most elected officials serving as President, members of Congress and state governors are members of these two main parties.

The Republican Party is normally thought of as being the more conservative of the two parties. Yet there are 'moderate Republicans', 'right-wing Republicans' and 'Christian conservatives'. In the 2000 presidential election, George W. Bush popularised the term 'compassionate conservatives'.

The Democratic Party contains both 'liberal Democrats' (such as President John F. Kennedy, who pushed for civil rights for African Americans) and 'conservative Democrats'.

The Democratic Party agenda states that it is 'committed to keeping our nation safe and expanding opportunity for every American'. It ensures that this commitment is reflected by the following:

- strong economic growth
- affordable health care for *all* Americans
- retirement security
- an open, honest and accountable government
- securing the nation while protecting civil rights and liberties.

Democrat Presidents

- John F. Kennedy
- Bill Clinton
- Barack Obama

Figure 1.19 The donkey, symbol of the Democratic Party ↑

Democratic supporters

The Democratic Party tends to gain support from the poorer classes, ethnic minorities, women and people who strongly agree with their liberal views.

The Republican Party agenda states that 'The United States has been blessed with a unique set of individual rights and freedoms available to all'. Republicans share many of the party's main beliefs:

- People can succeed through hard work, family support and self-discipline.
- Helping people through voluntary giving and community support is worthwhile rather than taxation or redistribution.
- Government should never become too powerful and infringe on the rights of the people.
- A commitment to lower taxes.
- The armed forces should protect and defend our democracy.

Figure 1.20 The elephant, symbol of the Republican Party ↑

Republican Presidents

- Ronald Reagan
- George H. W. Bush
- George W. Bush

Republican supporters

The Republican Party tends to gain support from men, the middle and wealthier classes, whites and people with more conservative views.

Organisation and finance of campaigns

Campaigns are no longer organised by parties but by the candidates themselves. Candidates know that their own appeal counts more than the party label. Candidates develop their own organisations to manage their campaigns. Members of their own personal staff are responsible for:

● policy development
● itinerary
● promotion of their image.

In terms of finance, campaigns have also become candidate-focused with more money channelled directly to the candidate rather than to parties. Candidates will raise the huge sums of money required for their campaign from wealthy supporters and investors. It costs millions of dollars for members of Congress, senators and potential Presidents to be elected.

In the 2008 presidential election the two main candidates raised and spent millions of dollars.

Barack Obama
Raised – $532.9 million
Spent – $513.5 million

Figure 1.21 Barack Obama campaigning in 2008 →

John McCain
Raised – $379.0 million
Spent – $346.6 million

Figure 1.22 The Republican candidate John McCain campaigning in the 2008 presidential election →

This money was spent by the parties in identifying potential state victories. Their campaigns focused on advertising each candidate's main policy areas.

In 2008, there were approximately 304,059,724 people in the USA: that is a lot of potential voters for the whole host of different elections that take place in the USA. Registered voters can vote for different levels of government that affect their everyday lives, from State Governors to their President.

Presidential election 2008

The 2008 presidential election was one of most widely anticipated events in America and the rest of the world. The Republican Party, headed by George W. Bush, saw the end of its eight years in power. The 'need' for change was cited as one of the main factors in seeing the Democrats take over the White House.

It was the first presidential election since 1952 in which neither the incumbent President nor the incumbent Vice President was a candidate. This explains why, in January 2008, there were sixteen serious candidates, eight each from the two main parties. John McCain eventually won the Republican nomination. He had unsuccessfully contested the Republican nomination in 2000, losing to George W. Bush. He won the 2008 nomination despite being regarded as a maverick Republican and there being an issue over his age (he would have been the oldest elected President, at age 72) because the party respected his Vietnam war record and his integrity.

It was assumed that Hillary Clinton would win the Democrats' nomination. However, Obama's early victories in, for example, the Iowa caucuses gave him the momentum to hold off a late surge from Clinton. Obama defeated McCain and thus became the first black president.

Obama claimed:
- **365** electoral votes
- **52.5%** of the overall popular vote.

McCain claimed:
- **173** electoral votes
- **46%** of the popular vote.

Voting patterns

Democratic support is mainly concentrated in larger city areas and coastal areas, such as New York and California. Geographical support can overlap with the income situation of voters. Poorer people, traditionally blue-collar manual workers, tend to live in the inner-city areas and vote for the Democrats.

Republican support generally comes from the southern states, including Texas. Voters in small towns and living in rural and suburban areas tend to favour them. The middle class and higher classes tend to vote for the Republican Party, including the 'religious right'.

The 2008 presidential election shows that a large majority of voters in urban areas voted for the Democrats (73%), whilst just over half of voters living in suburban areas voted for the Republicans (53%).

In terms of income, the 2008 results show that a large majority of voters earning less than $15,000 per year voted Democrat (73%). Republican support in terms of income was not as predictable as usual. Having said this, just over half of those voters earning $100,000–150,000 per year voted for the Republicans (51%).

Table 1.2 **Geographical areas of voters in the 2008 presidential election**

Democrats	**Republicans**
Urban = 63%	Urban = 35%
Suburban = 50%	Suburban = 48%
Rural = 45%	Rural = 53%

Source: CNN exit poll

Table 1.3 **Income of voters in the 2008 presidential election**

Democrats	**Republicans**
Under $15,000 = 73%	Under $15,000 = 25%
$30,000–50,000 = 55%	$30,000–50,000 = 43%
$100,000–150,000 = 48%	$100,000–150,000 = 51%
>$200,000 = 52%	>$200,000 = 46%

Source: CNN exit poll

Traditionally women are more likely to vote for the Democratic Party than their male counterparts. In the 2004 presidential election, Democrats had a narrow majority of 51% female voters. Females accounted for 41% of all voters. In the 2008 election, the Republicans attempted to increase their share of the vote by fielding a female candidate for Vice President, Sarah Palin.

In general, ethnic minority groupings in the USA tend to favour the Democrats. However, while the minorities with liberal views may vote Democrat, those with more conservative views will tend to vote for the Republicans.

In the 2004 presidential election, 67% of non-white men voted for the Democrats; 75% of non-white women voted for the Democrats.

After the results of the 2008 presidential election had been announced, an exit poll was carried out. A staggering 95% of non-whites polled stated that they had voted for Obama and the Democrats and a mere four per cent voted in favour of McCain and the Republicans. Obama is the first black President. He is representing minorities in the USA and they voted accordingly.

Table 1.4 **Votes by race in the 2008 presidential election**

Democrats	Republicans
White = 43%	White = 55%
Black = 95%	Black = 4%
Hispanic = 67%	Hispanic = 31%
All other races = 64%	All other races = 32%

Source: CNN exit poll

In terms of gender, the male vote was very closely split between Democrats and Republicans, with only one per cent separating the parties. In contrast, 56% of women voted in favour of Obama with only 43% voting Republican. The number of women voting Democrat was a slight increase from the 2004 election.

Table 1.5 **Votes by gender in the 2008 presidential election**

Democrats	Republicans
Men = 49%	Men = 48%
Women = 56%	Women = 43%

Source: CNN exit poll

The voter turnout in the 2008 presidential election was 62.8%, the highest since the 1960s.

An estimated 23 million Americans under the age of 30 voted in the 2008 presidential election, an increase of 3.4 million compared with 2004. Barack Obama received strong support from 18–29 year olds; about two-thirds of their votes were cast for the Democratic Party. Young voters are more likely to define themselves as a 'Democrat'.

Figure 1.23 shows the preference of voters in terms of age in the 2008 presidential election. Voters aged 18–29 overwhelmingly favoured the Democratic Party which received 66% of the youth vote; the Republicans received a mere 32% of the votes. In stark contrast, the Republicans gained loyal votes from the 65+ category, winning just over half of their votes

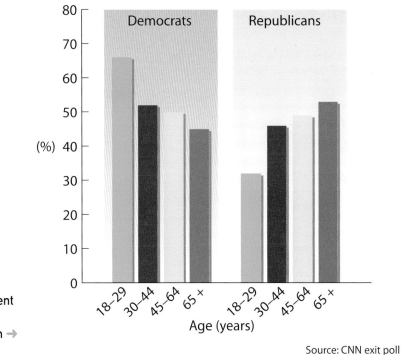

Source: CNN exit poll

Figure 1.23 Voting preference of different age groups in 2008 presidential election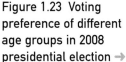

at 53%. This trend is as it has been in previous years as younger citizens tend to have more liberal views, such as the Democratic Party's stance on homosexual rights. Older voters may have more conservative views about traditional family values, which more closely reflect those of the Republicans.

Other influences

Religion: In the 2008 election a staggering 78% of voters who were Jewish voted in favour of the Democratic Party; 74% of voters who were Evangelistic Christians voted in favour of the Republican Party.

Gun owners: Voters who live in southern states or along the 'Bible belt' tend to vote for the Republican Party. Only 37% of gun owners voted in favour of Obama and the Democrats. Their Republican counterparts received more support from gun owners and gained 62% of their votes.

First-time voters: On an extremely interesting note, there were many first-time voters who participated in the 2008 election. Of these first-time voters, 68% gave their support to Obama. In contrast, only 31% of first-time voters used their first vote to support McCain.

Congress in 2008

Table 1.6 **Minorities in Congress in 2008**

	House of Representatives	**Senate**	**Total**
Hispanic	27	3	30
Black	42	1	43
Asian	6	2	8
Native American	0	0	0
Women	73	16	89
Men	382	84	466

Source: US Census Bureau

There was only one black senator, Roland W. Burris, in the 2008 Congress and he is a member of the Democratic Party. This is an extremely small figure considering that blacks make up 13% of the population. Although women make up over half of the population, they only account for 16% of the Senate and only 17% of the House of Representatives. This shows that women are largely under-represented in American politics. In comparison, there were 382 men in the House of Representatives out of a possible 453. In the Senate, there were 84 male members out of a possible 100. There were 27 Hispanic members in the House of Representatives, 24 of whom were Democrats, and only three were Republican.

All of the Asian and Pacific Islanders in Congress are Democrats.

Mid-term elections, November 2010

The November 2010 mid-term congressional elections resulted in the Republicans regaining control of the House with the greatest swing in votes between the parties since 1948. However, the Democrats maintained control of the Senate with the Democrat majority leader, Harry Reid, retaining his Nevada seat. Obama will find it very difficult to get his State of the Union January 2011 legislative programme through Congress. However, Bill Clinton, the Democratic President (1993–2001), did badly in his first mid-term elections but was re-elected as President for a second term two years later.

Black participation and representation

Roland W. Burris took over from Obama, when he was elected as the country's President, as the Democratic Senator of Illinois in 2008. He lost his seat in the 2010 elections and there are now no African American Senators. To date, six African Americans have served in the Senate. In 1993, Carol Moseley-Braun became the first black American woman to serve as a senator.

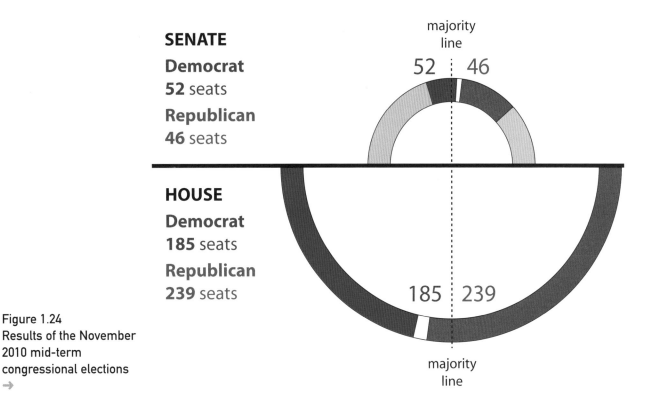

SENATE

Democrat
52 seats

Republican
46 seats

majority line

52 : 46

HOUSE

Democrat
185 seats

Republican
239 seats

185 : 239

majority line

Figure 1.24
Results of the November 2010 mid-term congressional elections
➜

Despite the lack of black representation in the Senate, progress is being made in the House of Representatives, which currently has 42 black members. Although progress is being made, it is fair to state that black Americans are not represented fairly in relation to their share of the total population.

The Black Caucus

The Black Caucus consists of all the black members of the House of Representatives. This group can prove influential when passing a bill through this chamber. There are 42 African American members of the House and if their votes are cast together they can deliver 20% of the votes required. The original thirteen members believed that a Black Caucus in Congress 'speaking with a single voice, would provide political influence and visibility far beyond their numbers.'

The Black Caucus provides a strong united front and requires that both Democrats and Republicans vote together. In the 40 years since its founding, Caucus members have been successful in gaining strategic places on House Committees to effect much-needed changes in federal policies. The members represent many of the largest and

Figure 1.25
Congresswoman Barbara Lee is the Chair of the Congressional Black Caucus for the 111th Congress ➜

most populated urban areas in the country, together with some of the most expansive and rural districts in the nation.

Majority–minority districts

US federal voting district boundaries tend to produce a proportion of constituencies with an African American or other minority in the majority.

Majority–minority districts are often the result of racial 'gerrymandering', in which the boundaries of the district are deliberately modified for electoral purposes. In such a district, the majority of constituents are ethnic minorities. Many of the majority–minority districts were created to enforce the Voting Rights Act. These districts were generated with the hope of increasing the opportunity for minorities to elect candidates of their choice. There has been a significant increase in the number of black representatives elected to the House of Representatives.

As of 2009, there are currently four states which are majority–minority:

- Hawaii
- New Mexico
- California
- Texas.

The Supreme Court recently outlined that there is a need to 'narrow the interpretation of the Voting Rights Act':

'The federal Voting Rights Act does not authorise vote dilution lawsuits in voting districts in which a particular racial or ethnic group comprises less than 50 per cent of the voting-age population.'

The case is important because it establishes ground rules that will apply nationwide during the redrawing of voting districts following the 2010 census. This could undermine the influence minority voters have over the outcome of the election, as minority voters will be concentrated in minority districts rather than distributed evenly, so will have little effect on the overall outcome.

Other factors that influence voting behaviour

Motor-Voter Law: The Motor-Voter Law was another aide in trying to increase the number of potential voters from ethnic minorities. The law did not become mandatory until 1995. The legislation enabled potential voters to register to vote at the same time as applying for or renewing their driver's license or applying for social services. The initial intention of the bill was to provide extra assistance to those who required it in order to register to vote. The lack of voter registration and turnout among the minority groups can affect the outcome of the election results. The Democrats hoped that with 'new potential voters' they would see an increase in their support. However, this was not the case as the Republican Party still remained the majority party in Congress.

Vote or Die: In the run up to the 2004 presidential election Sean (P Diddy) Combs became frustrated with the 'hustle of politics' and started a non-profit campaign that aimed to encourage the younger population to use their vote:

'Young voters in this country are throwing away their power to have a say about education, health care, and any issue that affects them. These things affect your life, so – Vote or Die!'

Figure 1.26 P Diddy supporting the 'Vote or Die' campaign →

In 2004, there were 42 million people in the USA aged 18–30. P Diddy recognised that this age group were unlikely to vote and wanted to change this as they accounted for 25% of the voting population. As a result, a whole host of popular famous faces were seen sporting the 'Vote or Die' merchandise. The campaign did not state allegiance to either party, although it was heavily criticised for aiming to 'swing' the result for a particular party.

The *Washington Post* claimed that the campaign was successful. It stated that the 'youth vote' increased dramatically between 2000 and 2004. In fact, the youth vote had climbed by 4.6 million votes since the 2000 election. However, although the campaign encouraged younger citizens to vote in favour of Democrat candidate John Kerry, George W. Bush still won the election and the Republicans gained another four years in office. Millions of younger voters were brought into the campaign but it could be argued that their vote made no real difference to the outcome.

Declare Yourself: Actress Jessica Alba is another of the famous faces in America who tried to encourage the younger generation to register and vote. Since 2004, the campaign 'Declare Yourself'

Figure 1.27 Jessica Alba took part in the 'Declare Yourself' campaign in 2008 →

has registered almost four million young people to vote via their online registration service. The campaign prides itself on the fact that in the 2008 presidential election there was a major increase in young voters; approximately 24 million young people used their vote.

Table 1.7 **Voter registration and turnout, 2008 presidential election**

	USA citizens who registered	USA citizens not registered	USA citizens who voted	USA citizens who did not vote	Total population who registered	Total population who voted
White	72%	28%	64.4%	35.6%	66.6%	59.6%
Black	69.7%	30.3%	64.7%	35.3%	65.5%	60.8%
Asian	55.3%	44.7%	47.6%	52.4%	37.3%	32.1%
Hispanic	59.4%	40.6%	49.9%	50.1%	37.6%	31.6%

Source: US Census Bureau

Comparing 2004 and 2008

In 2004, 64.4% of black Americans registered to vote in the presidential election. Only 56.3% of black Americans actually voted on the day of the election.

In the 2008 presidential election, 69.7% of black Americans registered to vote. On the day of the election, 64.7% turned out to vote.

Many believe that the main reason for the increase in black American voter registration and turnout was Barack Obama. This was the first time that an ethnic minority candidate had stood a good chance of becoming the President, and so this was seen to be a rare opportunity where voting would actually make a difference.

Why do black Americans tend to vote for the Democrats?

Black Americans are said to be one of the most conservative groups in the country, especially the older generation. Many are God-fearing and church-going, and are against abortion and homosexuality. They tend to stick to their traditional ways and they still believe in family, even though in some cases the father may be absent from the home. If this is the case, why then do black Americans vote Democrat? The Republican Party claims to be conservative because it stands for family, God and morality, does not support gay rights or the right to an abortion and believes in tradition and heritage. The difference between their conservatism and black conservatism is that they have power, wealth and influence, and they do not want any system to change their advantage. The conservatism of the Republicans is designed to maintain their culture, way of life, and most importantly their economic and political status. Black conservatism is more religious than cultural.

Hispanic representation and voting

Figure 1.28 Mel Martinez, Senator of Florida →

Hispanics are the fastest growing ethnic group in the USA. In both chambers, Hispanics are largely under-represented considering that there were approximately 46.9 million living in the USA as of 2009. In 2011 there were three Hispanics in the Senate and 24 in the House of Representatives (17 Democrats and 7 Republicans). In November 2010 Susana Martinez became the first Latina to be appointed as Governor of a State (New Mexico).

The Congressional Hispanic Caucus

Similar to the Black Caucus, the Hispanic Caucus aims to provide opportunities for their ethnic group to take part in politics and have a 'political voice'.

The Hispanic Caucus believes that there is a need to help the younger citizens because 87% of Hispanics do not have bachelor degrees, and nearly half leave school by the eighth grade (age 14). Currently, the Hispanic dropout rate is two and a half times higher than that of black Americans and three and a half times higher than that of non-Hispanic whites.

Figure 1.29 Nydia Velazquez, Chair of the Congressional Hispanic Caucus →

Additionally, the Caucus highlights the under-representation of Hispanics in elected office. Hispanics comprise only six per cent of the House of Representatives and there are only two in the Senate. Furthermore, it is thought that Hispanic representation is also lacking in most sectors of society, including higher education, business and the media.

Majority–minority districts

There are districts in large states such as California and New Mexico that have a high concentration of Hispanics. In states that do not have an overwhelming majority of Hispanics, the re-drawing of district boundaries, the creation of the so-called majority–minority districts, has increased their level of political representation and as a result, the number of Hispanics in Congress has increased over recent years.

The importance of the Hispanic vote

The attitude towards Hispanics has changed drastically over the last decade. The main political parties are now realising the importance of the Hispanic vote in assisting them to obtain key state victories. Both parties now go to great lengths and spend millions of dollars to win the 'Spanish vote':

- Party websites are translated into Spanish.
- Billboards, leaflets and posters are produced in English and Spanish.
- Latino media outlets including TV and tabloids are targeted.
- Instructions on ballot papers are written in both English and Spanish.
- Immigration is placed at the top of the list of priorities in political campaigns.

George W. Bush's outreach to Hispanic voters in the 2004 election

In January 2004 George W. Bush was campaigning for his second presidential term. His office introduced a big incentive to try and win over the majority of Hispanic voters. Bush unveiled a new immigration policy that included the creation of a Guest Worker Program, to 'bring the illegal immigrants out of the shadows' and allow them to seek work in the USA.

In reality, after his presidential victory, his intentions were exposed as a political scam. In 2005 he introduced tighter border controls to stop immigrants entering the country illegally. He also planned to allow 11 million guest workers into the USA on a temporary basis only, before they were forced back to their own country.

Comparing 2004 and 2008

In 2004, 34.3% of Hispanics registered to vote in the presidential election and 29.8% turned out to vote on the day of the election. In 2008, 59.4% of Hispanics were registered to vote in the presidential election. On the day of the election 49.9% of Hispanics used their right to vote.

In the space of four years the number of registered voters had almost doubled. The citizens who voted made a significant impact on the result. This is despite the fact that there are still millions of illegal immigrants living in the country who are unable to vote.

This increase further emphasises the importance of the Hispanic vote.

Hispanic political preference

Latino Evangelicals are twice as likely to vote Republican as Latino Catholics. This difference is far greater than would be seen in a white population with similar religious views. Another anomaly is that white conservatives generally vote Republican regardless of their religion, whereas Hispanic conservatives tend to lean towards the Democrats. While the Democrats have been the preferred party for Latinos traditionally, the Republicans have been narrowing this advantage in recent elections. In the 2000 and 2004 presidential races and in the 2006 mid-term elections the Hispanic vote for the Republican candidate has ranged from 30% to 40% on a national basis. Although the results show that religion is an important factor in shaping Hispanic preferences, Hispanics have been known to be 'swing voters' and so the political parties often target them in election campaigns.

Source: adapted from pewhispanic.org

Activities

1 Outline the key differences between the Democratic Party and the Republican Party.

2 What factors can influence the voting behaviour of USA citizens?

3 What conclusions can be drawn about the 2008 presidential election results?

4 Make notes on the aims of the Congressional Black and Hispanic Caucuses.

5 Explain why the majority of black Americans support the Democrats.

6 Describe the campaign methods that have been used to influence the Hispanic vote.

Social and economic inequality in the USA

The USA is arguably the richest country in the world, where many have worked hard to make money and achieve the American Dream. However, this is not true for all Americans. For many, reality is a life of poverty and discrimination reliant on welfare in a country where a capitalist ideology favours a strong independent work ethic and minimum state intervention. As a result, the USA is a very unequal country especially among the different family types and ethnic groups.

Poverty

In the USA the official measure of poverty is the Federal Poverty Level (FPL). It is estimated that around 40% of Americans find themselves below the poverty level at some point within any ten-year period. In 2010 The National Center for Children in Poverty reported that more than 13 million American children were living in families with incomes below the official federal poverty level of $22,050 a year for a family of four. It further reported that the number of American children living in poverty had increased by 2.5 million since 2000.

In 2008 there was an increase in poverty rates among families from 9.8% (7.6 million) to 10.3% (8.1 million). However, different types of families were affected differently. For example, in families with married couples the rate of poverty increased from 4.9% (2.8 million) to 5.5% (3.3 million) between 2007 and 2008, while in female-only households and male-only households rates remained the same.

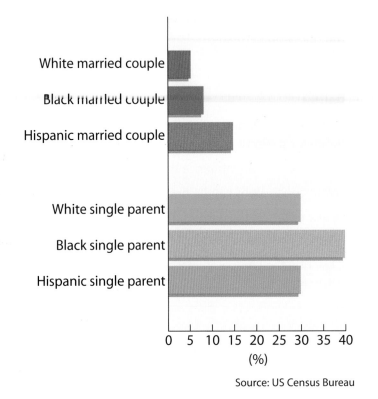

Figure 1.30 Poverty rates by ethnic group and family status, 2008 →

Source: US Census Bureau

While black Americans had the highest poverty levels and remained the most likely ethnic minority group to experience poverty, they were the only group whose poverty levels remained the same between 2007 and 2008, at 24.7%. Hispanics felt the biggest increase from 21.5% (9.9 million) in 2007 to 23.2% (11 million) in 2008, but were still below the level for black Americans. Next were Asians who increased from 10.2% (1.3 million) to 11.8% (1.6 million), while white Americans saw the smallest increase from 8.2% (16 million) in 2007 to 8.6% (17 million) in 2008.

Table 1.8 **Poverty levels in the USA by ethnic group, 1990–2008 (%)**

	1990	**2000**	**2008**
Black	31.9	22.5	24.7
Hispanic	28.1	21.4	23.2
Asian	12.2	9.9	11.8
White	9.4	7.4	8.6

Source: US Census Bureau

Table 1.9 **Poverty rates for native- or foreign-born residents**

	2007		**2008**	
Native-born	11.9%	31.1 million	12.6%	33.3 million
Foreign-born	16.5%	6.2 million	17.8%	6.5 million

Source: US Census Bureau

Today, black and Hispanic Americans are more likely to be living in poverty and therefore experience social and economic inequality compared to either Asian or white Americans. Black and Hispanic Americans are three times more likely to be living in poverty than white Americans and twice as likely as Asian Americans. Asian poverty levels are marginally higher than white poverty levels.

The reasons for the relatively high levels of black and Hispanic poverty are different. Black Americans have suffered systemic and long-term discrimination and have faced barriers to progress, and they have subsequently fallen victim to the poverty cycle. The poverty cycle has been described as a situation where poor black families become trapped in poverty for generations. This leads to limited access to, and in some cases exclusion from, education and employment opportunities that can affect subsequent generations.

Black community

For the last 50 years of the twentieth century, the level of black poverty in the USA steadily decreased. However, in the last ten years the numbers of black people in poverty have begun to increase and black Americans at all levels continue to experience greater disadvantage than white Americans or any other ethnic group. In 2008, almost a quarter of black American families lived below the poverty level and the average black American income was $34,218, compared with $55,530 for white Americans.

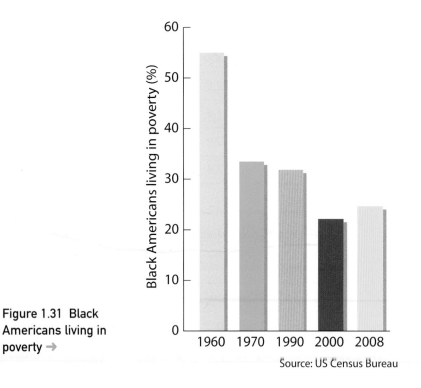

Figure 1.31 Black Americans living in poverty →

Source: US Census Bureau

This has resulted in a black underclass living in ghettos where they find it more and more difficult to get proper education, employment, homes, health facilities and even justice in the law courts. Their persistent exposure to the detrimental effects of poverty has led to rising crime and substance abuse in the ghettos. Another barrier to progress and employment opportunities is that life in the ghetto for many families means life as a single-parent family. Therefore the opportunities for work are restricted and most rely on welfare benefits for income. However, recent welfare reforms have meant that many have seen their benefits cut and their income drop. Black Americans are by far the biggest ethnic group reliant on welfare in the USA.

At the same time, America has seen a rise in a black middle class. Recent government initiatives to improve educational opportunities for ethnic minorities and affirmative action programmes have enabled many black families to move upward and outward from the urban ghettos to the residential suburbs. Today many black Americans are moving into better homes and in some cases second homes. Housing barriers are gradually disappearing and white Americans are no longer fleeing at the arrival of black people in the neighbourhood.

However, black people still tend to cluster together, whether in the cities or suburbs. Like other ethnic groups, they still prefer the company of other black Americans. No longer feeling the effects of social exclusion and identification by the colour of their skin, they have integrated into white middle-class neighbourhoods and have developed their own black middle-class neighbourhoods. The city of Atlanta, for example, has a large black community. Some of America's wealthiest black people live in the suburbs of Atlanta. Communities such as South Dekalb in Atlanta and Baldwin Hills in Los Angeles are thriving, and few white-owned homes are more luxurious than the black-owned mansions in these areas.

Case Study: Black middle class

In the middle-class Queens area of New York, the average income among black households (nearly $52,000 a year) was higher than that of white households in 2005. The gains among these black households were driven largely by the growth of two-parent families and the successes of immigrants from the West Indies. Many live in tidy homes in neighbourhoods like Cambria Heights, Rosedale and Laurelton.

Figure 1.32 The black middle-class ⬆

Today middle-class black America is well established as a separate community and does not have to live side by side with lower-income black Americans left behind in the ghetto. It is understandable for the middle class to escape the conditions of the ghetto as soon as they can afford to, just as other ethnic groups have done. But by doing so they leave behind those who cannot escape the ghetto to its more predatory and violent gangs, aggravating the spread of crime and decay.

Source: adapted from blackdemographics.com

The reasons for poverty among Hispanics are different than for black Americans. For Hispanics the cause is mainly the rise in immigration, especially from Central and South America. However, poverty levels between Hispanic groups are not evenly distributed. Mexicans and Puerto Ricans have higher numbers living in poverty than Cubans. These two groups tend to account for the majority of poor economic migrants and are mostly unskilled and looking to escape poverty in their own country. They merely add to the levels of Hispanic unemployed and increase their levels of poverty. In contrast, the Cubans have a more stable population and many have achieved the American Dream through working hard as business people and entrepreneurs.

For example, many Cuban migrants have settled in southern Florida, mostly in and around Miami, where the Cuban section has become known as 'Little

Havana'. Cuban immigrants are fully integrated into every level of society in Miami, where they make up one-third of the population and have become successful in the business sector, high finance and banking.

Income

As you have seen, poverty levels are related to income. Due to the world recession in the last few years, the median household income for all ethnic groups in the USA fell by 3.6%, from $52,163 to $50,303, between 2007 and 2008. In 2008 the average annual incomes of Asian households was the highest of all and almost double that of black Americans. In the Long Beach area of Los Angeles, the average Asian household income was more than $65,000 a year, more than $10,000 greater than that of white Americans.

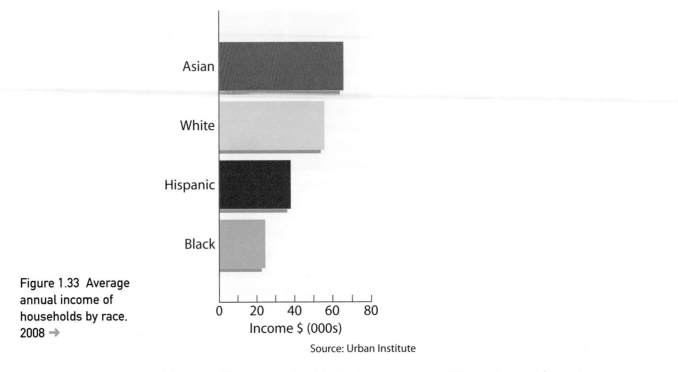

Figure 1.33 Average annual income of households by race, 2008 →

Source: Urban Institute

The overall result is that black Americans and Hispanics are three times more likely to be poor than white Americans, that black people earn 62 cents for every dollar white people earn and that the family median net worth of white Americans in 2007 was $170,400 compared with $27,800 for black Americans and Hispanics.

Fact File

Welfare USA-style

Personal Responsibility and Work Opportunity Reconciliation Act (PRWORA)
This federal law was signed in 1996 and overhauled the nation's welfare system, establishing the Temporary Assistance for Needy Families (TANF) block grant.

Temporary Assistance for Needy Families (TANF)
This grant programme replaced an outdated welfare funding system to give states more administrative/programme flexibility to move people from welfare to work. The funding goes to states in the form of block grants, which they use to provide cash grants to eligible recipients and to fund related state programmes.

Child Care and Development Block Grant (CCDBG)
This is federal funding to the states for child-care assistance to low-income families. Along with TANF allocations, the CCDBG has become a primary source of additional funding for state child-care subsidies.

Food Stamp Program (FSP)
This is a federal Department of Agriculture programme that provides funding to help those on low incomes purchase food, often through bank-style debit cards rather than paper coupons or stamps.

Source: Whitehouse.gov

Unemployment

Unemployment is one of the major causes of poverty and its effects are not shared equally. All ethnic groups saw a sharp rise in unemployment levels throughout 2007 to 2010 as the worldwide recession began to bite. Banks and industries collapsed and many workers lost their jobs. Changes in unemployment during the recession showed a rapid rise in the rates for Hispanics and black Americans. The unemployment rates for both of these groups saw the biggest change from 2007 to 2010 but the level of unemployment increased at a much faster rate for black people. Since 2000, the unemployment rates for black people have increased by roughly double those of both Asians and white Americans.

By 2010 the unemployment rate for black Americans was over 17%, compared with around nine per cent for white workers – this is almost double. In 2010, the unemployment rate for both black Americans and Hispanics reached double figures and for black people it was at its highest for 25 years.

Another barrier to progress for black Americans comes down to location, location, location. Many black Americans live in cities like Cleveland or Detroit which prospered during the heyday of heavy manufacturing but now struggle as old low-tech industries have been replaced by new high-tech ones.

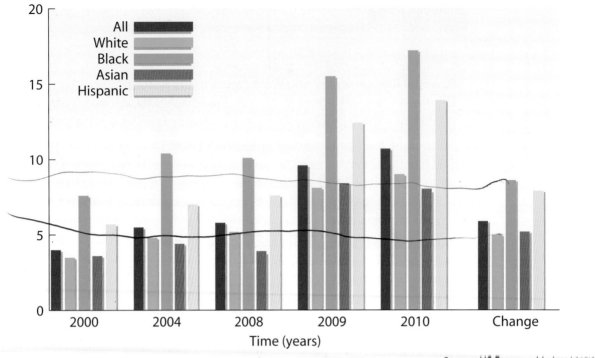

Figure 1.34 Unemployment levels, 2000 to 2010 (%) ↑

Source: US Bureau of Labor Statistics

In addition, those black Americans who do find themselves in areas with strong economic growth like Los Angeles or Atlanta have historically been isolated to areas with little or no opportunities.

Black people and Hispanics have felt the biggest rise in unemployment, mainly because they have been disproportionately employed in sectors hardest hit in the recession – manufacturing and construction. For example, in 2010 the unemployment rate for black Americans was 27% in Michigan, which has shed many jobs in the motor car industry. Other states with black unemployment levels above 20% include Alabama, Illinois, Ohio and South Carolina. In Nevada, the level of Hispanic unemployment reached 22.2%, as a result of the dramatic slowdown in construction.

Black and Hispanic Americans were far behind white people in employment levels even when the economy was booming. However, throughout the recession, the unemployment rate has grown much faster for both of these ethnic groups than for white people.

Employment

There are around 154 million people in the workforce in the USA. In 2010, 2.3 million fewer people were employed than in 2009. Among the ethnic groups, only the native-born Hispanics have seen a rise in employment levels. This is due to the rising numbers of them seeking employment, and when workers retire or leave employment they are increasingly more likely to be replaced by native-born Hispanics.

Table 1.10 **Employment sectors by race, 2008** (%)

	Asian	**Black**	**Hispanic**
Management and professional	6.3	8.3	7.1
Service occupations	4.6	15.9	20.2
Sales	4.2	11.5	12.3
Construction	1.9	6.9	25
Production and transport	3.8	14.5	20.4

Source: US Bureau of Labor Statistics

The numbers of people living on a low income and facing the effects of poverty in the US vary significantly for the different ethnic groups. In 2010, over 13.4 million families with children fell into the low-income category. Most of these families were from ethnic minority groups. Four million low-income families (or 30% of the total) were Hispanic, 2.9 million (22%) were black, and about 800,000 (6%) were other non-whites including Asians.

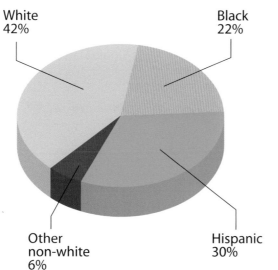

White 42%
Black 22%
Other non-white 6%
Hispanic 30%

Figure 1.35 Low-income families by ethnic group, 2010 (%) →

In the first decade of this century, US social policies underwent significant changes in an attempt to encourage greater work effort, with the expectation that full-time employment along with some social support would enable families to earn enough to provide for themselves and their families.

Income is dependent on whether anyone in the household is in work. In the US around 72% of all low-income families with children have at least one employed adult, though not all are working full time. However, there is clear inequality when this is broken down by ethnic group. For example, Hispanic families are most likely to have an adult who is working full time (55%), while black and white families are equally likely to have a family member working full time (44% and 43%, respectively). Black families are most likely to have no employed members (27%) and least likely to have a self-employed member (4%).

Another determinant of employment status is the type of family. Low-income Hispanic and other-race families are most likely to be in married-family households (53%). Of white families 42% are in married-family households, but this figure goes down to only 18% for black families. This means that black families are the most likely to be lone-parent families (83%), which might make it more difficult to balance work and family responsibilities.

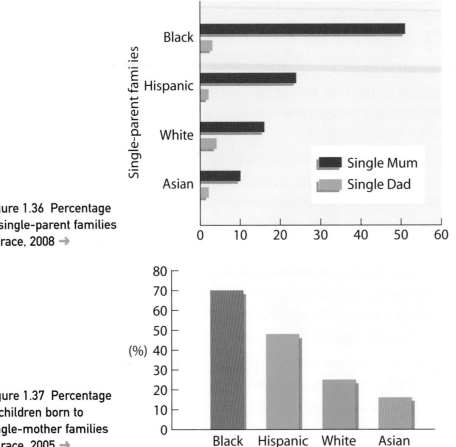

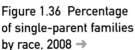

Figure 1.36 Percentage of single-parent families by race, 2008 →

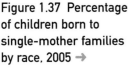

Figure 1.37 Percentage of children born to single-mother families by race, 2005 →

Low-income black families are more likely to experience poverty than all other families. More than half of low-income black families (53%) are poor, compared with 44% of Hispanics and 42% of other-race families. A quarter of low-income black families have incomes below 50% of the poverty level and live in deep poverty, compared with around 17% of white and Hispanic low-income families.

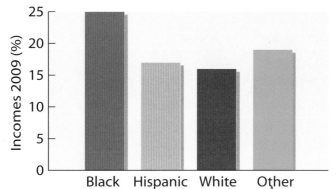

Figure 1.38 Percentage of families with incomes below 50% of Federal Poverty Levels (FPL) by ethnic group →

For all ethnic groups, income or earning potential increases with educational attainment. Nevertheless Hispanics with a high-school education or better tend to have less income than those from other ethnic groups with similar educational attainment, while Hispanics with less than a high-school education earn more than those from other ethnic groups. Hispanics seem to make up for any lack of education through greater work effort, making the overall income gap between them and other ethnic groups insignificant. Among single-parent households, the effect of educational attainment is strong.

For Asians the situation is much brighter. Many Asians tend to seek out work that provides improved job security. For example, many Filipinos are employed as doctors, nurses and teachers, where the risk of losing your job is minimal. In fact, the health care and education sectors were the only economic sectors in the US to grow during the recession. Other Asians are employed in science and technology, banking and high finance with many others owning their own small businesses.

However, some Asians have not escaped the effects of the recession. Many are refugees struggling to survive on low incomes like those in the Hmong community in Minnesota, most of whom are not well educated and don't speak English well. Levels of unemployment rose sharply in Minnesota by 150% between 2007 and 2009. Also, many Chinatowns and Little Saigons in large cities are seeing a downturn as people stay at home and cut back on eating out in restaurants. In addition, small family businesses are being squeezed out by big chains.

Activities

1 Explain in detail what is meant by a black underclass in the USA.

2 Explain in detail what is meant by a black middle class in the USA.

3 Describe in detail the reasons for poverty among black Americans.

4 Describe in detail the reasons for poverty among Hispanics in the USA.

5 Critically examine the argument that all ethnic minority groups experience poverty to the same extent in the USA.

6 Describe the measures introduced by the US government in response to inequality in wealth among its citizens.

7 All Americans have an equal opportunity to secure employment. Discuss.

8 Describe the employment situation facing Asians in the USA today.

Education

There is a well-proven link between education and employment and income levels. In the US, educational achievement for ethnic minority children is just as much about the opportunity to access key educational resources, including skilled teachers and a quality curriculum, as a matter of ethnic background. It could be argued that the US educational system is one of the most unequal in the industrialised world, and pupils experience significantly different learning opportunities not only because of their race but also because of their social status. In the wealthiest 10% of US school districts, educational spending is almost ten times more than in the poorest 10%. Up until the 1960s most black, Hispanic and Native American pupils were educated in wholly segregated schools funded at rates many times lower than schools for white pupils, and they were excluded from many higher education institutions.

Hispanics tend to have high dropout rates and low college completion rates, with a significant and persistent educational attainment gap between them and white pupils. According to the Pew Research Center, the biggest reason for this gap is the financial pressure to support a family. Nearly three-quarters of young Hispanics under the age of 25 who cut their education short during or immediately after high school in 2009 did so because they had to support their family.

It is felt that having at least a high-school diploma is a critical step for avoiding poverty, and a college degree is a prerequisite for a well-paid job in the US. The costs of dropping out of high school are substantial and have risen over time, especially for black Americans and Hispanics, who find it almost impossible to earn an adequate income to take care of themselves and their families. It was estimated in 2010 that those without a high-school diploma have considerably lower earning power and job opportunities and that over a working lifetime they would earn $400,000 less than those who graduated from high school.

This means that around three in every ten Hispanic and one in every five black students drop out of high school in the USA.

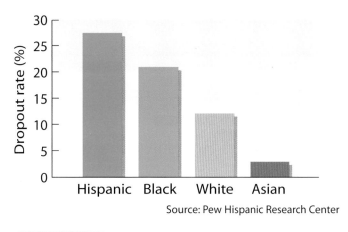

Figure 1.39 High-school dropout rates by ethnic group, 2010 (%) →

Source: Pew Hispanic Research Center

Fact File

Hispanics and education

Young Hispanics who have a high-school education gave the following reasons for not continuing their education.

- Nearly three-quarters (74%) say they need to help support their family.
- Nearly half (49%) say their English skills are limited.
- More than four in ten (42%) say they didn't like school.
- Four in ten (40%) say they cannot afford to go to school.
- Almost four in ten (39%) say they don't need more education for the career they want.
- More than two in ten (21%) say their grades were not high enough.

Source: Pew Hispanic Center

For black Americans living in the ghetto, educational aspirations can be smothered by a culture of educational apathy brought on in no small part by feelings of being left behind and disregarded.

Among all the ethnic groups it is Asians who have achieved the most. Asians account for about 4% of the US population yet in 2008 they accounted for 49% of college graduates, almost double that of whites. About 30% of Asians aged 25 and older have a bachelor's degree and almost 20% have a graduate degree, compared with only 17% and 10% for the whole of the USA. All other ethnic groups have a smaller share of college graduates: 18% of white Americans have a bachelor's degree and 11% have a more advanced degree while the figures are 12% and 6% for black Americans, and 9% and 4% for Hispanics.

More Asians than other ethnic groups are employed in management, professional and related occupations, jobs that require a higher level of education and have larger salaries. About 47% work in management or professional jobs compared with 35% for the US workforce as a whole. As a

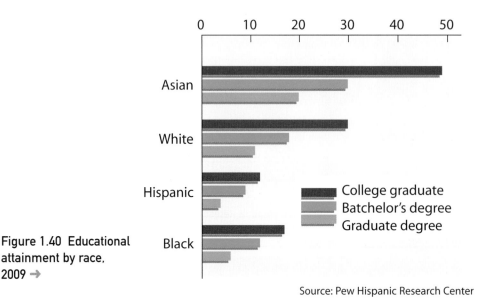

Figure 1.40 Educational attainment by race, 2009 →

Source: Pew Hispanic Research Center

whole, Asians make up 5% of US workers but make up a disproportionate share of computer software engineers (29%), computer programmers (20%), computer scientists and system analysts (16%).

The Asian population places great importance on education. In proportion to their percentage of population they are by far the most educated ethnic group and in the future it may lead to them earning the highest incomes and taking over as the wealthiest group in the USA. They already account for the highest percentage of top earners in the USA. Many have achieved great success through education in business and have a reputation for being ambitious and efficient. For example, many Koreans have set up businesses in deprived areas and ghettos, contributing to their regeneration and reducing unemployment even among the white population. Many have also excelled in science and technology and in education, as lecturers in colleges and professors in universities.

Table 1.11 Income of ethnic groups, 2007 (%)

	Under $10,000	$30,000–$34,999	$60,000–$74,000
Asian	3.4	3.7	10.4
White	3.6	4.6	11.6
Black	11.6	6.1	9.3
Hispanic	7.5	7.3	10.1
	$100,000–$149,000	$150,000–$199,000	$200,000 and above
Asian	20.4	9.4	3.8
White	16.1	16	2.7
Black	9	2.2	0.7
Hispanic	7.6	2.2	0.7

Source: Pew Hispanic Research Centre

What is more, there is a worrying rise in illiteracy in the USA, especially among ethnic minorities. It is estimated by literacy organisations that 20% of adults read at a level far below that needed to earn a living wage and around 40 million Americans are functionally illiterate. Half the people with the lowest literacy skills live in poverty and 70% are unemployed.

Housing

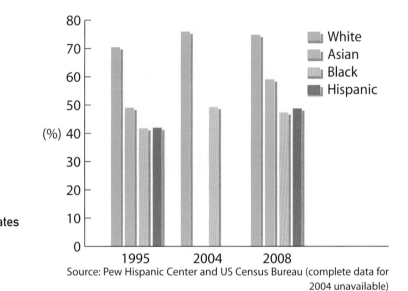

Figure 1.41
Homeownership rates
by ethnic group,
1995–2008 (%) →

Source: Pew Hispanic Center and US Census Bureau (complete data for 2004 unavailable)

Despite a reduction in the homeownership gap between white Americans and all other ethnic minority groups since 1995, a large gap persists. In 2008, 74.9% of white people owned their own home, compared with 59.1% of Asians, 48.9% of Hispanics and 47.5% of black Americans.

The total homeownership rate in the USA dropped by 1.2% from 69% in 2004 to 67.8% in 2008. Throughout these four years, the homeownership rate for black households decreased 1.9%, from 49.4% to 47.5%, reversing four years of increases. Similarly for Hispanics, their homeownership rate reached its highest level in 2005 only to fall by 2.6% from 56.2% to 53.6% in the following three years. It appears that the American Dream of becoming a homeowner is only true for less than half of black Americans and Hispanics.

Three-quarters of white people own their own homes compared to less than half of black Americans and Hispanics. Both black Americans and Hispanics can find it difficult to secure a mortgage, sometimes because of the area in which they live and want to buy property but more often because they are more likely to be unemployed or living on a low income and cannot afford it. The result is that they buy what they can afford or rent. This means they end up congregating in areas together and living in poorer quality housing, expanding the ghettos.

Figure 1.42 **The difference between rich and poor housing areas in the USA** ↑

Health

In contrast to the UK, America does not have a National Health Service that is free at the point of use. Instead, Americans need private medical insurance to pay for medical costs.

As a result there are ethnic health disparities where non-whites are more likely to lack health insurance, to receive lower-quality care, to suffer from worse health outcomes and to die prematurely. The causes of these disparities are broad and complex. They range from societal issues like poverty, racism and unhealthy environments, to health system factors like lack of health insurance, linguistic or cultural barriers, and limited access to health care facilities.

America's uninsured

Up to 46 million Americans are uninsured, because they are unemployed, because their employer does not provide cover, or because they do not qualify for existing government-funded health care. People aged 65 and older can qualify for Medicare, the poor can qualify for Medicaid, veterans and members of the military can qualify for Veterans Health Administration and TRICARE as part of the Military Health system, and children can be covered under a programme called the State Children's Health Insurance Program (SCHIP). However, many are overlooked by the system, including the young just entering the workforce, the self-employed, the unemployed and people who work for small businesses. In March 2010 Congress passed Obama's health care bill and it was signed into law by President Obama (see page 20).

Obama's health care plan

Health reform will make health care more affordable, make health insurers more accountable, expand health coverage to all Americans, and make the health system sustainable, stabilising family budgets, the federal budget and the economy.

- It makes insurance more affordable by providing the largest middle-class tax cut for health care in history, reducing premium costs for tens of millions of families and small business owners who are priced out of coverage today. This helps 32 million Americans afford health care who do not get it today – and makes coverage more affordable for many more. Under the plan, 95% of Americans will be insured.

- It sets up a new competitive health insurance market, giving millions of Americans the same choices of insurance that members of Congress have.

- It brings greater accountability to health care by laying out commonsense rules of the road to keep premiums down and prevent insurance-industry abuses and denial of care.

- It will end discrimination against Americans with pre-existing conditions.

Source: Whitehouse.gov

Ethnic group health highlights

Black Americans
- In 2008, 20% of black Americans (7.4 million) were uninsured, compared to 10% of white Americans.
- Although more than 80% of black Americans live in working families, only 53% are covered by employer-sponsored health insurance, compared to 73% of white Americans.

American Indians and Alaska Natives
- In 2003, American Indians and Alaska Natives had worse access to care than white Americans for about a third of access measures, including lacking health insurance.

Asians and Pacific Islanders
- In 2008, 16% of Asian Americans and Pacific Islanders (2.2 million) were uninsured, compared to 10% of white Americans.

Hispanics
- In 2008, 34% of Hispanics (14.8 million) were uninsured, compared to 10% of white Americans.
- The number of uninsured Hispanics increased from 10.8 million in 2000 to 14.8 million in 2008.
- Roughly one-third of Hispanics are uninsured, the highest rate among all ethnic groups and almost three times the rate for white people.

Overall health

When viewed as a group, ethnic minorities suffer from worse health compared to their white counterparts. For example:

- American Indians, black Americans and Hispanics are more likely to rate their health as fair or poor in comparison to white and Asian citizens.
- Among adults, death rates for black Americans are approximately 55% higher than they are for white people.
- Hispanics are more likely to be employed in high-risk occupations than any other racial or ethnic group. For example, although they comprise only 14% of the population, Hispanics account for 35% of all textile workers, 27% of building workers, 21% of construction workers and 24% of all workers in the farming, forestry and fishing industries.
- Black women have the highest death rates from heart disease, breast and lung cancer, stroke and pregnancy among women of all racial and ethnic backgrounds.
- Compared to the general US population, American Indians are 638% more likely to suffer from alcoholism, 400% more likely to contract tuberculosis, 291% more likely to suffer from diabetes, 67% more likely to have pneumonia or influenza and 20% more likely to suffer from heart disease.

Infant and maternal mortality

Infant mortality rates offer a vivid portrait of disparities in health. Even at birth, children from ethnic minorities suffer worse health outcomes, including a notably higher rate of death. For example:

- Infant mortality is more than twice as high for black infants as it is for white infants (13.9 deaths per 1000 live births versus 5.8 deaths per 1000 live births).
- The maternal mortality rate for black women is nearly five times the maternal mortality rate for white women.
- American Indians and Alaska Natives have Sudden Infant Death Syndrome (SIDS) rates that are twice those of the general US population.

Crime and the law

When you compare the ethnic makeup of the general population of the USA with that of the prison population it becomes clear that there is an ethnic imbalance. The connection between a person's ethnic background and their involvement in criminal activity has been long debated in the USA. This is especially so when you consider the disproportional representation of ethnic minorities, especially black Americans, at all stages of the criminal justice system, including arrests, prosecutions and prison sentences.

Most crime in America takes place in the inner cities and tends to be highly concentrated in economically disadvantaged areas with large black and Hispanic populations. America's inner cities contain the highest proportions of its immigrants, its poor, unemployed and unemployable.

Prison population and ethnic background

In 2009 more than 9.8 million people were held in penal institutions throughout the world, according to the International Centre for Prison Studies at King's College London. Most of the world's prisoners are in the USA – 2.29 million compared with 1.55 million in China and 0.87 million in Russia. The USA sends people to prison at a rate of 756 per 100,000 of the population. This means that the USA is the biggest user of prison in the world.

The state of Texas has the highest prison population in the USA. Its prison rate is more than 1000 per 100,000 residents. Around one in every 22 adult Texans is in prison or on probation or parole compared to one in 31 for the rest of the USA.

In 2008 around 40% of the prison population were black compared to 34% white and 20% Hispanic. For white Americans the rate of prison population is around 409 per 100,000 compared with 1038 per 100,000 for Hispanics and 4618 per 100,000 for black Americans. This means that one in every 22 people in prison are black compared to one in every 96 who are Hispanic and one in every 245 who are white.

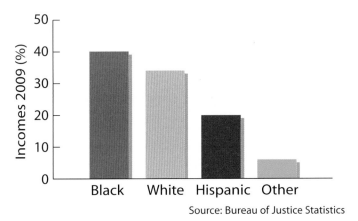

Source: Bureau of Justice Statistics

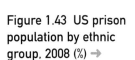
Figure 1.43 US prison population by ethnic group, 2008 (%) →

Many criminologists argue that this difference in prison population is linked to discrimination, especially when it comes to the handing out of prison sentences. In a study conducted by the Rand Corporation it has been estimated that black Americans and Hispanics receive longer sentences and spend more time in jail than white people who are convicted of similar crimes and with similar criminal records. For example, in California, sentences average 6.5 months longer for Hispanics and 1.5 months longer for black people when compared to white Americans.

Criminal offences and ethnic background

According to official US crime statistics, in 2008 of all those arrested for crimes 69.2% were white or Hispanic, 28.4% were black and the remaining 2.4% were from other ethnic groups.

Also, out of 16,277 murders that happened in 2008, 5334 were committed by white Americans, 5943 were committed by black Americans and Hispanics, 273 were committed by those of other ethnic groups and 4727 murders were committed by offenders whose race was not known.

According to the US Department of Justice, in 2008 the crime of rape was more likely to be committed by white Americans than by any other ethnic group. White people represented 65.2% of those arrested for rape, black people 32.2%, with American Indians and Asians around 1%.

White Americans were also more likely to commit hate crimes. In 2008 around two-thirds (61%) of those arrested for hate crimes were white and the majority of victims, almost three-quarters (73%), were black.

Murder

Black Americans are more likely than any other ethnic group to be arrested for murder; in 2008, 36% of all people arrested for murder were black. Since black Americans make up around 12% of the population of the USA, this is a significantly high ratio of total arrests made.

Black Americans are also more likely to be the victims of murder; 47% of all murder victims in 2008 were black. However, 95% of these were murdered by other black people. The same is true for white Americans; 83% of all white Americans murdered in 2008 were killed by other white people.

Table 1.12 **Offenders and victims of murder, 2008 (%)**

	Offender	**Victim**
Black	36.5	47.8
White	32.8	48.2

Source: Bureau of Justice Statistics

Violent crime

The biggest percentage of the population arrested for violent crimes tends to be white. In 2008 white people accounted for around 58% of arrests. However, when you consider that they make up around 80% of the total population, this is less than other ethnic groups in terms of arrests per percentage of population by ethnic group. Similarly, Asians, who make up around four per cent of the total population, were also significantly under-represented, making up only one per cent of total arrests. However, black Americans were significantly over-represented, making up around 12% of the population and more than 39% of all arrests.

Table 1.13 **Offenders of violent crime by ethnic group, 2008 (%)**

	Total	**Rape**	**Robbery**	**Assault**
Black	39.4	32.2	56.7	34.2
White	58.3	65.2	41.7	63.3
Native American	1.2	1.2	0.7	1.4
Asian	1.1	1.4	0.9	1.2

Source: Bureau of Justice Statistics

Fact File

Prison facts

- One in ten (10.4%) black males aged 25–29 was in prison or jail in 2007, as were one in 28 (3.6%) Hispanic males and one in 59 (1.7%) white males in the same age group.

- 40% of persons in prison or jail in 2006 were black and 20% were Hispanic.

- Black males have a 32% chance of serving time in prison at some point in their lives. Hispanic males have a 17% chance and white males have a 6% chance.

- In 1983, at the height of apartheid, South Africa imprisoned black males at a rate of 851 per 100,000. In 2003 in the USA under George W. Bush, black males were imprisoned at the rate of almost 5000 per 100,000. Hence Bush imprisoned black males at a rate of almost six times higher than the authorities in South Africa at the height of apartheid.

Source: Bureau of Justice Statistics

Fact File

Death penalty

In 96% of the states where there have been reviews of race and the death penalty, it was found that there was a pattern of either race-of-victim or race-of-defendant discrimination, or both.

- 98% of the chief district attorneys in death-penalty states are white and only 1% are black.

- A comprehensive study of the death penalty in North Carolina found that the odds of receiving a death sentence rose by 3.5 times among those defendants whose victims were white.

- A study in California found that those who killed white people were over three times more likely to be sentenced to death than those who killed black people and over four times more likely than those who killed Hispanics.

Source: US Death Penalty Information Center, 2010

What is Affirmative Action?

Affirmative Action emerged from the civil rights movement and calls for ethnic minorities to be given special consideration in employment and education. Organisations that exercise policies of Affirmative Action actively use recruitment policies, set-asides and preferential selections to attempt to redress the balance by ensuring diversity in favour of ethnic minorities who have suffered from discrimination. For example, during the recruitment process Affirmative Action would encourage the selection board faced with two similarly qualified applicants to choose the ethnic minority candidate over the white person. However, by law decisions taken through Affirmative Action should not be based on quotas and they should not give any preference to unqualified candidates.

Affirmative Action has been called America's most ambitious attempt to redress its long history of racial discrimination. Nevertheless, today it has aggravated rather than soothed divisions and inequality.

Those opposed to Affirmative Action argue that the battle to guarantee equal rights for all citizens has been fought and won and to continue favouring someone from one group over another now creates inequality and reverse discrimination.

On the other hand, defenders of Affirmative Action argue that there still exist inequalities among minority groups and continued action is required to ensure that a level playing field is created. If this comes by promoting modest advantages to ethnic minorities then it only redresses hundreds of years of discrimination and favouritism to white people.

The quota system has been declared unconstitutional by the Supreme Court and is no longer favoured by politicians. At the state level, universities such as the University of Michigan have been legally challenged over their admission policies. The debate still continues, and the then Senator Obama summed it up in 2008 when he said:

'I still believe in Affirmative Action as a means of overcoming both historic and potentially current discrimination, but I think that it can't be a quota system and it can't be something that is simply applied without looking at the whole person, whether that person is black, or white, or Hispanic, male or female. What we want to do is make sure that people who've been locked out of opportunity are going to be able to walk through those doors of opportunity in the future.'

Activities

1 Explain why Hispanics tend to have high dropout rates and low college completion rates in the USA today.

2 To what extent have all ethnic minority groups in the USA achieved success in education?

3 Describe in detail the inequalities that exist in housing between different ethnic minority groups in the USA.

4 Describe in detail the inequalities that exist in health between different ethnic minority groups in the USA.

5 Describe in detail the inequalities that exist in crime and law between different ethnic minority groups in the USA.

6 Describe what Affirmative Action is.

7 What are the two differing views on Affirmative Action today in America?

Essay questions

1 What evidence is there that the American Dream has been achieved by members of ethnic minority groups? (15)

2 All Americans have an equal opportunity to achieve the American Dream. Discuss. (15)

3 To what extent have minority ethnic groups made social and economic progress in the USA? (15)

The Republic of South Africa

The 'rainbow nation'

South Africa is a nation reborn. In 1994 the country elected its first democratic government after the end of white rule under a system known as apartheid. Nelson Mandela, the leader of the ANC (the African National Congress), became the first democratically elected President. Before Mandela, the white people had used apartheid to deny the non-white people political, social and economic rights: this has left a legacy of vast inequalities between the races which will be discussed later in this chapter. The new rainbow nation has made great progress in the creation of a more prosperous country for all, and in 2010 the football World Cup finals were held in South Africa. It was fitting that South Africa was the first African country to hold such a prestigious event.

Figure 2.1 One of the new stadiums built in South Africa for 2010's football World Cup →

Will World Cup stadiums change Africa's image?

South Africa's World Cup stadiums could change the image of Africa forever, or stand as spectacular monuments to extravagance and waste in a country still struggling to spread the fruits of majority rule.

South Africa has confounded sceptics who said the stadiums would never be finished in time for the soccer spectacular and managed to complete ten top-class venues that bear comparison with the world's best.

But while that controversy has passed, the debate has not diminished over whether Africa's first World Cup should have been more modest, freeing up millions of dollars to help an army of poor who live in squalor 15 years after the end of apartheid. When Pretoria won the right to stage the 2010 tournament back in 2004, it set the budget for stadiums at about R3 billion ($390 million). However, the addition of two extra venues pushed that figure to at least R13 billion ($1.7 billion). Critics say the money was wasted and should have been spent on alleviating poverty – which feeds South Africa's frightening rate of violent crime – building millions of new houses to replace apartheid-era informal settlements and combating HIV/AIDS. They charge that many of the stadiums will quickly become unused relics after the tournament.

Argument

But there is another side to the argument that says the World Cup gives Africa the chance finally to reverse stereotypes of famine, pestilence and war that still blight the continent.

Nobel peace prize laureate and anti-apartheid hero Archbishop Desmond Tutu has said the World Cup will have as big an impact for black people as the election of US President Barack Obama and will give new pride to a still divided nation.

'With all the negative things that are taking place in Africa, this is a superb moment for us. If we are going to have white elephants, so be it,' he said.

Economists also say World Cup construction has cushioned South Africa from the global recession and will contribute close to R56 billion ($7.3 billion) to the economy. 'It has been a huge blessing for South Africa in view of the recession' said Gillian Saunders of business consultants Grant Thornton.

Nevertheless, the stadiums' spectacular style can perhaps be seen as going way beyond football – the affirmation of the capabilities of a young, democratic country in the face of doubts and cynicism both at home and abroad. 'For the many little boys kicking a ball in the streets of the world's townships and squatter camps, football is the stuff of dreams,' said commentator Tinyiko Sam Maluleke.

Source: adapted from *The Mail* and *Guardian*, 29 December 2009

The land and the people

South Africa is five times the size of the United Kingdom with a population three-quarters that of the UK. Due to its size, it has different climates and landscapes in different parts of the country. Much of the west of the country is desert, while the south, around Cape Town, has a Mediterranean climate. South Africa is divided into nine provinces (see pages 66–67).

Its population of 49 million is made up of numerous ethnic groups and this is reflected in the recognition of 11 official languages. Black South Africans make up 79% of the population (see Table 2.1 on page 64).

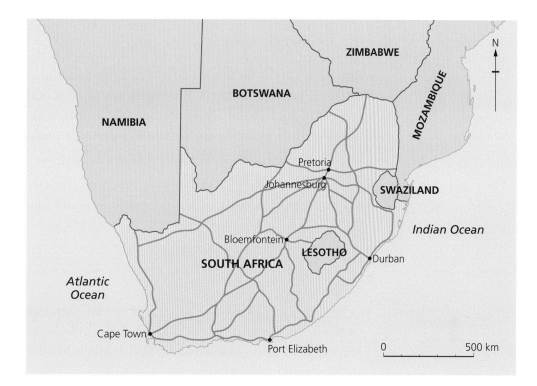

Figure 2.2 Southern Africa →

Boers, British and Africans

In 1752 a settlement was established by the Dutch East India Company to supply fresh provisions for their trading ships.

By 1806 the British government had decided to control Cape Colony and consequently took it over. The resultant increase in immigration from Britain established two distinct white communities: the Afrikaners (Boers) and the English-speaking whites (Anglos). With the discovery of diamonds and gold, Britain proceeded to annexe the Afrikaner republics of Transvaal and the Orange Free State. This eventually led to the Boer War (1899–1902), in which the Boers were defeated.

British dominance ended in 1948 when the Afrikaner National Party won the election and began its policy of apartheid and total white control of all aspects of life.

South Africa's economy

South Africa is a middle-income emerging economy with an abundant stock of natural resources. It is served by a modern infrastructure ensuring an efficient distribution of goods to major urban areas .The country has well-developed financial and legal sectors with a stock exchange that ranks among the top ten largest in the world. Unemployment is still a problem, with about 50% of the population living below the poverty line. Massive economic inequalities still exist between the white population and the new black middle class and the majority of black South Africans. South Africa is one of the most unequal societies in the world alongside the USA, China and Brazil, in terms of wealth distribution among its citizens.

South Africa is the wealthiest country in sub-Saharan Africa in terms of natural resources and its manufacturing industry. It is the world's largest producer of gold. Large-scale commercial farming ensures an abundant supply of food. In the less fertile areas pastoral farming dominates, with sheep rearing and cattle ranching particularly strong.

South Africa is the region's economic superpower. It accounts for 85% of southern Africa's energy consumption and 90% of its Gross Domestic Product (GDP).

Ethnic groupings

South Africa is made up of four ethnic groups.

1 The dominant group is the black indigenous population, who are sub-divided by tribal group. The two main tribal groups are Xhosa (former Presidents Nelson Mandela and Thabo Mbeki) and Zulu (current President Jacob Zuma).
2 Whites are divided into English-speaking and Afrikaans-speaking.
3 The coloured population are of mixed race.
4 Asians, or Indians, are descended from workers who were brought from India to work, especially in Natal, in the nineteenth century.

Table 2.1 indicates that South Africa's population is fast approaching 50 million. In 2009 the coloured population overtook the white population – an estimated 800,000 white people have left South Africa since 1994. With a higher birthrate than the other races, the African population has increased by almost 8 million from 1996 and will soon reach 80% of the population.

Table 2.1 **South Africa's population**

	1996 Population (millions)	**%**	**2009 Population (millions)**	**%**
African	31.3	76.8	39.1	79.3
White	4.7	11.4	4.47	9.0
Coloured	3.3	9.0	4.48	9.1
Asian	1.2	2.8	1.2	2.6
Total	**40.5**	**100**	**49.3**	**100**

Source: Statistics South Africa, Mid-Year Population Estimates, 2009

While there are significant inequalities in South Africa based on race, there are also significant inequalities between urban and rural areas. The 2001 Census, published in July 2003, highlights the fact that regional inequalities are still a feature of South Africa.

Illegal immigrants

Official figures detailing South Africa's population fail to include the millions of Africans who have flocked to the country to escape poverty and persecution in their home nations. It has been estimated by the South African Institute of Race Relations that around five million immigrants are living illegally in South Africa. It is ironic that while highly skilled and educated white people leave the country for better jobs abroad (around 800,000 are thought to have left since 1994) and educated black South Africans flock to London to take up jobs in health and education, South Africa is being left with an unskilled and uneducated workforce, which the country, with its unemployment rate of 40%, does not need.

Most refugees originate from the Democratic Republic of Congo, Rwanda, Mozambique and Zimbabwe (see Figure 2.2). Around two million Zimbabweans are thought to be currently living in South Africa, although many may return home if peace and stability return to Zimbabwe. Illegal immigrants face great hostility from South Africans. The view in 2004 of the then Home Affairs Minister, Chief Buthelezi, still reflects public opinion and explains the xenophobic violence which took place in 2008. He stated 'the presence of illegal aliens impacts on housing, health services, education, crime, drugs and transmissible diseases.'

The vicious attacks against foreign immigrants began in May 2008 in townships around Johannesburg and spread to Cape Town. In all 60 people were killed and tens of thousands were left homeless. Further riots against foreigners flared up in Mpumalanga in January 2010.

Activities

1 Outline the benefits and criticisms of South Africa holding the World Cup.

2 Describe the main racial groups in South Africa and discuss what conclusions can be reached about population change.

3 Create a brief profile of the nine provinces.

4 Why are many South Africans hostile to illegal immigrants?

Profile of the provinces of South Africa

Province/Capital   **GAUTENG/Johannesburg**

Population   10.5 million (21.4% of total)

Area km²   18,810 (1.6% of total)

% of GDP   38

Agriculture and industry   Gauteng is South Africa's engine room, where about 40% of the country's GDP is generated. Gauteng means 'Place of gold' and this is a highly urbanised and industrialised area. It is a magnet area for a large inflow of migrant labourers who settle in the townships such as Soweto and shanty towns.

Comment   Pretoria, the administrative capital of South Africa, is situated in the province.

Province/Capital   **NORTHERN CAPE/Kimberley**

Population   1.1 million (1.9% of total)

Area km²   361,800 (29.7% of total)

% of GDP   2

Agriculture and industry   Extremely rich in mineral wealth – including copper, manganese and marble.

Comment   It covers the largest area in South Africa and has the smallest population. It is a semi-arid region with low summer rainfall and is the home of the San (bushmen) people who live in the Kalahari area of the Northern Cape.

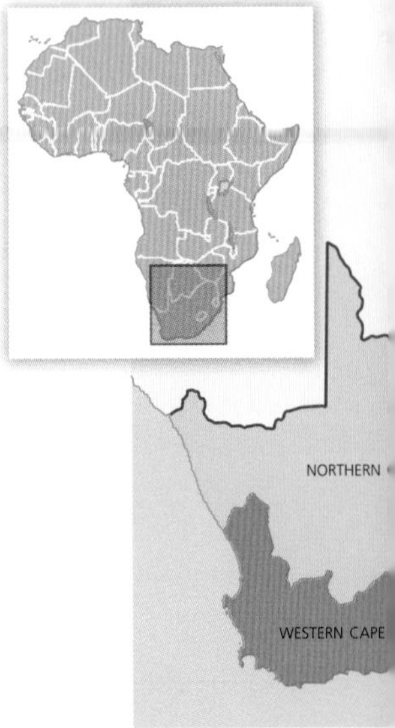

Province/Capital   **WESTERN CAPE/Cape Town**

Principal language   Afrikaans (55%), English (20%), isiXhosa (23%)

Population   5.3 million (10.9% of total)

Area km²   129,379 (14.4% of total)

% of GDP   14.4

Agriculture and industry   Food basket of South Africa with a harvest of top-grade fruits, vegetables and meats. The head offices of many South African businesses are in Cape Town. Some 96% of its population is urbanised.

Comment   Cape Town is the legislative capital of the country. Western Cape has the highest literacy rate in the country.

Province/Capital   **FREE STATE/Bloemfontein**

Population   2.9 million (6.0% of total)

Area km²   129,480 (10.6% of total)

% of GDP   5.5

Agriculture and industry   'The granary of the country' with 31% of the potentially arable land of South Africa. Its main economic base is mining.

Comment   It lies in the heart of South Africa and is the third-largest province.

Province/Capital   **NORTH WEST/Minabatha**

Population   3.4 million (7.1% of total)

Area km²   116,190 (9.5% of total)

% of GDP   5.5

Figure 2.3 South Africa's nine provinces ↑

Agriculture and industry	Its main economic base is mining with its major agricultural products being maize and sunflowers. High unemployment levels in the province contribute to the poverty experienced by many of its citizens.
Comment	It is developing its tourist industry through national parks.

Province/Capital	**EASTERN CAPE/Bisho**
Population	6.6 million (13.5% of total)
Area km²	169,600 (13.9% of total)
% of GDP	8.1
Agriculture and industry	Not rich in minerals but includes rich agricultural and forestry land. The urban areas of Port Elizabeth and East London are based primarily on manufacturing.
Comment	Includes the former Homelands of Transkei and Ciskei.

Province/Capital	**LIMPOPO/Pietersburg**
Population	5.2 million (10.6% of total)
Area km²	123,280 (10% of total)
% of GDP	3.7
Agriculture and industry	Extremely rich in minerals including coal, copper and platinum. Unemployment is high. The per capita income is by far the lowest in the country. Contains the three former Homelands of Venda, Gazankulu and Lebowa.
Comment	The province is the country's gateway to the rest of Africa as it shares borders with Botswana, Zimbabwe and Mozambique.

Province/Capital	**MPUMALANGA/Nelspruit**
Population	3.6 million (7% of total)
Area km²	78,370 (7.3% of total)
% of GDP	8.1
Agriculture and industry	Produces sub-tropical fruits and its tree plantations supply half of the country's total timber needs. It is rich in coal reserves and the country's three biggest power stations are based in the area.
Comment	Mpumalanga (formerly Eastern Transvaal) means 'place where the sun rises'. The province attracts migrant labour from neighbouring states, especially refugees from Mozambique. Suffers from extreme levels of poverty and low levels of literacy.

Province/Capital	**KWAZULU-NATAL/Pietermaritzburg/Ulundi**
Principal language	isiZulu (79%), Afrikaans (2%), English (16%)
Population	10.4 million (21.2% of total)
Area km²	92,180 (7.6% of total)
% of GDP	16.7
Agriculture and industry	Rapid industrialisation in recent times. Durban is one of the fastest growing urban areas in the world. Huge gap between the urban and rural per-capita income.
Comment	The only province with a monarchy specifically provided for in the 1993 Constitution. Ulundi is the traditional capital of the Zulu monarchy.

Source: SA Government Yearbook 2009

sotho is not a province; is a nation

N

LIMPOPO

MPUMALANGA

GAUTENG

EST

REE STATE

KWAZULU-NATAL

LESOTHO

ERN CAPE

0   500 km

The apartheid years: 1948–94

Apartheid is an Afrikaans word which means 'separate development' and it was used by the National Party in 1948 to enable the white minority to deny the non-white population their political, social and economic rights. This created vast inequalities between the races and this legacy still haunts South Africa today.

Dividing the population and land

The first step in the National Party's development of apartheid was to define the races to which people belonged. This was done through the Population Registration Act (1950) which decreed that all people were to be racially classified into three main groups – black, white and coloured – with subdivisions.

Figure 2.4 Racial segregation in action →

The majority black South African population was divided into eight tribal groups. The coloured population comprised two main groups: the Cape coloureds, descendants of relationships between white people and the original African inhabitants of the Cape (the San and Khoikhoi); and the Asians, or Indians, descended from Indian workers who were brought from India to work in the nineteenth century. White people were divided into English-speaking and Afrikaans-speaking, with the latter controlling the country.

Coloured people were not given a homeland to live in. They were forced to live in coloured towns and cities. By 1980, over 116,000 coloured and Indian families had been forced to leave their homes and move to these designated areas.

The 1950s saw the creation of the Homelands policy, which defined the territory which white South Africans considered to be the traditional land of the black South Africans. It was in these Homelands or Bantustans that the black South Africans would be entitled to exercise citizenship rights.

Homelands and townships

The Homelands comprised no more than 13% of the total land area of South Africa, but were expected to support almost 73% of the population. The largest, Bophuthatswana, had a large amount of desert and semi-desert. Only 6–7% was suitable for growing crops, with the remainder only suitable for grazing livestock.

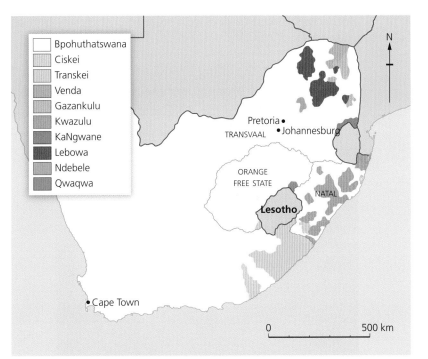

Figure 2.5 A map of the Homelands →

Due to the shortage of land and employment many black South Africans had to seek work outside the Homeland. Thus the Homelands were left with a disproportionately large number of children, women, elderly and sick people.

Most black South Africans who qualified to stay in 'white South Africa' under Section 10 regulations were housed in one of the many townships. These were housing areas for the black South African labour force which was required by local industry, and they were usually located on the outskirts of an urban area. Soweto, situated 12 miles south-west of Johannesburg and housing well over one million black South Africans, was an example of one such township.

Modernising apartheid, 1978–94

The Soweto riots of 1976–77 were crushed by the security forces with an estimated 700 deaths. Many young black South Africans fled the country to prepare for armed resistance and were determined to return with bullets, not stones.

In 1978 P. W. Botha became the new President of South Africa and promised to introduce reforms. 'We must adapt or die' was his message to the white electorate. P. W. Botha hoped to create a larger non-black minority by giving the vote to the coloured and Asian communities. He hoped his economic reforms would create a black middle class which would benefit from the apartheid system.

Botha's reforms were condemned by the black majority and even by the coloured and Asian communities. The townships once again exploded and

Botha was forced to declare a state of emergency before order was restored in 1989.

In August 1989, the ailing President Botha was replaced by F. W. de Klerk who, within a year, had brought apartheid to an end. He released Nelson Mandela from prison, legalised the ANC and other political parties in February 1990, and scrapped the remaining apartheid laws. Negotiations began for peaceful transition from white minority to black majority rule.

Figure 2.6 F. W. de Klerk with Nelson Mandela →

Fact File

Timetable to freedom

1990	
2 February	The ANC and other political parties are legalised.
11 February	Nelson Mandela walks out of Victor Verster Prison to freedom.
1991	Hated apartheid legislation, such as the Group Area Acts and the Population Registration Act, is repealed.
1993	
July	The Inkatha Freedom Party (IFP) and the white Conservative Party promise to boycott the April 1994 elections.
1994	
19 April	Fighting continues in KwaZulu-Natal between Inkatha and ANC supporters, forcing de Klerk to declare a state of emergency. Inkatha agrees to take part in the elections and civil war is avoided.
27 April	The elections take place without disruption.

Election day

Finally, in April 1994, the silent political voice of the African people roared into life as millions of non-whites turned up to vote for the first time.

Nelson Mandela, leader of the ANC, stated without exaggeration that 'Today is a day like no other before' as 20 million fellow voters waited patiently in long excited queues to cast their votes.

1994 Election analysis

- It was a triumph for democracy with the election remaining free from intimidation, fraud and violence.
- As expected, the ANC dominated the election, winning over 12 million votes and just failing to receive two-thirds of the votes (which would have enabled it to create a new constitution without consulting the other political parties). At the provincial level the ANC won seven of the nine provinces with narrow defeats in the Western Cape and KwaZulu-Natal.
- The New National Party, by winning the support of white, coloured and Asian South Africans, gained an impressive 20.4% of the vote and thus a post of Deputy President. Its best performance was in the Western Cape where it won the provincial election. The Democratic Party, a white party that had always opposed apartheid, did badly.
- The Inkatha Freedom Party (IFP) gained a narrow victory over the ANC in KwaZulu-Natal and won control of the province. The results reinforced the status of the IFP (and the New National Party) as regional rather than national players. While the IFP gained 1.8 million votes in KwaZulu-Natal, its combined vote in the eight other provinces was only 214,000.

1994 Election results

Table 2.2 **A breakdown of the election results**

Party	Number of votes cast	Percentage of the vote	Seats won
African National Congress (ANC)	12,237,655	62.6	252
New National Party (NNP)	3,983,690	20.4	82
Inkatha Freedom Party (IFP)	2,058,294	10.5	43
Freedom Front (FF)	424,555	2.2	9
Democratic Party (DP)	338,426	1.7	7
Pan Africanist Congress (PAC)	243,437	1.2	7
African Christian Democratic Party (ACDP)	88,104	0.5	2
Votes counted	19,533,456		

Percentage poll 87%

The main political parties, 1994

Political party	Description
African National Congress (ANC)	The ANC, with its history of struggle against apartheid and the leadership of Nelson Mandela, had the overwhelming support of the black South Africans. It was a broad organisation which had strong ties with COSATU (trade unions) and the SACP (South African Communist Party). It had some support from the white and coloured communities. The ANC fought the election on the slogan 'A Better Life for All'. Inevitably, promises were made such as to build one million low-cost homes by 1999, which raised the expectations and hopes of the black South Africans.
New National Party (NNP)	The National Party, led by F. W. de Klerk, changed its name to the New National Party and declared that it was now a party for all the people of South Africa. Its main support came from white and coloured South Africans. It came a respectable second with 20% of votes. Its leader became Deputy President and joined the Government of National Unity (GNU). This was the highpoint for the NNP; ten years later the party disbanded in disarray and merged with the ANC.
Inkatha Freedom Party (IFP)	The IFP, under the leadership of Chief Buthelezi, only agreed to participate a week before the elections. Its main aim was to establish an independent Zulu state and it was unhappy with the Constitution which limited the powers of the provincial governments. It joined the GNU.

Nelson Mandela on being sworn in as South Africa's first black President in 1994:

'We shall build a society in which all South Africans, both black and white, will be able to walk tall, without any fear in their hearts – a rainbow nation at peace with itself and the world. We must act together as a united people, for national reconciliation, for nation building.

Let there be justice for all.
Let there be peace for all.
Let there be work, bread, water and salt for all.'

Nelson Mandela

Nelson Mandela was born on 18 July 1918, the son of a tribal chief of the Xhosa nation. He graduated from the University College of Fort Hare and later set up a legal practice with Oliver Tambo in Johannesburg. Both men were leaders of the ANC Youth League which supported boycotts, strikes and acts of civil disobedience.

The introduction of apartheid in 1948 and the brutal use of force by the white regime made him question the ANC's policy of non-violence. In 1961, Mandela went underground to organise the military wing of the ANC. On 2 August 1962 he was sentenced to life imprisonment for attempting to overthrow the government by violent revolution. It was not until 11 February 1990 that he gained his freedom, when he was released from prison by President de Klerk. He was reunited with his wife, Winnie, but their marriage ended and they were divorced in 1996. Nelson Mandela was elected President of the new democratic South Africa in 1994 and retained this post until 1999, when he retired from politics. Mandela preached reconciliation between the races and worked hard to create a new 'rainbow nation'.

Activities

1 Briefly outline the action taken by the National Party to impose apartheid.

2 Explain the terms Homelands and Townships, and discuss why they were criticised.

3 Outline the main political parties who participated in the 1994 election and their performance.

Social and economic issues in South Africa

Legacy of apartheid

The provision of the vote to all citizens ensured that the black South African people would run their own country. The political legacy of apartheid was removed by this action. Much more difficult for the new ANC government would be the removal of the social and economic inequalities between the races. In its 1994 election manifesto, the ANC promised 'a job, a decent home and a chicken in every pot'. Seventeen years on, many Africans are still waiting for this to be achieved. The legacy of apartheid, which created vast inequalities between the races, is outlined in the statistical survey and comments which follow.

Archbishop Desmond Tutu, 1994

'Apartheid has left a ghastly legacy. There is a horrendous housing shortage and high unemployment; health care is inaccessible and not easily affordable by the majority; Bantu education has left us with a massive educational crisis; there is gross maldistribution of wealth and an inequitable sharing of resources with which South Africa is so richly endowed. Some 20% of the population owns 87% of the land. Then there is the hurt and anguish of those who have been victims of this vicious system, those who were forcibly removed from their homes, nearly 4 million people. Those whose loved ones were detained without trial or banned, or who died mysteriously in detention, such as Steve Biko, or at the hands of death squads.'

Figure 2.7 Desmond Tutu ↑

Education

The population growth within the black South African community is one of the challenges facing the government. Sixteen million of the 39 million black African population are under the age of 16. The paradox which South Africa faces is that while it has an unemployment rate of 40%, it is desperately short of skilled and educated black South Africans.

The culture of violence, with 'no education before liberation' being the slogan for a generation of young black South Africans, contributed to the decline of educational standards. This was reflected in the low matriculation results achieved by black South African students (see Figure 2.8). Overcrowded classrooms and few resources were also factors which help to explain poor educational performances and low African literacy rates (see Figure 2.9).

Health

Table 2.3 Health inequalities, 1990

	Infant mortality rate (per 1000 births)	Life expectancy (at birth)
Black	65	60
Coloured	35	62
Asian	14	67
White	8	72

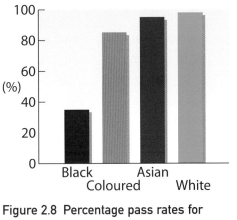

Figure 2.8 Percentage pass rates for high school leaving examinations by race, 1993 ↑

Source: SA Department of Education

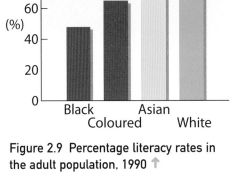

Figure 2.9 Percentage literacy rates in the adult population, 1990 ↑

Source: SA Department of Education

While the white South Africans enjoyed an excellent health service, the non-white population was condemned to a second-rate one which struggled to cope. In 1994 there was a white doctor for every 400 white people and an African doctor for every 44,000 Africans. The situation was worse in the rural areas of the Homelands. Poverty, hunger and disease, combined with the lack of doctors and nurses, explained the high level of malnutrition and undernourishment among rural children.

The existence of a strong private health care sector also created inequalities between the races. In 1994, 90% of the white community relied on private medical care, while the vast majority of black people could not afford private care.

Land

As Archbishop Desmond Tutu highlighted, almost four million non-white people were forcibly removed from their homes by the apartheid regime. The Homeland and Township systems created squatter camps, shanty towns and sprawling townships such as Soweto, where the majority of dwellings lacked basic amenities such as electricity and proper sanitation. In the rural areas many black South Africans were forcibly settled in arid lands which could not sustain them. The outcome was malnutrition, disease and abject poverty.

Cyril Ramaphosa, then ANC General Secretary, stated in 1993 that 'unless we settle the land question we tear South Africa to pieces'. As part of the 1994 peace agreement between de Klerk and Mandela, the white farmers were guaranteed that their land would not be taken from them through nationalisation or expropriation policies.

Activities

1 Refer to the comments made by Archbishop Desmond Tutu in 1994. What evidence does he give to support his statement that 'apartheid has left a ghastly legacy'?

2 Outline the vast inequalities between the races that existed in 1994 in terms of: education, health and land.

Reducing social and economic inequalities

As indicated earlier, all ANC governments since 1994 have faced the apartheid legacy of vast social and economic inequalities and widespread poverty. President Mandela gave hope and raised expectations (1994–99), President Mbeki created disillusionment (1999–2007) and the current President, Jacob Zuma, again promises improvement.

RDP and GEAR

The Reconstruction and Development Programme (RDP) and Growth Employment and Redistribution (GEAR) have been central policies in bringing wealth to the African population and reducing poverty. The government was prepared to upset the trade unions and the South African Communist Party by selling state-owned enterprises, such as electricity and gas, to the private sector. This policy of privatisation provided income to enable the government to improve services. The downside was that private firms raised prices and consumers have had to pay higher charges for essential services. This has placed a heavy financial burden on the poorer sections of society.

GEAR encouraged growth and employment by providing economic stability which encouraged foreign investment. GEAR also promoted a black enterprise culture. 'Wealthy, black and proud of it' is the slogan of the government.

Has GEAR succeeded?

The government highlights that GEAR has brought inflation down and has reduced the budget deficit from 8% in 1997 to 1.5% in 2008.

Every year since 1994 the economically active population available for work increases by about 4% and the available workforce now stands at about 17 million (compared with 11.5 million in 1994). This explains why the official unemployment figure remains at 25%.

The worldwide economic recession has impacted on the economy's growth in 2009–10. However, the 2010 World Cup has help to protect the economy through the massive expansion programme which involved the building of new highways, stadiums and surrounding infrastructure.

A better credit rating and a more stable currency have drawn more private money into South Africa.

The Congress of South African Trade Unions (COSATU) has protected the wage levels of their members but workers who are not in unions suffer from low wages.

Strikes are a common occurrence in South Africa and tension remains between the Triple Alliance of the ANC, SACP (South African Communist Party) and COSATU (see page 115). They accused President Mbeki of 'talking left and acting right'. They were opposed to Mbeki's free-market GEAR policies and supported Zuma in his struggle against Mbeki (see page 115).

Mbeki was aware of the need to transform South African society. The shift of power which took place in the political field must now cover all aspects of economic and social life. To try to narrow the huge gap between black and white, the government embarked on a programme of Affirmative Action.

Affirmative Action

Mandela did not wish to antagonise the white population and did not pass the legislation to compel employers or institutions to discriminate in favour of non-white people. His successor, Thabo Mbeki, used Affirmative Action legislation to speed up the 'transformation of South Africa's economic life'.

There are two major pieces of Affirmative Action legislation – the Employment Equity Act and the Black Economic Empowerment Act.

The Employment Equity Act

The Employment Equity Act, 1998, set up a directorate called 'Equal Opportunities' to ensure that organisations 'democratically represented' the black people of South Africa. The Act decreed that the correct balance of a workforce should be 75% black, 52% female, 5% disabled. The Act promoted reverse discrimination which meant that black South Africans were entitled to preferential treatment in hiring, promotion, university admission and the awarding of government contracts.

Any company which has more than 50 employees is covered by this Act and can be fined up to £100,000 if it does not meet its terms. In an effort to strengthen monitoring and enforcement of the legislation, a National Roving Inspectorate Unit was set up in November 2005.

The Black Economic Empowerment (BEE) Act

The Department of Trade and Industry (DTI) states that 'Our BEE strategy is not affirmative action, although employment equity forms part of it. Nor does it aim to take wealth from white people and give it to blacks. It is essentially a growth strategy, targeting the South African economy's weakest point: inequality. The purpose of BEE is to stimulate economic growth and creating employment.'

The South African government accepts that a review of BEE is necessary to try and include disadvantaged Africans. President Zuma has dismissed calls from the Afrikaner Freedom Front Party to end the discrimination towards young white people as they were not responsible for the inequalities created by apartheid. He stated that 'it was unthinkable for the ANC to abandon it'.

Views of the opposition party, the Democratic Alliance (DA)

The DA is fully behind broad-based black economic empowerment. It believes that if properly implemented, it will pull people into the economy, reduce unemployment and stimulate growth. But there is a view that BEE only benefits the ANC elite and ignores the millions of disadvantaged Africans. The DA supports the favouring of a black, coloured or Indian candidate over a white candidate where candidates are of equal merit.

The controversial fabulous four

It is significant that former ANC leaders who fought against apartheid have crossed over from politics to the boardroom to become millionaires. The four who symbolise the new black elite are Cyril Ramaphosa, once touted as Mandela's successor, Tokyo Sexwale, former ANC provincial premier, Saki Macozoma, former political prisoner, and Patrice Motsepe who is married to an ANC minister. They are aware of the growing criticism coming from fellow black South Africans, but they argue that

Figure 2.10 Cyril Ramaphosa ↑

their goal is to create a million black capitalists. However, Moletsi Mbeki, an economic analyst, claims that BEE has struck 'a fatal blow against the emergence of black entrepreneurship by creating a small class of unproductive, but wealthy black crony capitalists'.

BEE: achievements and criticism

Achievements	Criticisms
The African middle class is now about 3 million and growing. Their new wealth has led to a consumer explosion. Their spending power is now far greater than that of their white counterparts. The number of black middle-class families living in the former white suburbs has increased from 20% in 2004 to 50% in 2009.	Many black-owned firms win government contracts despite submitting higher bids (the government rule is that bids from previously disadvantaged individuals, PDIs, can be up to 10% higher than others). Having won the contracts they sub-contract the work to their losing competitors. In effect the PDI/10% rule constitutes a special tax on all taxpayers with the proceeds going to the black businessmen who win the contract.
In 2005 Anglo American, the mining group, appointed Lazarus Zim as its first black Chief Executive in charge of all its South African operations. State-owned industries such as Eskom now have black majorities on their boards.	Several high-profile black empowerment businesses such as the African Bank and Community Bank have collapsed. Eskom, the state-owned power company, is regarded as inefficient and incompetent, and numerous power cuts took place in 2009. In November 2009, the board's white chairman stood down. The ANC Youth League had denounced him as a racist.
To achieve government contracts, firms must now file a BEE scorecard to prove that they are promoting 'previously disadvantaged individuals' including black, coloured and Asian South Africans. The government spends R12 billion a year on government contracts, much of which benefits black businesses and the black workforce.	Many BEE activities simply enrich a small number of individuals and do not offer any economic benefits to the black majority. White businessmen give directorships and shares to black business people to conform to BEE regulations. Eric Molobi, the chairman of Kagiso Trust and former ANC activist, has been appointed deputy chairman of the Imperial Group, which had revenues of $3 billion a year.

The gap is closing

In a controversial speech in 2004 the then President Thabo Mbeki referred to South Africa as being a land of two nations – one white and rich, the other black and poor. While there are still significant inequalities between the races, progress has been made through the BEE project. There is now a rich African middle class, referred to as the 'Black Diamonds'.

The divide is now not so much based on race but on social class.

White poverty

It is true that rich, white South Africans have retained their wealth since apartheid ended, but many poorly educated white people have sunk into poverty and white beggars are a common sight in South African cities. In 2008 Jacob Zuma, then leader of the ANC, visited a poor white community in Bethlehem in Pretoria. Bethlehem has no electricity, running water or sewage system and the people survive by selling vegetables they grow near the shacks. Solidarity, a union whose base is among white workers, claims that white poverty has increased from 3% in 1994 to 13% today and that their plight had been ignored by Mbeki. One Bethlehem resident stated 'When we tried to apply for food aid and social security payments, we were told by black social workers that you whites can suffer now. When we applied for jobs, we were turned away because of our colour. We are now the victims of the new apartheid.'

'Black Diamonds'

Figure 2.11 A 'Black Diamond', one of South Africa's new black elite →

Evidence of the emergence of a black elite can be found in the number of black people now living in the wealthiest suburbs of South Africa's cities, once the exclusive domain of white citizens. Houghton, the grandest suburb in Johannesburg, has among its growing number of black residents Nelson Mandela and former Regional Premier Tokyo Sexwale. The new black elite now live in their walled estates and in luxury homes with a BMW in the driveway. Their children go to the middle-class mixed-race state schools or to the best private schools. These 'Black Diamonds' are categorised as educated, professional African workers who earn at least R7000 a month. They now number about 3 million and make up nearly a third of the country's buying power. Black Diamond women now represent 40% of all female consumer spending power.

The coloured and Asian community

As stated previously, the coloured community are now the second largest racial group in South Africa (see page 64). Eighty-five per cent of the 4 million coloured people live in the Western Cape, especially around Cape Town, and in the Northern Cape. The majority speak Afrikaans and many feel that they are being ignored by successive ANC governments and that their lives have not improved since 1994 (see box on page 81).

Many of the 1.2 million South African Indians have established themselves as successful businessmen, traders and professionals. Their economic and educational success over the last 40 years and their strong cultural beliefs have brought them at times into conflict with the African majority. In 2002 an African playwright wrote a song called 'Amandiya' which urged Africans to rise against the Indian community. The Indian and coloured communities feel that the policy of Affirmative Action discriminates against them: 'Under apartheid we were not white enough, now we are not black enough'.

Case Study: Rainbow Nation still divided along colour lines

They call it the 'border': the broad snaking railway track cutting through a grimy section of the Cape Flats townships. On one side live black South Africans, on the other the mixed-race coloured community. Dumped here by the apartheid government under segregation, little has changed to integrate communities where grinding poverty is the only common denominator.

According to Winston Baadjies little has changed 15 years after the world hailed a new democratic South Africa as the Rainbow Nation. 'Basically it's still the same. Nobody is coming together, they are still living separately, blacks on that side, coloureds on this side and whites more in the upper-class area'.

Today desegregation has happened fastest in the millionaire and middle-class suburbs where the new black section of the middle class is moving in.

Meanwhile in Gugulethi, the black township, barefoot children in threadbare clothes play with tyres and marbles amid rubble and mud. Across the track in Manenberg, the coloured township, children play surrounded by overcrowded blocks of shoddy flats.

Source: adapted from *The Mail and Guardian*, April 2009

What progress has been made with transformation since 1994?

Distribution of income

Despite declining poverty levels and sustained economic growth, national income inequalities have not reduced. The GINI International index, which measures wealth inequalities, has increased from 0.64 in 1995 to 0.69 in 2007. The gap between the rich and poor in all race groups has grown since 1994. The richest four per cent of South Africans, a quarter of whom are black, now earn a hundred times more than the average person.

The growth in inequality is linked to the emergent black middle class and growing unemployment among the lower deciles of the black population (unemployment increased from 36.2% in 1994 to 46.6% in 2007).

Table 2.4 Percentage total working population aged 16+ by income group and race, 2008

	% of total workforce	Up to R50,000	R50,000–100,000	R100,000–300,000	R300,000–500,000	R500,000–750,000	Above R750,000
Black	75.3	83.0	65.9	47.1	29.9	20.3	16.3
Coloured	8.8	8.3	14.3	9.0	5.6	3.0	2.1
Indian/Asian	2.8	2.2	4.0	5.4	5.1	8.4	4.3
White	13.0	6.5	15.7	38.5	59.5	68.4	77.4
Total workforce	100	75.5	10.1	10.7	2.3	0.8	0.6

Source: SA Government

Fact File

The following facts illustrate how the income has been redistributed between the races over the period 1975 to 2007:

- The black share of income rose from 22% to 42%.
- The white share of income declined from 67% to 45%.
- The coloured share of income increased from 7% to 9%.
- Indian income increased from 2.8% to 4%.

A growing black middle class

- The emergent black middle class is the largest component in an increasingly multiracial national middle class.
- The public service has made substantial progress in achieving employment equity goals.
- Black representation in the public services increased from 76% in 1995 to 88% in 2007.
- In the private sector, white South Africans still hold 65% of senior posts.
- Among the 295 companies listed on the Johannesburg Stock Exchange (JSE) black people comprise 36% of directors.

Activities

1 What is GEAR? Outline its achievements and criticisms.

2 What is Affirmative Action and why was it introduced?

3 Describe the main features of the Employment Equity Act.

4 Outline the benefits and criticisms of BEE.

5 What evidence suggests that social class rather than race is the main cause of wealth and poverty in South Africa?

Tackling poverty

The Presidency Report of 2008 entitled *Towards a Fifteen Year Review* concluded that income poverty had declined in South Africa over the last 15 years and that there had been a significant decline in child poverty. The report stated:

'When using the R322 per person (per month) poverty line, in 1995 about 53% of households was living below that line. In 2009, that figure has decreased to 41%.'

Social grants have played a very critical role in this regard. In 1999, 2.5 million people benefited from grants. By 2009 this figure had risen to over 13 million. The social grants system is the largest form of government support for the poor. Most is given in the form of the child support grant, which reached 7.8 million families in 2007 compared to only 34,000 in 1999.

In February 2009, the then Finance Minister, Trevor Manuel, stated that 'South Africa, proportionally one of the world's biggest spenders on social grants, will spend an extra R13.2 billion on benefits in 2009/10 to help protect poor South Africans during the credit crunch slowdown. The benefit system currently supports 13 million people'. South Africa spends about 12% of total government spending on social protection. President Zuma is considering increasing the eligible age for the child support grant to 18 years of age, subject to affordability.

Despite the decrease in the number of poor people, the report found a widening inequality gap in the country. 'While many poor South Africans were lifting themselves from abject poverty, the rich in South Africa, especially the new black middle classes, were getting richer, most likely due to access to economic opportunities.'

Case Study: Poverty in Mthatha and Mvezo, Eastern Cape

The ANC has done little to improve life in communities like Mthatha and Mvezo in the Eastern Cape. In Mthatha, 43% of the population are unemployed and most depend on social grants from the government. In such poverty violence flourishes. The *South African Medical Journal* concluded that Mthatha's murder rate was 133 per 100,000, more than three times the South African average (see Crime, pages 100–101).

In Mvezo, the village where Mandela was born and an hour's drive from Mthatha, disillusionment with the ANC is widespread. Vincent Ntswayi, 53, sums up his despair: 'My life was better during apartheid, I had employment. Freedom turned out to be just a word. Real freedom, real power, that comes from money and I haven't got any money'.

Education

Under Mandela and Mbeki much has been done to improve the horrendous legacy of African education from the time of apartheid. The government is aware that education and training are crucial for the creation of economic prosperity. There is a shortage of skilled and highly educated black South African workers, yet an abundance of poorly educated, unskilled black South Africans who face a lifetime of formal unemployment.

In 2009 the government invested 21% of the entire budget in education. At over 6% of the country's GDP, this is one of the highest rates in the world. Yet while much has been achieved, such as the introduction of the 'Mandela sandwich' (see page 92), there are still major shortfalls. Fighting the culture of non-attendance and resistance to learning, the pressures caused by population growth, and the legacy of apartheid in terms of provision of resources between the races is a long uphill struggle, but one which is essential to enable South Africa to end poverty, unemployment and illiteracy among its people. Another major problem is the incompetence of many of the officials employed in provincial education departments. Appointment is not based on merit but on racial quotas (see BEE pages 77–79). Again corruption is a major issue. This partially explains why the massive investment in education (spending in 2006 was R12.4 billion, by 2009 it had increased to R19.7 billion) is failing to deliver a culture of learning (see page 85, School Crisis: Eastern Cape).

The new government of President Zuma has set a target to eliminate all mud huts in rural South Africa by 2012. The target in Eastern Cape is to do away with 835 dilapidated schools.

Figure 2.12 Inequality is still a problem in South Africa's school system →

Case Study: School crisis: Eastern Cape

In April 2009 the National Department of Education had to take over the running of the Department of Education in the Eastern Cape. Money allocated to schools never reached teachers and pupils and in some districts, the teacher vacancy rate was 80%.

Conditions at Zandise Junior Primary School in rural Eastern Cape are disgraceful. The 87 children are taught in the shade of a tree with only a blackboard as a resource. The school principal stated that 'When it rains very few children come to school'. The local community is building a mud hut to provide shelter for the pupils as the previous mud hut had collapsed. The school now has four teachers but this is to cover eight school years. Only one teacher taught all the grades.

According to a survey carried out by *The Mail and Guardian* newspaper in June 2009, five of the nine provincial education departments are 'in an administrative and financial mess, seriously undermining learning and teaching'. Excluding Eastern Cape, the following problems were identified:

- The Free State education department had overspent its budget by almost R1 billion.
- Teachers' posts had been frozen in Mpumalanga because of widespread corruption in the department. Three high-placed officials were dismissed for fraud and negligence.
- In Limpopo, Free State and Gauteng teachers and support staff are often paid late.
- In Northern Cape, schoolchildren have no transport because bus operators have not been paid.

Source: *The Mail and Guardian*, June 2009

Table 2.5 **Enrolment in school by age (%)**

	2002	**2007**
5 year olds	40	60
6 year olds	70	88
7–15 year olds	96	98

Source: SA Department of Education

South Africa's education system

South Africa has a single national Education Department and system. Provincial legislatures and local governments have substantial powers to run educational affairs (excluding universities and technikons, further education colleges) subject to a national policy framework.

The South African Schools Act, 1996, ensures that no state schools are racially segregated. While former white schools now take in pupils of all races, many former black South African and disadvantaged schools have no white pupils and have the highest number of matriculation failures. The Act also provided compulsory education for learners between the ages of 7 (Grade 1) and 15 (Grade 9). The first year of education, Grade R, and the last three years are not compulsory. From Grade 10 to Grade 12, students either attend school or engage in Further Education and Training (FET). In 2008 students were presented for the new National Senior Certificate. Under the new system all students have to take seven subjects, including maths, and have to pass six in order to matriculate. Candidates have to achieve 40% in three subjects and 30% in the remaining three to pass. The number of students sitting for the Certificate in 2008 was 560,000, 150,000 more than in 2003. However, the rise in presentations is not reflected in performance and concern has been expressed about the low pass rate (see Table 2.6 on page 88).

South Africa's education system accommodates more than 13 million learners and there is a sizeable and growing private sector. National norms and standards for school funding have been set to address the inequalities between the races. Schools are divided into five categories based on needs: the poorest 20% receive 35% of the resources and the richest 20% receive 5% of the resources. Education is not free in South Africa for most pupils and school fees are paid by parents. This explains why many pupils from the poorest communities (and those who are disadvantaged most in their quality of life) do not attend school. The Department of Education now exempts the poorest 40% of schools (all black South African) from fees. The target is to increase this figure to 60% in 2010. However, provincial education departments do not always provide the poorest schools with the money to cover the non-payment of fees. South Africa has a teacher shortage, made worse by the low number of qualified teachers who actually teach and the number who have died from HIV/AIDS. It is estimated that 50,000 teachers have died from AIDS over the last 5 years.

Matriculation results

The pattern of matriculation results, while highlighting significant progress since 1994, still reflects large inequalities in performance in spite of a more equitable allocation of resources across schools and provinces. Despite the massive investment in education, exam results are falling, although it is difficult to make a clear comparison as the 2008 exam is argued to be more demanding. The only province to have witnessed improvement is Free State. The Western Cape has the best results at 78.6% and Eastern Cape the poorest at 50.0% – clear evidence of massive regional inequalities which also cover wealth and health.

The Institute for Justice and Reconciliation (IJR) states that nearly 80% of high schools are failing their children and that the overwhelming majority of children in the failing schools are black African. The IJR also states 'the best schools are those that were reserved exclusively for white children prior to 1994 and these schools today should enrol the poorest children'. The IJR also argued that the 400 Dinaledi schools should be expanded as these schools were on the way to excellence. The Dinaledi project is a partnership between state schools and the business sector with the emphasis on maths and science. The Afrikaans Teachers' Union argues that the education system is in crisis and that the culture of teaching and learning has disappeared in many rural and township schools (in these areas 43% of the population live below the poverty line). At its 2009 conference its general secretary Chris Klopper stated: 'In 1995 1.5 million pupils started Grade 1 and only 360,000 completed matriculation in 2007. The same happened with the 1996 intake and matric results in 2008. There were 1.2 million pupils who got lost on the way. We want to know what happened to them.' (See Case Study: The Impact of Poverty on Education, page 88.)

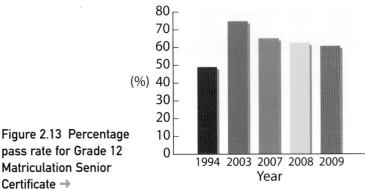

Figure 2.13 Percentage pass rate for Grade 12 Matriculation Senior Certificate →

Source: SA Department of Education

In January 2010 the 2009 matriculation results were published and made depressing reading. Most provinces experienced further decline in the pass rate, with Northern Cape suffering a massive 11% decline. As always, regional inequalities were apparent with the three poorest provinces having the worst results (see Table 2.6).

As well as regional inequalities, racial inequalities are still apparent (see

Figure 2.14). Despite making up less than 10% of the population, more white students pass mathematics than African students.

Table 2.6 **Grade 12 Matriculation Senior Certificate results (provincial results, %)**

Province	2003	2008	2009
Western Cape	87.1	78.6	75.9
Northern Cape	90.7	72.6	61.6
Free State	80.0	62.5	60.1
Gauteng	81.5	76.4	71.8
KwaZulu-Natal	77.2	57.8	57.0
Limpopo	70.0	54.0	48.6
North West	70.5	72.6	72.1
Eastern Cape	60.0	50.0	50.0
Mpumalanga	56.0	51.8	47.9

Source: SA Department of Education

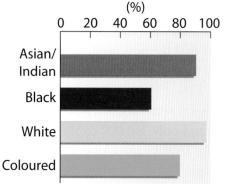

Figure 2.14 2007 matriculation results pass rates by race (based on schools in Mpumalanga Province) →

Source: Department of Education and Independent Examination Board. (These statistics are not totally reliable as they rely on candidates self-classifying themselves; some refuse.)

Case Study: The impact of poverty on education

Ibhongo High School consists of run-down buildings littered with broken glass in the centre of Soweto. Its 2008 matriculation pass rate was 33%. Its headmaster explains why: 'Some learners stay in shacks on their own, some children have nothing to eat, some stay with a parent that is very sick because of AIDS. Three or four out of ten girls get pregnant and drop out of school. It is not that our pupils are not willing to learn, but because of social and health reasons, they lose the interest to learn.'

Table 2.7 Education level, selected provinces, 1996–2008 (%)

	EC	WC	MP	GP	LP
1996 no schooling	20.9	6.7	29.4	9.5	36.9
2008 no schooling	12.4	3.2	17.9	5.0	18.8

EC Eastern Cape, WC Western Cape, MP Mpumalanga, GP Gauteng, LP Limpopo

Source: SA Department of Education

Modernisation of schools

Successive governments have placed the upgrading of schools as a priority and progress has been made in providing basic infrastructure within schools, such as electricity, water and sanitation. However, as the situation in Ibhongo High and Zandise Junior Primary School indicates, much still needs to be done.

A 2008 survey found that a quarter of the country's 29,000 schools were in a poor condition, while 61% of rural schools had no sanitation.

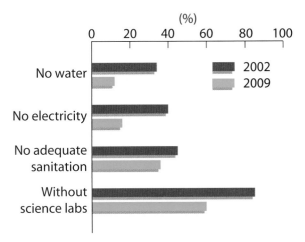

Figure 2.15 The infrastructure of schools →

Source: National Education Management Infrastructure, 2010

University and technikon students

Despite the shortcomings in attainment, a significant change has taken place in higher education. There is clear evidence of progress. Black South Africans now make up more than 65% of university and technikon students. Under BEE legislation all higher-education institutions must have equity targets to ensure that African students are not under-represented. White students argue that they are being discriminated against but can take no action as the Constitution supports 'Black Transformation'.

The former Afrikaans University of the Free State reflects the racial diversity in higher education. The student population is made up of 57% African and 36% white, mainly Afrikaner. In October 2009 the University elected its first ever African Vice Chancellor. However, racial tension and controversy haunt the University. In 2007 a video recording of four white students tormenting and humiliating African university catering staff shocked the nation. Among other humiliations, the workers were shown on their hands and knees, forced to eat food the students had apparently urinated on. All four students were suspended or expelled and all face human rights charges in the Equality Court.

The following statistics illustrate the progress made.

- The number of black students enrolling at universities and technikons increased by almost 101% between 1996 and 2006. By 2002 they were 60% of the total – compared with 40% in 1993.
- In contrast the number of white students enrolled went down by 20% between 1996 and 2006 with their share of the total declining sharply from 46% to 26.5%.
- At the other end of the educational spectrum, the government's Adult Basic Education and Training (ABET) programme has led to a steady increase in the literacy rate of adults which now stands at 75%. The Kha Ri Guide (*Let us Learn*) mass literacy campaign was launched in 2008. The Government has pledged to spend R6 billion over five years to enable 4.7 million South Africans to achieve literacy by 2013. However, significant provincial inequalities remain. Provinces with the largest number of illiterates are KwaZulu-Natal, Limpopo and the Eastern Cape. The lowest numbers occur in the Western Cape and the Free State.

Activities

Tackling poverty

1 Outline the main findings of the *Towards a Fifteen Year Review*.

2 What evidence supports the view that poverty has declined but inequalities have widened?

Education

1 What evidence supports the view that the incompetence of education departments is to blame for shortfalls in education provision?

2 Describe the South African education system and new exam reforms.

3 To what extent has progress been made in exam results, modernisation of schools and African entry to further and higher education?

Health

Under Mandela and Mbeki significant progress has been made in improving primary health care (PHC) in both urban and rural areas. For those not covered by medical aid schemes, free health care is provided at public PHC facilities such as clinics and community health care centres. Some 40% of all South Africans live in poverty and 75% of these live in rural areas where health services are least developed. Regional inequalities reflect the urban–rural divide. Gauteng and Western Cape are highly urbanised and have the best health provision. Malnutrition is a major problem in rural areas alongside recent outbreaks of cholera in KwaZulu-Natal and tuberculosis in the Eastern Cape. Since 1996, eleven state-of-the-art hospitals have been built to tackle the poor hospital facilities available in provinces such as the Eastern Cape.

A key weapon against ill health and disease has been the availability of a clean water supply. Over the last 15 years, 11 million South Africans have been provided with a clean water supply. As with other things, regional inequalities still exist in the percentage of households with no toilet facility. Child mortality rates double when there is no access to clean water.

South Africans' use of the health service has doubled over the last 8 years and in 2008–09 health expenditure reached R15.1 billion, its highest ever figure.

There is a very strong private health service which inevitably reflects a racial imbalance in favour of white people and ensures that they have access to better health provision. The private sector consumes R33 billion and serves 8 million people, while the public sector spends R33 billion and serves over 40 million people. In short, over 40 million South Africans are uninsured. At present hospital patients who do not have private insurance pay for examinations and treatment on a sliding scale in accordance with their income and number of dependents. Those who meet the 'poverty criteria' have their fees paid by the provincial government.

Figure 2.16 Health care in South Africa →

State health provision faces severe problems. Under the previous president, Thabo Mbeki, state hospitals were under-funded despite the burgeoning AIDS epidemic (see pages 93–96). This was reflected in the low pay of state health care workers including doctors. Many health care workers have moved to the private sector or have gone abroad to countries such as the UK. This has led to staff shortages including 11,000 vacant doctors' posts and an estimated 50% shortfall in nursing staff at the country's 386 hospitals. Health unions claim staff morale is low and that there is a shortage of vital medical equipment.

President Zuma recognises the crisis in the state health system. In his first State of the Nation address in 2009, he stated 'salaries, working conditions and management skills need to be improved'. A new salary structure has been agreed; however, some authorities have been slow to implement it, leading to further industrial action from doctors in KwaZulu-Natal and the Free State.

Table 2.8 **Doctors per 100,000 of the population, by province (selected), 2008**

Province	Doctors
Western Cape	36.8
Gauteng	34.5
Eastern Cape	12.2
Limpopo	9.5
North West	12.1

Source: SA Health Statistics, 2008

Primary health care

The primary health care programme offers a comprehensive range of services delivered by health professionals and associated organisations, such as school and nutritional services. Water and sanitation services, both of which have an obvious connection to health, are also included.

The strategy embraces health education, nutrition, family planning, immunisation, screening for common diseases, HIV/AIDS education and counselling, maternal and child health, oral health and the provision of essential drugs.

Projects such as the National Primary School Nutrition Project for needy primary school children have improved educational achievement as well as health standards. Every day about 6 million children in over 18,000 schools munch on a 'Mandela sandwich'. This has increased attendance at school and improved concentration and alertness levels.

Immunisation against tuberculosis, whooping cough, diphtheria, polio and measles is available free of charge to all children under the age of six. Such has been the success of this programme that South Africa has been declared polio-free by the Global Certification Commission.

Alongside the free health care programme for children under six and pregnant women, an impressive clinic building and upgrading programme has been implemented. Around 3500 primary health care clinics have been built and more than 700 mobile clinics set up, providing basic health care in the most remote and isolated areas.

HIV/AIDS

The one regret Nelson Mandela has of his period in office was his failure to tackle the outbreak of HIV/AIDS in South Africa. Unfortunately his successor, Thabo Mbeki, was very slow to react to the crisis. HIV/AIDS is the biggest health and social issue facing South Africa today and Mbeki was criticised, even by Nelson Mandela, for his failure to accept that AIDS is caused by HIV. For this reason Mbeki initially refused to give free anti-AIDS drugs to all HIV-positive pregnant women and their children.

In November 2001, a small group of AIDS activists, the Treatment Action Campaign (TAC), took the government to the highest court of the land, the Constitutional Court, to force it to provide the anti-AIDS drug, Nevirapine, free to mother and child at birth. The Court ruled in favour of TAC and, in October 2002, the government announced that it would investigate ways of providing the anti-retroviral drugs that keep people alive – a dramatic reversal of policy. The nationwide civil disobedience campaign, led by TAC leader Zackie Achmat, had been successful.

TAC was especially critical of the then Minister of Health, Dr Manto Tshabalala-Msimang, who continually downplayed the AIDS epidemic and the use of anti-AIDS drugs. In June 2005 she argued that AIDS sufferers should use traditional remedies such as garlic and olives. ANC sources had accused TAC of serving the interest of the pharmaceutical companies. In December 2009, Dr Tshabalala-Msimang died, and to the anger of many received an official state funeral. Dr Stephen Lewis, the United Nations' special envoy for HIV/AIDS in Africa until 2007, said that the policies of Tshabalala-Msimang and Mbeki were 'wrong, immoral and negligent, more worthy of a lunatic fringe than a concerned and compassionate state'. Independent studies from Harvard University claim that about 350,000 people had died because of the delay in providing anti-retrovirals to AIDS patients.

Fact File

AIDS pandemic: the present and the future?

- Life expectancy has dropped from 62 to 47.
- Over 60,000 children aged between 1 month and 5 years die each year.
- 35% of deaths among pregnant women are caused by AIDS.

- Nearly 5 million children will be orphaned by 2016.
- Just under 1000 South Africans die every day from AIDS.
- Almost 40% of women aged between 25 and 29 are infected by HIV/AIDS.
- 500,000 people are infected each year.

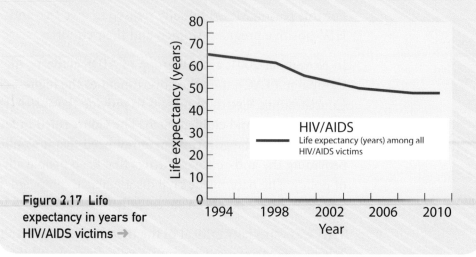

HIV/AIDS
Life expectancy (years) among all HIV/AIDS victims

Figure 2.17 Life expectancy in years for HIV/AIDS victims →

Figure 2.18 Nkosi Johnson ↑

'I want people to understand AIDS – to be careful and respect AIDS. You can't get AIDS if you touch, hug or hold hands with someone who is infected. Care for us, and accept us, we are all human beings, we are normal. We have needs just like everyone else. Don't be afraid of us. I just wish the government would give anti-AIDS drugs to all HIV-positive pregnant women and their children.'

These are the words spoken by 11-year-old Nkosi Johnson at an International AIDS Conference held in Durban in South Africa in July 2000. Nkosi had been born HIV-positive and had been abandoned by his mother. He was sent to a hospice to die. There he was adopted by a white woman, Gail Johnson, and so he outlived both his parents (who died of AIDS). Within a year after the conference he was dead. Such was the impact he had made on the world community that his death was mourned around the world.

Figures of death

Health professionals and the South African government have been locked in a bitter struggle over the real scale of the HIV/AIDS epidemic. There is still a stigma attached to AIDS and many AIDS-related deaths have been diagnosed as being other illnesses such as tuberculosis and influenza. This attitude is slowly changing, helped by the actions of political leaders such as Chief Buthelezi and Nelson Mandela. Both leaders publicly stated that their children had died of AIDS. In August 2004, Buthelezi buried both a son and a daughter and in January 2005 Mandela's son died of the disease.

The National HIV Survey 2007 indicated that KwaZulu-Natal, Mpumalanga and the Free State have the highest HIV prevalence and that among the races, Africans had the highest HIV prevalence (see Table 2.9). According to government figures, 5.7 million South Africans suffer from HIV/AIDS and it is women in their mid- to late twenties who are the hardest hit. In January 2009 Statistics South Africa reported that between 1997 and 2007 the annual number of registered deaths of women aged 25–34 had quadrupled and for men aged 30–39 had doubled. This explains why life expectancy in South Africa is far below what it was during the apartheid era (see Figure 2.19).

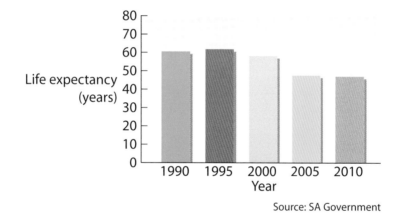

Source: SA Government

Figure 2.19 Life expectancy in South Africa (years) →

The resignation of President Mbeki in December 2007 (see page 109) led to greater urgency in tackling the AIDS crisis through treatment and prevention. In December 2009 on World AIDS Day, President Zuma announced ambitious plans to expand the free treatment for HIV-positive babies and pregnant women by April 2010. Zuma had already appointed Dr Aaron Motsoaledi as his health minister, described by AIDS activists such as TAC as 'a man who trusts science and is willing to learn from past mistakes'. Zuma's Government had earlier set a target of getting 80% of those who need AIDS drugs on them by 2011. In response to a plea by Zuma, the USA announced it would give South Africa $560 million in 2010 to fight AIDS.

Table 2.9 Estimated figures for HIV prevalence among South Africans aged 2 years and older by sex, race and province (selected)

Sex and race	Prevalence (%)
Male	8.2
Female	13.3
African	13.3
White	0.6
Coloured	1.9
Indian	1.6
Province (selected)	**Prevalence (%)**
KwaZulu-Natal	16.5
Mpumalanga	15.2
Guateng	10.8
Northern Cape	5.4
Western Cape	1.9

Source: SA Department of Health, 2009

Activities
Health and HIV/AIDS

1 Outline the progress which has been made in the provision of primary health care and other health improvements.

2 What evidence supports the view that health inequalities are a major problem? (Refer to regional inequalities and the role of the private sector.)

3 Why was President Mbeki criticised over his handling of the HIV/AIDS crisis and what action has President Zuma taken?

4 What evidence suggests that HIV/AIDS is the biggest health crisis in South Africa?

Land and housing

Mandela was aware of the enormous task his government faced in order to provide adequate housing. There was a distinct racial and urban–rural divide. These differences were still obvious in 2001 (see Table 2.10 and Figure 2.20). The situation was not helped by an influx of people into the cities from the rural areas.

It became clear that the 1994 election promise to deliver 1 million new homes over a 5-year period was unrealistic. This figure was retained but was extended over a 10-year period with many of the houses being 'starter homes' rather than fully completed units. The target was achieved by December 2000 but still left a housing backlog of 3 million homes. Since then a further 2 million homes have been built. The creation of an African middle class has led to a growth in the number of homes provided by the private sector. Between 1998 and 2008 the number of black property owners increased by just under 70%. Townships such as Soweto now have their middle-class area and a shopping mall was opened several years ago. In the Diepkloof neighbourhood of Soweto new cars are parked next to elegant houses protected by their security gates.

Progress has been made in providing basic amenities such as electricity and running water. The electrification programme has seen 3.6 million homes electrified between 1994 and 2008. Those on a low income receive a free monthly allocation of 50KWh.

The Community Water Supply Programme has brought clean water to over 9 million mainly rural homes. Unfortunately, a culture of non-payment of rents and amenities charges still persists. The situation has not been helped by the privatisation of services which has led to an increase in charges. The government provides 6000 litres of water per household per month free of charge to more than two-thirds of South Africa's population. While this is welcomed, the Anti-Privatisation Forum (APF) argues that an average family of six needs about 20,000 litres of water each month. Pre-paid water meters are being installed in the townships and this has created unrest among many residents. In Soweto and Johannesburg police had to protect workers installing pipes.

A significant number of the new black middle class have moved into the former exclusively white areas. They live in mansions with spacious grounds or luxury apartments with controlled entry and security guards. In contrast those black South Africans who live in informal settlements (squatter camps) have witnessed little progress since 1994. Their makeshift homes lack electricity and sanitation provision, crime is high and health is poor. Schooling is basic; many of the children do not complete secondary school and do not have the skills to contribute to or benefit from the BEE programmes. Gauteng and North West have the largest number of informal settlements (see Figure 2.20). There has been a shift from rural to urban areas. Twenty per cent of people in the main urban areas are new migrants.

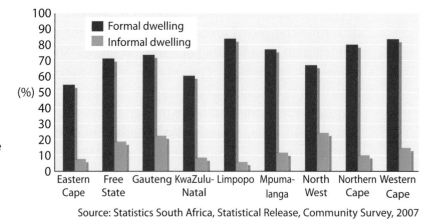

Figure 2.20 Percentage of households living in formal and informal dwellings, 2007 →

Source: Statistics South Africa, Statistical Release, Community Survey, 2007

Table 2.10 **Access to basic services (%)**

Households	1996	2001	2007
Using electricity			
For lighting	58	70	80
For cooking	47	51	67
For heating	45	49	59
Water			
Equivalent to or above Reconstruction and Development Programme (RDP) standard (200m to communal tap)	62	74	88

Source: SA Community Survey, 2009

Land reform

Land reform, especially in the countryside, is a major issue. A new Department of Land Affairs was created in 1994 with responsibility for developing and implementing a policy of land reform. The plan involves:

- Compensating those who lost their land because of apartheid laws.
- Redistributing the productive land to those who were disadvantaged.
- Creating an independent Commission on Restitution of Land Rights as well as a Land Claims Court. Any claimant will have to prove that he or she was dispossessed after 1913 without financial compensation or alternative land being provided.
- Setting up the Land Reform Pilot Programme to 'establish mechanisms for state-assisted entry into the land market for the most disadvantaged sectors of rural society'.
- Giving tenants the right to buy the land on which they farm and protection from eviction.

The original Reconstruction and Development Plan (RDP) promise of redistribution of 30% of agricultural land within 5 years was totally unrealistic. The revised target date of 2014 will not be achieved at the present rate of progress; R70 billion is needed to meet that target and the provisional amount allocated over the next four years is only R30 billion. Black ownership of land has increased from 13% in 1994 to 18%. Unless the government were to resort to mass confiscation as Mugabe has done in Zimbabwe, it has virtually no hope of doubling black ownership of the land. The government would argue that its record on dealing with the 80,000 redistribution claims is excellent. By July 2009, 75,000 land cases costing R4.4 billion had been settled by the Chief Land Claims Commission at a cost of R16 billion. Most people in urban areas prefer cash compensation to land redistribution. This therefore partly explains the limited increase in black land ownership.

Under a separate land-restitution programme to compensate victims of forced evictions during the apartheid years, a further 2.5 million hectares have been returned to those who were dispossessed. However, more than half of these new black farms have failed, usually due to a combination of lack of money and skills. A recent failure was an ostrich farm near Pretoria. The group of small-scale black farmers abandoned the starving animals. The government stepped in and applied for the first time a 'use it or lose it' policy and claimed back the land for use by new black farmers. Much more successful has been the partnership between 70 white farmers in the Eastern Cape, the University of Fort Hare and black farmers. The Fort Hare Dairy Trust is a BEE initiative whereby ownership is shared between the white farmers (35%) and 600 black dairy farmer workers. The University contributes research and scientific knowledge to the farm and the Land Bank has provided loans.

The 'willing buyer–willing seller' principle has been at the core of South Africa's land settlement, guaranteeing that land will be acquired by the state at fair prices and given to the landless black population. The government has the power to force a compulsory sale if the white farmer rejects the original offer. This policy, despite its good intentions, has had an adverse effect on agricultural production. White farmers are reluctant to invest in improvements, while others have abandoned their farms. Agri SA, the white farmers' union, claims that about 700 of its members have responded to offers from neighbouring African states and are now farming in these countries. Since 2007 South Africa has become a net importer of food, after decades of self-sufficiency.

Fears of white farmers

The Afrikaner farming community is concerned that events in Zimbabwe, where the government orchestrated nationwide land invasion of white farms, will encourage further attacks on their property. Since 1994 about

3000 farmers and their families have been murdered and more than 10,000 attacked. Farmers claim that this is an organised attack on white farms with unemployed black people being paid £200 a time to ambush and kill. A government enquiry denied that this is the case and claimed that the high murder rate of farmers reflects South Africa's high murder rate – over 25,000 South Africans are murdered every year.

At the grassroots level there has been a significant increase in militancy with the formation of the Landless People's Movement and a series of threatened land invasions. The Pan Africanist Congress (PAC) regards Mugabe as an African hero and encourages land invasions. Supho Makhombathi, representing landless impoverished farm labourers, urges action: 'We are still living in slavery. We have given the government an ultimatum to give us land or we will simply follow the examples of our brothers in Zimbabwe and invade.'

The government has reassured white farmers that there will be no seizure of their farms. In May 2005, the Constitutional Court, in a landmark judgment, upheld farmers' property rights after squatters had invaded a white farm.

Crime

The fear and impact of crime is one issue that unites all races. While many white people and rich Africans seek safety in their walled estates, ordinary black and coloured South Africans protect their families as best they can. The availability of guns is a major problem. You can buy an AK47 rifle in any taxi queue for £30. On average, 50 murders take place every day. Of these, 27 are caused by guns.

Case Study: Why has there been a crime explosion in South Africa?

- The dismantling of the rigid controls imposed by the security forces in the apartheid years has brought crime into the former white suburbs.

- The apartheid years created a culture of violence at the political level between the ANC and Inkatha in KwaZulu-Natal.

- The association of law enforcement and the rule of law with the apartheid regime have created a lack of respect for the police within the black community.

- The vast inequalities in terms of wealth in South Africa have created a 'war' between the 'haves' and the 'have nots'.

- Massive influxes of poor people from the countryside to the towns and the arrival of illegal immigrants (estimated at 4 million) from other African countries have created a group in society who ignore its laws.

Official government figures clearly indicate that South Africa is a less violent country than previously. The number of murders has declined by 30% since 1994 – the 2009 figure is 18,148 per year. The number of attempted murders has also declined over the past five years from 30,076 to 18,298. However, this still represents 50 murders a day, making South Africa one of the most dangerous places to live. This figure equates to 37 murders per 100,000 South Africans (see Figure 2.21). The Democratic Alliance argues that many crimes are not reported as the public have little faith in the culprits being caught. In a 2008 opinion poll, 57% of the public believed that crime levels had increased. Crimes of rape and aggravated robbery at residential premises have increased and this explains the fear factor experienced by South African citizens.

In 2009, President Zuma promised tough action against criminals to ensure a peaceful 2010 World Cup Finals. He appointed Bheki Cele as National Commissioner of police. Cele replaced Jackie Selebi who was charged with corruption (see pages 119–120). The new Commissioner promised to shake up the police and root out corruption. He stated 'the pool of ugliness will be the number of police who are arrested because they are corrupt'. The target is to increase the police force to 183,000 well-qualified officers.

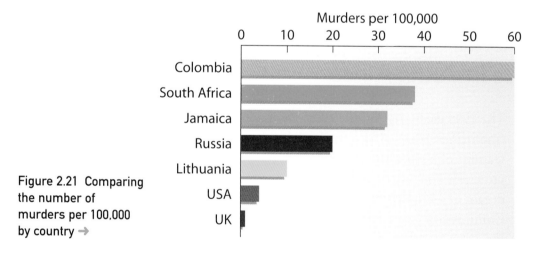

Figure 2.21 Comparing the number of murders per 100,000 by country →

The new hardline policy extends to police being allowed to shoot to kill if a suspect is armed. In October 2009, Police Captain Charl Scheepers from the Brooklyn police station in Pretoria was shot dead after shouting three times to a criminal to drop his gun. However, critics of this policy highlight the high number of individuals shot dead by the police. In the period 2008–9, 556 suspects, including 32 innocent bystanders, were shot and killed by the police. This figure is not far off the 1976 figure of 653 shot dead by the apartheid police during the black student protests.

Activities

Land and housing

1 Describe the progress made in the provision of adequate housing and basic services.

2 Outline the government's policy on land reform.

3 Outline the fears of white farmers.

Crime

1 Why has there been a crime explosion in South Africa?

2 What action has the government taken and with what success?

Essay questions

1 South Africa is a land of two nations – one white and rich, the other black and poor. Discuss. (15)

2 To what extent has the Black Economic Empowerment (BEE) Act reduced inequalities? (15)

3 Critically examine the view that inequalities exist only between different racial groups. (15)

Political issues in South Africa

The 1994 elections and the creation of a liberal, progressive Constitution tranformed South Africa into a stable multi-party democracy with all the features of a pluralist society including a free press and an independent judiciary. Four successive elections have been held and Nelson Mandela's dream of a rainbow nation has been achieved. The Truth and Reconciliation Commission (see page 103) has brought closure to the horrors of apartheid. Yet some fear that the dominance of the ANC and the corrupt activities of some of its members are turning the country into a one-party state where criticism of the government, especially when Mbeki was President, is seen as white racism or if by blacks, as a betrayal of fellow Africans. Jacob Zuma's comment in 2008 that 'the ANC will rule South Africa until Jesus returns' horrified many South Africans for its arrogance.

While South Africa has on paper a federal system of government, the reality is that the central government totally dominates the provinces. Only in Western Cape is there an alternative to ANC rule; in 2009 the Democratic Alliance (DA) gained overall control of the province. However, there is concern that the ANC will attempt to further reduce the powers of the provinces to weaken the power of the Western Cape provincial government.

The Truth and Reconciliation Commission, 1996–2002

The Truth and Reconciliation Commission (TRC), chaired by retired Archbishop Desmond Tutu, was set up to establish as complete a picture as possible of the 'causes, nature and extent of the gross violations of human rights committed between 1960 and 10 May 1994'.

The Commission travelled round South Africa listening to the heartbreaking stories of those who had lost their loved ones. The Commission had the power to grant an amnesty to anybody whose crime had a political objective as long as they admitted their wrongdoing.

In general, the black South African population, with the exception of supporters of Chief Buthelezi, welcomed the Commission. The white community had their reservations, especially supporters of the NNP and extreme right-wing white organisations. Victims of apartheid had the opportunity to share their grief with the nation and to discover what had happened to their loved ones. Ordinary white people could no longer pretend that apartheid was simply a bad system which had made mistakes. The hearings, aired on television, shocked and horrified the nation. The revelations damaged the National Party and led to the resignation of de Klerk.

In October 1998 the Commission presented its interim findings. While the report accused the National Party, especially P. W. Botha, and the Inkatha Freedom Party of being responsible for the bulk of the apartheid-era atrocities, it also accused the ANC of human rights abuse. The only member of the ANC directly named was Winnie Madikizela-Mandela.

In 2002 the TRC's final two reports were given to President Mandela with a request that the government carry out its legal obligation to provide reparation to the 22,000 victims who testified to the Commission. Finally, in April 2003 the government announced that it would give victims a £30,000 payment, which fell short of what the Commission had recommended. The government also stated that it would not take out any lawsuit against corporations or support any taken out by victims of apartheid.

The Constitution of South Africa

The Constitution includes a Bill of Rights which guarantees an extensive range of human rights. This includes equality before the law, the right to life including the abolition of the death penalty, and freedom of speech and religion.

The Constitution provides for an independent judiciary. The Constitutional Court is the highest court in the land. It deals with the interpretation, protection and enforcement of the Constitution. It deals exclusively with constitutional matters. The Constitutional Court plays a crucial role in upholding the rights of the citizens of South Africa. There are eleven judges including the Chief Justice. One of its most recent decisions was to uphold the right of South African citizens living abroad to vote in the 2009 national elections.

The Constitution makes clear reference to the need to address the inequalities created by apartheid. Article 9.2 states: 'To promote achievement of equality, legislative and other measures designed to protect or advance persons or categories of persons disadvantaged by unfair treatment may be taken.'

Central Government

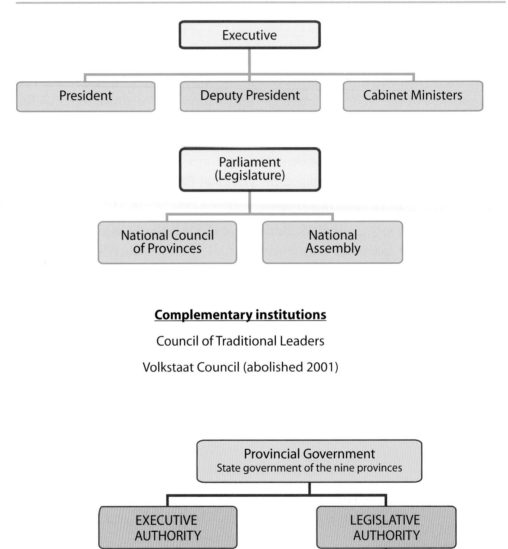

Complementary institutions

Council of Traditional Leaders

Volkstaat Council (abolished 2001)

Parliament

South Africa has a bicameral (two-chamber) parliament consisting of a National Assembly (400 members) and the National Council of Provinces (NCOP). The council has two roles, both as an upper house and also as a body with special responsibilities to protect provincial interests. The NCOP consists of 90 delegates (ten from each province) and ten delegates representing local government. Elections for both houses are held every 5 years based on a system of proportional representation.

Figure 2.22 The South African Parliament in Pretoria →

The President and the Cabinet

The President is elected by the National Assembly from among its members. He or she is the executive head of state and leads the Cabinet. The President may not serve more than two 5-year terms in office.

The Cabinet consists of the President, the Deputy President and 25 Ministers. The President appoints the Deputy President and Ministers, and may dismiss them. Thabo Mbeki dismissed his deputy, Jacob Zuma, in 2008.

Table 2.11 **Presidents of South Africa since the apartheid era**

President	Terms of office
Nelson Mandela	1994–99
Thabo Mbeki	2000–08 (forced to resign)
Kgaleme Motlanthe	2008–09
Jacob Zuma	2009–present

Law making

Legislation may be introduced in the National Assembly only by Cabinet members, Deputy Ministers or a member of a National Assembly committee.

Bills amending the Constitution require two-thirds majority in the National Assembly as well as a supporting vote of six of the nine provinces represented in the NCOP. Any bill amending Section 1 of the Constitution, which sets out the state's founding values, requires a 75% majority in the National Assembly.

Volkstaat Council

The Volkstaat Council consisted of twenty members elected by the MPs who supported the establishment of an Afrikaner Homeland (Volkstaat). In 1996 it made its submission on self-determination for the Afrikaner people. President Mbeki abolished this Council in 2001. Afrikaners have set up a 'white homeland' in Orania, Northern Cape. It is a thriving community of over 800 Afrikaners who do not wish to be part of the rainbow nation.

Provincial government

All nine provinces have their own legislature and government led by a Premier. In 2009 eight of the nine premiers were appointed by Jacob Zuma. This ensures that the ANC leadership controls the provincial parties and weakens the powers of the provincial governments. Provincial constitutions and laws must correspond with the National Constitution as confirmed by the Constitutional Court. Provinces have legislative powers over agriculture, cultural affairs, education except higher education, environment, health services, housing, local government, police, welfare services, and urban and rural development.

Local government

There are 283 local councils referred to as municipalities, and large cities such as Cape Town and Johannesburg have their own metropolitan municipalities. The Zuma Government is at present reviewing the role of local government as many municipalities are failing to deliver basic services.

The South African Constitution:

Maintains unitary government. **The Constitution of South Africa shall provide for the establishment of one sovereign state, a common South African citizenship and a democratic system of government committed to achieving equality between men and women and people of all races.**

Supports cultural identity. **The diversity of language and culture shall be acknowledged and protected, and conditions for their promotion shall be encouraged.**

Offers limited powers to the provinces. **The powers granted to the provinces are to be used to improve the well-being of their inhabitants in accordance with the policies and priorities of the National Government.**

Elections

National elections take place every 5 years using a closed-list, proportional representation system known as the National List, where the percentage of votes cast for a political party closely match the percentage of seats won by a political party. The voters do not vote for a particular candidate but vote for a party. This ensures strict party loyalty as the party leader can remove a candidate from the list. It also encourages the formation of new parties: in 2004 Patricia Lille created the Independent Democrats and in 2008–09 supporters of Thabo Mbeki left the ANC and formed the Congress of the People (COPE). This weakens the formation of a strong opposition to the ANC as it only takes about 35,000 votes to obtain a seat in the National Parliament. Tony Leon, then leader of the Democratic Alliance, called it 'the cannibalisation of the opposition'.

Figure 2.23 People queuing to vote in a South African election →

A further concern has been a decline in registration and in voting turnout (see Figure 2.27, page 113), although turnout was higher in the 2009 election with the emergence of COPE. While turnout is significantly higher than turnout in the UK, it is clear that a sizeable number of South Africans are disillusioned that the promises made in 1994 have not been delivered and they see no point in registering. Many Africans do not choose to vote for the ANC based on their policies or their record, but base their support on their loyalty to the party of liberation and Nelson Mandela.

There have been three further successful elections since 1994. Here is a brief summary of the 1999 and 2004 elections won by the ANC leader Thabo Mbeki and the 2009 election won by ANC leader Jacob Zuma.

The 1999 election

The election result was a personal triumph for Thabo Mbeki. The ANC increased its support, winning 66.3% of the vote and just failing to achieve a two-thirds majority which would have enabled the ANC to change the

Constitution. In contrast, the election was a disaster for the New National Party and a disappointment for the new party, The United Democratic Movement. The Democratic Party emerged as the official opposition, benefiting from the collapse of the New National Party.

The ANC once again controlled seven of the nine provinces and shared power in KwaZulu-Natal with Inkatha. In the Western Cape, the former stronghold of the National Party, the ANC won the most votes but a coalition between the New National Party and the Democratic Party prevented the ANC from taking office. The Afrikaans-speaking Freedom Front witnessed a significant decline in support, dropping from nine to three members of the National Assembly.

As stated, the election was a disaster for the New National Party with its support falling from 3.9 million in 1994 to 1.9 million in 1999. The party which ruled South Africa from 1948 to 1994, and had been part of the Government of National Unity, was now reduced to the status of a minority party. It also lost overall control of the Western Cape and was forced to form a coalition with the Democratic Party.

The Democratic Party, traditionally the home of white, English-speaking liberals, achieved a huge increase in its vote from the 2% gained in 1994. Its leader, Tony Leon, had displayed a high profile in the Mandela parliament. The Democratic Party criticised the ANC for not doing enough to combat South Africa's high crime rate and unemployment rates, and promised to act as a watchdog over a powerful ANC.

The 2004 election

The election result in 2004 was a further personal triumph for Thabo Mbeki. The ANC won a landslide victory, gaining almost 70% of the vote in South Africa's third democratic election, its biggest win in ten years of power. For the first time ever it was the largest party in all of the nine provinces; only in KwaZulu-Natal and the Western Cape did the ANC not achieve absolute majorities and in these provinces the ANC ruled in coalition governments. Most importantly, the ANC gained control of KwaZulu-Natal, ending ten years of IFP rule in the province. The Democratic Alliance consolidated its position as the official opposition while the NNP suffered electoral annihilation, with its support falling from 3.9 million in 1994 to 251,000 in 2004, even losing out to the newly formed Independent Democrats. In 2005 the NNP disbanded and merged with the ANC, much to the anger of many Afrikaners, including former President F. W. de Klerk. The vote for the Inkatha Freedom Party continued to fall and, for the first time, the party lost control of KwaZulu-Natal.

As the ANC had gained a two-thirds majority in the National Assembly, it was able to change the Constitution if it so wished. Consequently, the party encouraged President Mbeki to consider changing the Constitution to enable the President to run for more than two terms.

Figure 2.24 Chief Buthelezi, leader of the Inkatha Freedom Party →

Thabo Mbeki, President 1999–2007

Thabo Mbeki replaced Nelson Mandela as President of South Africa and achieved two impressive election victories. He was chief architect of the country's economic recovery and his achievements of reducing inflation, boosting economic growth and allocating significant funds to public spending persuaded the international community to accept South Africa's bid to host the 2010 football World Cup. Yet his party colleagues forced him to resign in humiliating circumstances in 2007 as they switched their support to Zuma. Mbeki lacked the charisma of Mandela and Zuma, and his intolerance of criticism and the centralisation of power in his own hands made him unpopular. The ANC's trade union and communist allies felt ignored and Mr Mbeki's resistance to the scientific evidence on HIV/AIDS was a disaster for the country (see page 93).

His dismissal of his deputy Zuma in 2005 and his decision to run for a third term against Zuma was the last straw. The party faithful preferred Zuma, despite the corruption charges against him.

Figure 2.25 Thabo Mbeki →

The 2009 election

The 2009 election result was a personal triumph for Jacob Zuma and the ANC. Corruption charges against Zuma had been thrown out on a technicality but respectable figures such as Archbishop Desmond Tutu questioned his suitability as a leader. Tutu stated prior to the election: 'At the present time, I can't pretend to be looking forward to have him as President.' The ANC had suffered internal dissent in September 2008 when the ANC National Executive Committee forced Thabo Mbeki to resign as President. Supporters of Mbeki announced the formation of a breakaway party, the Congress of the People (COPE), led by former ANC defence minister Mosiuoa Lekota and former Gauteng leader Mbhazima Shilowa. The creation of this party galvanised the ANC and under the leadership of the charismatic populist Jacob Zuma they fought a professional and expensive electoral campaign.

The result was an overwhelming victory for the ANC, who won almost 66% of the votes, just failing to gain the two-thirds majority necessary to change the Constitution. Their greatest triumph was in KwaZulu-Natal where Jacob Zuma used his Zulu heritage against the Inkatha Freedom Party. Zuma traversed Northern KwaZulu-Natal, drawing more than 15,000 people to rallies in IFP strongholds. The IFP could no longer cast itself as the guardian of Zulu culture and the ANC as a group of Xhosas (Mandela and Mbeki were from the Xhosa tribe) out to destroy Zulu culture. Significantly COPE, dominated by Xhosa leaders, only gained 1.5% of the votes in KwaZulu-Natal. The ANC, however, failed to retain control of the Western Cape provincial government.

Figure 2.26 Helen Zille, leader of the Democratic Alliance →

The Democratic Alliance further increased its support to 17% of the national vote and achieved an outstanding victory in the Western Cape. Its leader Helen Zille continually reminded voters of past allegations of corruption and racketeering against Zuma and denounced the ANC as presiding over a 'failed state'. The DA had widened its racial support from white South Africans to embrace the coloured and Indian communities of the Western Cape. The

Indian community switched its support from the (Asian) Minority Front to the DA. The results in the Western Cape reflect that voting in South Africa is based on race. While black people account for almost 80% of the whole population, they comprise only 30% of the population of the Western Cape. Helen Zille declared that 'The Western Cape is leading South Africa towards democracy. The voters here have shown the nation that democracy is not just about the right for everybody to vote, but about the regular change of government through the ballot box.' She further declared that 'the DA is the most non-racial party in South Africa'.

The first action of the official opposition would be to oppose Amendment 17, a constitutional change which would limit the revenue-raising powers of provinces and municipalities.

For a party that had launched only 129 days before election day, the performance of the Congress of the People (COPE) was satisfactory. It gained 30 seats in the National Assembly and came second in four of the nine provinces, with its best result in the Eastern Cape where it gained 13% of the vote. On reflection, its early expectations of challenging the ANC were unrealistic. The party which had been created as a result of dissent within the ANC quickly descended into internal leadership squabbles. The party could not agree on who would be their presidential candidate and so appointed the lightweight Bishop Mvine Dandola. While the ANC spent a vast amount on the election, COPE ran out of money. In addition, COPE accused the South African Broadcasting Corporation (SABC) of blatant bias in favour of the ANC (see The media, pages 121–122). While the ANC received extensive coverage of its final election rally, COPE's final rally could not be televised because of 'technical problems'. COPE also suffered from its links to former President Thabo Mbeki and his free-market policies. The African poor of South Africa, especially in KwaZulu-Natal, preferred to identify with Jacob Zuma, despite his trial for rape and accusations of corruption. They saw him instead as a man of humble Zulu roots and the champion of the poor.

The Inkatha Freedom Party (IFP) continued to suffer heavy electoral losses. For a party which dominated KwaZulu-Natal from 1994 to 2004, it suffered the humiliation of being routed by the ANC. In 1994 the IFP received 1.8 million votes in KwaZulu-Natal; in 2009 they received only 780,000. The ANC had lost votes in all of the other eight provinces, but KwaZulu-Natal was the exception: Zuma's '100% Zulu Boy' campaign had sunk the IFP.

The Democratic Alliance has recently made progress in trying to form an alliance with other minority parties. In July 2010 Patricia de Lille, leader of the Independent Democrats, attended the DA's party congress. Both parties have agreed to create a formal agreement to co-operate at the 2011 municipal elections and to merge in time for the 2014 general election. Talks have also taken place with COPE, although internal dissention within COPE threatens its future existence. The IFP is also engaged in a bitter dispute over who will replace the leader Chief Buthelezi.

Table 2.12 **National Assembly election results for the main political parties: 1999, 2004, 2009**

Party	Seats			Votes		
	1999	**2004**	**2009**	**1999 (%)**	**2004 (%)**	**2009 (%)**
ANC	266	279	264	66.3	69.9	65.9
Democratic Alliance (DA)	38	50	67	9.6	12.6	16.7
Inkatha Freedom Party (IFP)	34	28	18	8.6	6.9	4.5
Congress of the People (COPE)	—	—	30	—	—	7.4

Table 2.13 **National Assembly distribution of votes and seats, 2009 (selected parties)**

Party	Votes	Seats	
		2009	**2004**
ANC	11,650,748	264	279
Democratic Alliance (DA)	2,945,829	67	50
Congress of the People (COPE)	1,311,027	30	–
Inkatha Freedom Party (IFP)	804,260	18	28
Independent Democrats	162,915	4	7
United Democratic Movement (UDM)	149,680	4	9
Freedom Front Plus	146,680	4	4

Table 2.14 **Voting support in selected provinces, 2009 (%)**

Province	ANC	DA	COPE	IFP
Limpopo	84.8	3.4	7.5	0.1
Western Cape	31.5	51.4	7.5	0.1
Eastern Cape	68.8	9.9	13.6	0.1
KwaZulu-Natal	62.9	9.1	1.3	22.4
Gauteng	64.4	21.9	7.8	1.5

Table 2.15 Election results for the province of KwaZulu-Natal (selected parties), 2004–09

Party	2004		2009	
	Votes	Seats	Votes	Seats
ANC	1,287,823	38	2,192,516	51
Inkatha Freedom Party (IFP)	10,098,267	30	780,027	18
Democratic Alliance	228,857	7	318,559	7
Minority Front	71,540	2	71,567	2

Table 2.16 Election results for the province of Western Cape (selected parties), 2004–09

Party	2004		2009	
	Votes	Seats	Votes	Seats
ANC	709,052	19	620,918	14
Democratic Alliance	424,832	12	1,012,568	22
New National Party	170,469	5	–	–
Congress of the People	–	–	152,356	3
Independent Democrats	122,867	3	92,116	2
ACDP	53,934	2	28,995	1
UDM	27,489	1	–	–

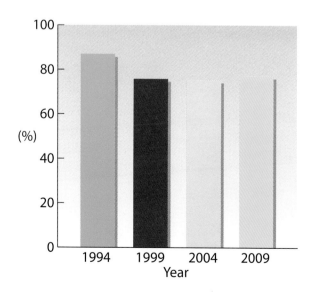

Figure 2.27 Turnout of registered voters, 1994–2009 (%) →

Activities

South African Constitution

1 Outline the findings of the Truth and Reconciliation Commission.

2 Describe the main features of the South African Constitution. Refer to the Bill of Rights, an independent judiciary, a unitary government, limited power to the provinces and Article 9.2.

3 Describe the political structure set up by the 1996 Constitution. Refer to Parliament, the President, the Cabinet and provincial governments.

4 What was the Volkstaat Council?

Elections 1999–2009

1 'The 1999 and 2004 elections were a triumph for the ANC, a success for the Democratic Alliance and a disaster for the New National Party and Inkatha FP.' To what extent is this statement correct?

2 Assess the impact of the 2009 elections (national and provincial) on the four major parties.

Jacob Zuma, 'The People's Man'

Figure 2.28 Jacob Zuma →

The new president of South Africa is a controversial figure. For some he represents the unacceptable face of democracy, a man accused of massive corruption and of a lavish lifestyle, supporting his six wives and his 20 children. On the other hand, his humble rural background and his lack of formal education make him highly popular among the majority of black South Africans who are poor. He is a '100% Zulu Boy' who offers hope to those who live in poverty.

The 67-year-old ANC leader is a populist who spent 10 years in prison during the apartheid years. The uneducated Zulu outmanoeuvred the university-educated Mbeki to gain control of the party in 2008. His supporters claim that 'he will improve the lives of the great unwashed, those whom other classes look down upon'. These supporters regard the corruption charges against him as an 'Mbeki plot' and ignore the strong evidence of his wrongdoing. All that matters to them is that the National Prosecution Authority (NPA) dropped all charges against him and that he is their President. The next five years will determine whether he is the saviour of the poor or whether he becomes the leader who makes South Africa 'a failed state'. The February 2010 disclosure that he had fathered an illegitimate child has disturbed many South Africans. He has been accused of presidential promiscuity and of weakening the fight against the spread of HIV/AIDS.

Tension within the ANC

The ANC dominates South African politics (see Table 2.12) and, as stated previously, the African people display intense loyalty to the party. The 'Triple Alliance' between the ANC, SACP (South African Communist Party) and COSATU (Congress of South African Trade Unions) remained solid despite criticisms of Mbeki's free-market economic policies. However, the government's attempt to control wage rises, to restructure public services and to introduce privatisation of essential services, such as electricity, has heightened tension. Life in the black townships has deteriorated over the last eight years and the fruits of Affirmative Action programmes have not been distributed to the poorest sections of society in South Africa.

The ANC's relations with COSATU were further strained by the escalation in strike action by public-sector workers in September 2010. The Secretary General of COSATU, Mr Vivi, stated that 'workers have little reason to celebrate the gains of democracy as the rich have become richer and the poor poorer'. It is not surprising, therefore, that COSATU and SACP backed Zuma in his power struggle with Mbeki and were duly rewarded when their respective leaders received key posts in Zuma's cabinet. These appointments led to tension between the moderate wing of the party and the socialist left. The moderate wing is especially concerned that the chairperson of the SACP, Gwede Mantashe, is also the ANC Secretary General and is pursuing a socialist agenda. The creation of COPE reflected the division within the ANC. Zuma hopes that his leadership will provide unity.

Opposition to the ANC

As discussed in the section on Elections, the National List proportional representation system encourages the formation of political parties which can weaken the opposition. Aware of this fragmentation, opposition parties have discussed forming a multiparty group with a new name to contest the 2011 municipal/local government elections. The parties involved would be the

Democratic Alliance (DA), the Independent Democrats (ID), the Congress of the People (COPE) and the United Democratic Movement (UDM). The parties would not merge but rather join forces. The ANC has tried to undermine the DA by calling Helen Zille a white racist. In return, opponents of the ANC might argue that ANC now stands for African/Nepotism/Corruption.

The Afrikaner community

The Afrikaner community felt threatened by the Mbeki Government. Their desire to establish their own Volkstaat – white homeland – had totally failed. Mandela had set up a Volkstaat Council to discuss Afrikaner self-determination but this was abolished by Mbeki in 2001. The collapse and dissolution of the New National Party in 2005 further weakened their political influence. The last white president of South Africa, and former NNP leader F. W. de Klerk, condemned the decision to merge with the ANC.

President Zuma has made conciliatory gestures to the Afrikaner community. He has acknowledged the existence of white poverty (see page 79) and he referred to the Afrikaner people as being the real white South Africans. He also appointed Pieter Mulder, the leader of Freedom Front Plus, to his Cabinet in 2009.

Figure 2.29 Pieter Mulder, leader of Freedom Front Plus →

There is deep anger and frustration among the Afrikaner community over the erosion of their culture, especially the Afrikaans language. Only one per cent of all schools in South Africa are now single-medium Afrikaans schools. Stellenbosch University and other Afrikaans universities have lost their status as Afrikaans-medium institutions.

In the Western Cape, Afrikaans is the language of the large coloured population as well as the Afrikaans-speaking white community. The Afrikaner community is concerned about the events in Zimbabwe and the government's measures to reduce their rights to hold arms. The attacks on white, mostly

Afrikaner, farms continue (see pages 99–100). The changing of place names from Afrikaans names to African names has also infuriated the whites. In 2005, the South African National Geographical Names Council approved the name change of the area around Pretoria to Tshwane.

Dan Roodt, an Afrikaner journalist, stated, 'What nation-building really means in South Africa is the complete destruction of Afrikaans culture and the Afrikaner identity.' This frustration and anger led to the re-emergence of white, right-wing terrorist attacks in 2002. A group called Warriors of the Boer Nation set off nine bombs in Soweto, killing one black South African woman. The government's reaction was swift: over 30 Afrikaners were arrested.

The murder of Eugene Terreblanche

In April 2010, Eugene Terreblanche, the leader of the paramilitary extreme Afrikaner group the AWB, was savagely murdered on his farm by two black farm workers. Terreblanche had consistently demanded the creation of an Afrikaner Volkstaat. After his murder, Pieter Steyn, one of the AWB leaders, stated 'All we want is a piece of land in South Africa where we can settle ourselves and call it our own and govern ourselves with our religion and laws.'

Terreblanche had been jailed for 3 years in 2001 for the attempted murder of a black farm worker. His death once again raised the issue of a so-called campaign of terror against the 40,000 white farmers; since 1994 over 3000 white farmers have been murdered (see pages 99–100). The white community blame Julius Malema, head of the ANC Youth League, for his death. In March 2010, Malema opened an ANC rally by singing 'Dubula Ibhunu' (Shoot the Boer). This song was banned by the high court as being an incitement to racial hatred and violence.

Figure 2.30 Eugene Terreblanche →

Inkatha Freedom Party (IFP)

The IFP demand greater autonomy for the Zulu nation and are against the dominance of the ANC. The bitter rivalry between the two parties has not been confined to the ballot box and each accuse the other of using violent methods. The IFP's poor showing in the 2004 and 2009 elections highlighted divisions within the party and there has been constant criticism of Chief Buthelezi's tight control of the party. The end of the party's participation in the Government of National Unity (GNU) and the loss of control in KwaZulu-Natal are clear evidence of the erosion of party support, especially in urban areas. However, the growth of urbanisation, creating a less deferential population, has led some party activists to demand that the party modernises and considers a change in leadership (Buthelezi is over 75 years old).

The 2009 result shocked the party leaders; KwaZulu-Natal was the only province in which the ANC increased its share of the vote. Between 2004 and 2009, the ANC and the IFP had shared power in the province, forming a KwaZulu provincial government coalition. The ANC government had spent significant funds on improving the living standards of the rural communities in the province and this, along with Zuma describing himself as '100% Zulu Boy', explains their success in persuading rural voters to switch from the IFP to the ANC. The IFP Youth Wing demanded radical reform of the party and called for the old guard to resign. The party declined the offer of two deputy ministerial posts in the national Cabinet.

The IFP can no longer cast itself as the guardian of Zulu culture. In his January 2010 wedding to his sixth wife, Zuma dressed as a Zulu chief. The IFP could no longer cast the ANC as a party dominated by Xhosas.

Towards a one-party state or a successful democracy?

In 2002 Chief Buthelezi stated 'I am very worried … if we are not careful we are going to become a one-party state.' This worry is shared by many. The emphatic victory of the ANC in the 2004 election followed by the dissolution of the NNP in 2005 gave the ANC over 70% of the seats in the assembly (286 seats to the DA's 50). This gave it the power to rewrite the Constitution and enabled President Mbeki to consider running for a third term. One of the only provinces which offered an alternative to the ANC and a protection of minority rights, KwaZulu-Natal, is now under the complete control of the ANC after the 2009 elections. Only in the Western Cape Province is there an alternative to the ANC.

To what extent is South Africa a successful democracy?

Table 2.17

Arguments for	Arguments against
1. South Africa is a stable model of democracy for Africa. There have been four peaceful elections based on PR. Over 35 political parties participated in the 2009 elections with thirteen parties sitting in the National Assembly. The PR system encourages the formation of new political parties.	1. There is a fear that South Africa is becoming a one-party state. The ANC controls eight of the nine provinces. Only in Western Cape is it in opposition. The NNP merged with the ANC in 2004. The ANC has 264 of the assembly seats. In contrast, the official opposition, the DA, has 67 seats.
2. A peaceful transition from Mandela to Mbeki occurred. The power struggle between Mbeki and Zuma was resolved peacefully with the resignation of Mbeki as President in September 2008.	2. There is an issue of corruption with leading ANC members such as Tony Yengeni being sent to jail. Zuma was under investigation for 8 years over charges of corruption. The charges were dropped in April 2009 in controversial circumstances.
3. South Africa has a federal system of government with powers divided between central and provincial governments. Local government structures provide local services. The Western Cape is controlled by the Democratic Alliance and this has prevented the ANC from totally dominating politics. Helen Zille, leader of the DA, called her victory 'a triumph for democracy'.	3. The federal system exists only on paper. Minority rights, such as Afrikaner and Zulu culture, are under threat. Zuma appoints all eight premiers of the provinces under ANC rule and there is a lack of democracy within them. The people do not directly choose the President or premiers of the provinces.
4. South Africa has a liberal Constitution guaranteeing freedom to its citizens. It provides for an independent judiciary. The Constitutional Court ordered Mbeki to provide drugs to combat AIDS. There is a free press and civil society able to criticise and monitor the actions of the government. The success of the Truth and Reconciliation Commission highlights the openness of South African society.	4. Mbeki was intolerant of criticism. He accused critics of being racists and even attacked Archbishop Tutu. The policy of Transformation Politics could threaten the independence of judges and the rights of non-black South Africans. The South African Broadcasting Corporation (SABC) is regarded as being the mouthpiece of the ANC. Zuma could threaten the independence of the judiciary through new appointments to the Constitutional Court.

Corruption

Every country has its corrupt politicians and the dominance of the ANC in every walk of life inevitably provides opportunities for politicians and officials to enrich themselves. Standards of public auditing are abysmal and every year huge sums of public money are stolen. A recent report from South Africa's anti-corruption body, the Special Investigating Unit (SIU), said it had identified 400,000 civil servants getting welfare payments to which they were not entitled. Many leading ANC leaders have been found guilty of corruption including Tony Yengeni, Chief Whip of the ANC, and Winnie Madikizela-Mandela. President Zuma has promised to root out corruption but he himself had been accused of taking bribes from foreign firms when he was Deputy President. His financial adviser, Mr Shaik, was found guilty, but controversially Zuma was pardoned by the new President in January 2010. The most recent trial for corruption has been that of the former chief of police, and a senior ANC figure, Jackie Selebi. In August 2010 he was jailed for 15 years for accepting bribes.

In January 2010, the wife of the Minister of State Security, Siyabonga Cwele, was arrested and charged with drug trafficking.

Kaleme Motlanthe, the country's Vice President, has stated that 'corruption was far worse than anyone imagines at all levels of government and too many ANC comrades regard election to public office as simply a chance to get rich'.

Figure 2.31 Jackie Selebi →

In 2009 Transparency International ranked South Africa as the fourth-cleanest state of Africa's 53 countries and 54th out of the 180 countries it judges worldwide. South Africa has an excellent record on tackling corruption and is ranked well above most other African countries by corruption monitors. However, most South Africans would wish to be measured alongside developed democracies rather than failing states in the developing world.

The judiciary and the media

Critics of those who argue that South Africa is now moving towards a one-party state highlight not only the democratic electoral system and the numerous political parties, but also the existence of an independent judiciary, a free press and active pressure groups such as TAC (see page 93) and COSATU. They rightly claim that South Africa is not Zimbabwe.

Administration of justice

As highlighted on page 103, the Constitution grants judicial authority to its courts which are independent and subject only to the Constitution and the law. The Constitutional Court has already played an important part in monitoring the activities of the government. (See availability of the anti-AIDS drugs, page 93, and the land rights of white farmers, pages 98–99).

An issue of concern to many commentators is the future independence of the judiciary. The dominance of white judges in the higher levels of the judiciary, especially the Constitutional Court, has led to demands from the ANC that the judiciary must reflect 'the racial and gender composition of South Africa'. This campaign of white judge-bashing was witnessed in the trial of Mr Shaik and during the investigations into corruption charges against Jacob Zuma when the judges were called 'white racists' by members of the Communist Party which is affiliated to the ANC.

The decision in 2009 to drop all charges against Jacob Zuma has again raised concern over the future independence of the judiciary. Helen Zille, leader of the DA, accused the Zuma Government of using the transformation of the judiciary (55% are now black) as a smokescreen to control the judges. She stated 'It [the Zuma Government] wants a bench that is subservient to the racial ideology, policies and political control of the party-state'. Further concern was raised when Zuma stated, in a pre-election address, that judges were not gods, and he was accused of trying to undermine the independence of the judiciary. Desmond Tutu also criticised the appointment of a discredited Zuma loyalist, Menzi Simelane, to the post of National Director of Public Prosecution. Four vacancies in the Constitutional Court enabled Jacob Zuma to appoint new judges and to appoint a new Chief Justice, Sandile Ngcobo.

The media

South Africa has a thriving free and independent press with liberal newspapers such as *The Mail and Guardian* keeping a close and critical watch on the actions of the government. (The newspaper was a fierce critic of the apartheid government in the 1980s.) Ironically, an article which highlighted the R11 million of taxpayers' money being given to the ANC for its 2004 election campaign by oil company Imvine failed to appear in print. A 'gagging order' by the courts prevented the newspaper from printing the article. The ANC is proposing a new Protection of Information bill which would place restrictions on access to government information backed up by severe punishment of up to 25 years in jail. In September 2010 on ANC spokesperson stated that, 'the media can be a serious obstacle to advancement'. In a democracy dominated by one party a free press is essential to highlight abuse of power by the government.

Television plays an important role in maintaining the culture and languages of South Africa. The impartiality and independence of the South African Broadcasting Corporation (SABC) is an issue of major debate in South Africa. Its previous white executives have been replaced by black employees committed to the goals of black transformation. Tony Leon, a prominent South African politician, has accused the SABC of 'becoming a virtual propaganda arm' of the ANC. COPE also complained that the SABC failed to provide live coverage of its final rally before the 2009 elections, and refused to accept that it had been a technical fault.

Activities

1 Why is Jacob Zuma a controversial politician?

2 Describe the division within the ANC between 2005 and 2009 and outline the outcome.

3 What is the Triple Alliance and why is there tension within it?

4 Explain why the Afrikaner community feel threatened by the ANC?

5 Why is the future of the IFP bleak?

6 With reference to Table 2.17, outline the arguments for and against South Africa being a successful democracy.

7 What evidence suggests that South Africa has a corruption problem?

8 Outline the role of the judiciary in South Africa.

9 To what extent is there a 'free' media in South Africa without government interference?

Essay questions

1 To what extent is South Africa a successful and stable democracy? (15)

2 'South Africa is moving towards a one-party state.' Discuss. (15)

The Politics of Development in Africa

Economic, political and social factors affecting development

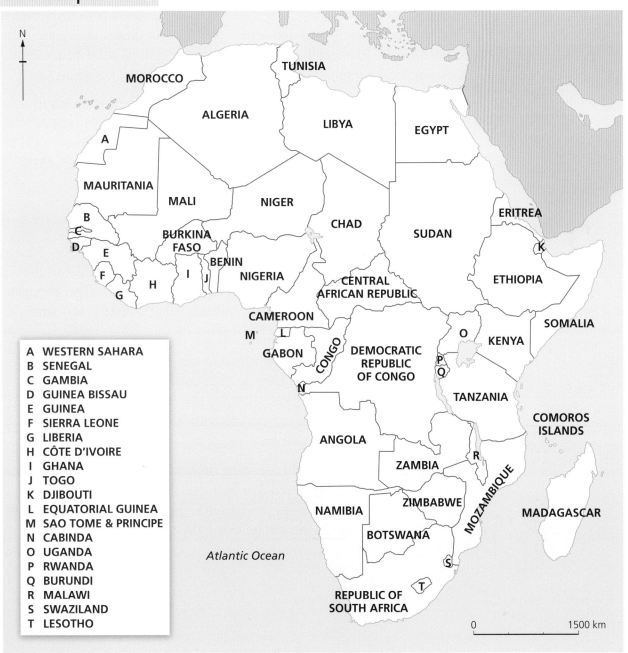

A WESTERN SAHARA
B SENEGAL
C GAMBIA
D GUINEA BISSAU
E GUINEA
F SIERRA LEONE
G LIBERIA
H CÔTE D'IVOIRE
I GHANA
J TOGO
K DJIBOUTI
L EQUATORIAL GUINEA
M SAO TOME & PRINCIPE
N CABINDA
O UGANDA
P RWANDA
Q BURUNDI
R MALAWI
S SWAZILAND
T LESOTHO

Figure 3.1 Africa ↑

Africa is a continent of approximately 690 million people made up of 53 independent countries; amongst these are 15 of the least developed nations in the world. Seventy per cent of Africa's population subsist on less than $2 a day, yet Africa abounds with natural resources – minerals, land and sea ports. How can this be?

There is no simple answer. A complex combination of economic, political and social factors interact to impede development. Some of these factors operate outside Africa while others operate within. No one factor explains the situation. Natural disasters hit the headlines and lead us to believe that nature alone is the cause of the desperate situation facing many African people. Undoubtedly drought, flooding, crop failures and climate change play a major part in creating wide-scale food shortages, but it is the inability of countries to cope with these natural disasters that is the major challenge facing the countries affected. The inability of social, economic and political structures within a country to respond to these natural disasters is the key issue.

A comparison between the profiles of the African country the Democratic Republic of Congo (DRC) and the United Kingdom (UK) reveals stark contrasts and provides a vivid insight into the gulf that separates the industrialised developed world from the developing world (see page 125).

Economic factors

The effects of debt

Africa has a $200 billion debt burden which creates a major obstacle to the continent's development. African countries spend almost $14 billion annually on repaying debt which results in vital resources being diverted away from essential social programmes.

Many African governments have borrowed money from the International Monetary Fund (IMF) or World Bank to finance development. Changes in interest rates, fluctuating market prices for goods sold abroad and the dependency on a limited range of cash crops has meant it has been difficult, if not impossible, to repay these debts.

The IMF attaches conditions when lending money, which can lead to extreme hardship for the countries involved. For example, the IMF can insist that education programmes and health programmes are cut to reduce government spending. If such conditions are not followed, then finance can be stopped.

Profile – Democratic Republic of Congo (DRC)

Education
Male literacy: 73%
Female literacy: 50%
Primary school enrolment: Boys 53%; Girls 47%
Secondary school enrolment: Boys 24%; Girls 13%

Economy
*GNI per capita: $100
*GDP per capita: growth minus 6.4% per annum
Percentage of the economy spent on defence: 18%

Health
Life expectancy: 42 years
People with HIV/AIDS: 4.2%

Immunisation levels:
TB 68%
Polio 55%
Measles 54%

Children protected by a malaria net: 12%

Women
Risk of death in childbirth: 1 in 3
Percentage with a skilled birth worker present at childbirth: 61%
Percentage with access to HIV education: 45%

Profile – United Kingdom (UK)

Education
Male literacy: virtually 100%
Female literacy: virtually 100%
Primary school enrolment: Boys 99%; Girls virtually 99%
Secondary school enrolment: Boys 97%; Girls 99%

Economy
GNI per capita: $42,740,350
GDP growth: 2.4% per annum
Percentage of the economy spent on defence: 7%

Health
Life expectancy: 79 years
People with HIV/AIDS: 0.2%

Immunisation levels:
TB virtually 100%
Polio 91%
Measles 80%

Women
Risk of death in childbirth: 1 in 3800
Percentage with a skilled birth worker present at childbirth: 99%
Percentage with access to HIV education: virtually 100%

*GNI: This is the average value of goods produced by a worker in a year for a country.

*GDP: This is the average value of goods and services produced in a year by a worker.

The inability of African governments to invest in social services and promote economic development is the enduring consequence of the debt burden. Nobel Laureate Wangari Maathai commented at the World Social Forum in January 2007, 'The debt burden continues to make it impossible for many governments to give services to the people'. Augustine Mkandawire, a research and monitoring consultant for the *African Monitor*, said in May 2007, 'The repayment of debt is robbing developing countries of the millions that they could be investing in creating employment and making progress in human development … Time is of the essence when it comes to saving lives.'

In recent years, some African countries have begun to receive debt cancellation. The resulting benefits have been considerable. After receiving partial debt cancellation, Malawi has been able to train 4000 new teachers per year while Cameroon plans to build some 1000 new health facilities over the next 6 years and build more than 2000 new schools. These examples indicate the progress that could be possible if debts owed by African countries were cancelled.

The Paris Club

The Paris Club is an informal group of government creditors who work together to find sustainable solutions to payment difficulties experienced by nations in debt. The UK is a permanent member of the Paris Club. The Paris Club has arrived at just over 400 agreements (with six in 2007 and six in 2008) with 85 debtor countries.

The effects of currency speculation and interest rates

In the global market in which we live, decisions or actions taken thousands of miles away can have profound and unexpected consequences on African countries. The finance market is one such example. It is estimated that over $1.85 trillion changes hands every day in the finance markets. Speculators buy and sell currency for profit. One morning the UK pound might be worth 1.15 euros but by afternoon it may have gone down to 1.01. A person who bought £100 worth of euros in the morning and sold them for pounds in the afternoon when the rate was 1.15 euros would make a profit of about £13. Imagine the profits that can be made when millions of dollars are traded.

Unfortunately, such speculation can have disastrous effects on the economies of African countries. If dealers fear a currency, such as that of an African country, is losing value, a herd instinct can take over with dealers trying to offload that particular currency quickly. Consequently, the value of the currency drops, resulting in imports being more expensive for the African country involved and the value of vital exports being worth less.

In Kenya during 1997–8, high interest rates on treasury bills (30%) attracted many investors. This inflow of foreign currency boosted the Kenyan economy, but when the interest rates fell, the money left the country virtually overnight, leaving Kenya with considerable financial problems. This is a typical example of the problems faced by many African countries.

The effects of cash crops and terms of trade

One of the conditions of receiving a loan from the World Bank or IMF may be the requirement to grow crops to sell on the open market for profit. This seems an eminently sensible way for a country to generate income but there are associated drawbacks.

Mozambique was once the world's leading producer of raw cashew nuts. In the 1970s its government banned the export of raw cashews in favour of selling the processed variety. However, in the 1990s the World Bank abolished restrictions in the cashew market and Mozambique could not compete in the world market. The cashew nut industry collapsed and 90% of those employed in the industry lost their jobs.

The case of Mozambique highlights the precarious situation of relying too heavily on one or a few cash crops. In times of overproduction, prices drop as the law of supply and demand comes into play. The production of cash crops is a controversial issue. It is true that income is generated but smaller farmers can lose out to larger concerns and the land available to grow food for domestic consumption becomes ever more limited.

Terms of trade

Africa's share of world trade dropped from 6% in 1985 to 2% in 2005. Half of all food produced had rotted by the time it reached the marketplace as a result of inadequate infrastructures. African producers do not compete on equal terms in world markets. The World Trade Organisation (WTO) insists on free markets, therefore subsidies by African governments to their food producers are not permitted and nor are import taxes that would inhibit free and equal trade.

Case Study: The US cotton trade

The US government pays its cotton producers around $3.4 billion in subsidies, a figure which is more than it gives in aid to the whole of Africa. American farmers receive approximately 70 cents per pound of cotton produced.

These subsidies encourage the US cotton industry to over-produce. As supply increases, the world price drops which directly affects African cotton farmers. As a result of subsidies, America can sell its cotton at an artificially low price, thereby undercutting their African competitors.

Cotton is Mali's second most important export, and thousands of Africans depend upon it for their survival, but cotton farmers in Mali are facing catastrophe. Unlike the USA, Mali is forbidden from supporting its cotton industry as a consequence of conditions attached to its loans from the IMF and World Bank. Therefore Mali cannot compete on equal terms with the USA. A Malian farmer commented to a Christian Aid worker, 'If we don't earn money from cotton, we won't be able to buy food. If any of our family members fall ill, we won't be able to take care of them. If any of our vehicles need repairing, we won't be able to do this.'

Figure 3.2 ➜

Activities

1 What is the extent of debt faced by African countries?

2 What problems does debt cause for African countries?

3 What have been the benefits of cancelling debt for the countries concerned?

4 Explain in detail how cash crops, terms of trade and currency speculation affect development in Africa.

Political factors affecting development

The effects of armed conflict

Along with HIV/AIDS and malaria, armed conflicts are now a leading cause of world hunger. Armed conflict leads to food shortages on a large scale and for long periods of time, destroying any prospect of economic and social development. In 2008, The Democratic Republic of Congo, Somalia, Sudan and Chad were all involved in armed conflicts. The following African countries have also recently experienced violent conflict: Sierra Leone, Liberia, Rwanda, the Ivory Coast, Angola and Mozambique. The effects of armed conflict are catastrophic for the countries involved and it can take decades to reconstruct after the conflict has ceased.

A recent report produced by the International Action Network on Small Arms, Saferworld and Oxfam revealed the enormous impact of armed conflicts in many African countries. The report demonstrated that the cost to the continent's development over a 15-year period was nearly $300 billion. In addition, African countries involved in conflict have, on average, '50 per cent more infant deaths, 15 per cent more undernourished people, life expectancy reduced by 5 years, 20 per cent more adult illiteracy, 2.5 times fewer doctors per patient and 12.4 per cent less food per person'. The report goes on to say that the cost of conflict was equal to the amount of money received in aid during the same period.

Fact File

The results of armed conflicts

- Millions of people can be uprooted from their homes and land, destroying any prospect of being self-sufficient.

- Vast numbers of refugees are created who are without food, water, shelter and medical support.

- Emergency aid can be severely disrupted or temporarily stopped because of the dangers caused by shooting, fighting, attacks and highjacking of aid trucks.

- Food becomes a weapon with soldiers destroying food and livestock, adopting a scorched-earth policy whereby they burn to the ground any crops or food supplies they have not plundered. Wells are often contaminated or mined which forces farmers off the land.

- Food production is seriously affected by armed conflict with areas affected suffering annual losses of more than 12% of production, although this figure varies widely from country to country. In the extreme case of Angola, food production was reduced by 44%.

A possible solution?

The biggest problem in the majority of armed conflicts lies in poor control and regulation of arms across borders. Approximately 95% of Africa's most commonly used conflict weapons come from outside the continent. A solution therefore could lie in international governments and African governments applying tighter arms controls, thus ensuring that the weapons needed to pursue armed conflict are not readily available.

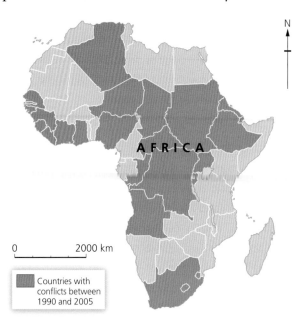

Figure 3.3 African countries with conflicts between 1990 and 2005 →

The effect of bad governance and kleptocracy

The Commission for Africa Report (2005) is unambiguous in identifying bad governance as a key issue in explaining lack of development in many African countries: 'A key difficulty for Africa in the past 40 years has been the weakness of governance.' Bad governance means that the police cannot be trusted, taxes are not efficiently collected, the government cannot be trusted to deliver key services, there is corruption, human rights are abused and the legal system is not independent.

Kleptocracy can go hand in hand with bad governance. Kleptocracy describes a situation where an elite group, and/or a dictator, exercises power to the benefit of themselves at the expense of the population at large. Funds or aid are diverted to equip the military who will ensure the government remains in power. Corruption is ignored because this keeps officials content with the present ruling elite as their well-being is linked to those in power. Those who support the regime are rewarded while those who do not suffer. Essential services are denied the money needed because funds are used to maintain the corrupt political system. In Nigeria, the late dictator General Sani Abacha succeeded in stealing between $1 billion and $3 billion in only 5 years.

Case Study: Somalia

There has been longstanding armed conflict in Somalia. The situation in 2009 was one of anarchy, no effective government and warring groups competing for resources and power.

Thousands still flee from the combat zone that defines the capital city of Mogadishu. Uprooted people seek refuge with relatives or other families or settle in temporary camps. In 2009, 75,000 displaced people from Mogadishu were living in such camps in southern and central Somalia.

In the north of the country, 36,000 displaced people rely on food aid, while 120,000 other displaced people in various parts of the country also rely on assistance from Non Governmental Organisations (NGOs) such as the Red Cross.

Figure 3.4 Armed soldiers in Somalia ⬆

Figure 3.5 Somalia ⬆

Case Study: Zimbabwe

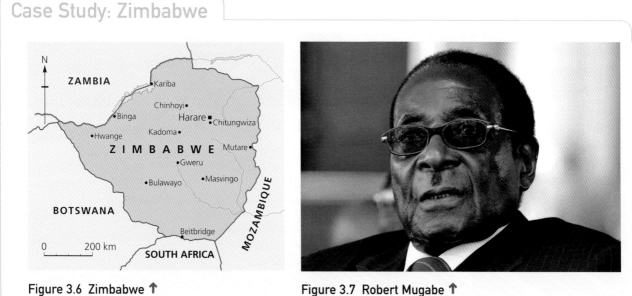

Figure 3.6 Zimbabwe ⬆

Figure 3.7 Robert Mugabe ⬆

Case Study: Continued

Zimbabwe was once the economic leader in Africa and a successful exporter of food but as a consequence of government mismanagement, the country has experienced a series of economic disasters. Since 2000, the country has been unable to feed itself adequately. President Mugabe introduced a land distribution programme that resulted in most white farmers being driven off their land, crippling commercial farming. In December 2007, the World Food Programme (WFP) estimated that as a result, 4.1 million people in Zimbabwe would need food aid by April 2008.

Zimbabwe faces staggering economic problems that result largely from the actions of the government. The IMF has suspended financial assistance because of the government's failure to meet budgetary goals. The exchange rate has fallen dramatically and the rate of inflation stood at 231,000,000% in 2009, making the currency effectively useless. A loaf of bread that cost Z$500 (Zimbabwe dollars) in August 2009 cost Z$10,000 in September. In May 2004 Mugabe refused food aid claiming that Zimbabwe had enough food to feed its people. Independent analysts estimated that more than 5 million people faced famine.

In 2009 corruption was reported to be 'pervasive' by a Zimbabwean journalist working outside his country. He went on to say 'Zimbabwe ranks 150 out of the world's most corrupt countries. Top officials hand-pick multiple farms (that have been acquired by the government under its policy of expropriating farms from white farmers) and register them in the names of family members to evade the official one-farm policy.'

The general election held in 2008 contained irregularities, however opposition leader Morgan Tsvangirai won in the presidential polls. In the lead up to the election in late June 2008, Mugabe's supporters committed considerable violence against opposition party members. Evidence of vote tampering and ballot-box stuffing resulted in international governments condemning the process. Difficult negotiations over power sharing followed and an agreement was finally agreed in February 2009 which allowed Mugabe to remain in power as President but created the new position of Prime Minister for Morgan Tsvangirai.

Figure 3.8 Morgan Tsvangirai ↑

The economic and social decline of Zimbabwe

- In 2009 the unemployment rate stood at 85%.
- Per capita income was lower in 2009 than in 1980.
- Life expectancy fell from 54 years for men in 1994 to 37 years in 2008.
- The population below the poverty line is 70%.
- There is no freedom of speech or right of assembly.
- Child mortality rose more than 50% between 1990 and 2003. Currently, Zimbabwe has the fastest rise in infant mortality in the world.
- The rate of HIV infection is one of the highest in the world with 25% of the population being infected. Every week 3500 people die from a combination of HIV/AIDS, poverty and malnutrition.
- Foreign investment and tourism have collapsed.
- There is an extreme shortage of medicines and medical equipment which caused major problems during the cholera outbreak of 2008.
- Out of a population of 12 million, over 4 million have emigrated abroad, many of whom are the skilled and educated people Zimbabwe needs.

Activities

1   Explain how bad governance hinders development in some African countries.

2   Explain in detail how armed conflict creates social and economic problems in some African countries.

Zimbabwe case study

1   Give examples of actions taken by Robert Mugabe that have led directly to problems faced by the people of Zimbabwe.

2   Give six examples of the social and economic decline of Zimbabwe.

Social factors affecting development

Health issues

HIV/AIDS

There is an HIV/AIDS epidemic in Africa; HIV/AIDS is one of the three major killers in Africa. An estimated 22 million adults and children were living with HIV in sub-Saharan Africa at the beginning of 2008. During 2007, an estimated 1.5 million Africans died from AIDS. The epidemic has left behind approximately 11.6 million orphaned African children. The Fact File below demonstrates in horrific detail the scale of the problem. HIV/AIDS is one of the biggest challenges confronting many African countries.

Fact File

HIV/AIDS in Africa

- AIDS could slash the wealth of some African countries by as much as 20% according to an International AIDS Conference held in Durban in 2000.
- 75% of all people in the world infected by AIDS live in Africa.
- In some African countries, AIDS is the major cause of children being orphaned.
- Half of all people with HIV become infected before they are aged 25.
- HIV/AIDS undermines the caring capacity of families and communities by deepening poverty as a result of a loss of labour and the high costs of medical treatment and funerals.
- Food is often the main need of poor families living with HIV/AIDS. Malnutrition increases as HIV progresses.
- Without good food, the anti-retroviral drugs used to treat the condition are not as effective as they could be.
- Seven million of Africa's farmers have died of AIDS.
- By 2020 it is estimated that HIV/AIDS will kill 20% of southern Africa's farm workers.

HIV/AIDS places huge burdens on societies in Africa. Medical services cannot cope with demand as around 50% of hospital beds in some countries have been given over to AIDS sufferers. The economy suffers and the social problems created are immense.

Countries in Africa have lost on average 10 to 20 years of life expectancy and the epidemic is worsening. Botswana, which has the world's second highest incidence of HIV with 36.5% of its population affected, faces a rapid increase in extreme poverty amongst its poorest households. Such households could face a decline in their income of at least 13%. Life expectancy is only 39 years while it would have been 72 if not for AIDS.

The vast majority of Africans living with HIV/AIDS are between the ages of 15 and 49 which is the prime of their working lives. The effects on the labour supply and the economy are dramatic with employers, schools, factories and hospitals having to constantly find and train staff to replace those who have become too ill to work.

Table 3.1 The HIV/AIDS epidemic in selected African countries

Country	People living with HIV/AIDS	Adult (15–49) rate, %	Women with HIV/AIDS	Children with HIV/AIDS	AIDS deaths	Orphans due to AIDS
Botswana	300,000	23.9	170,000	15,000	11,000	95,000
Malawi	930,000	11.9	490,000	91,000	68,000	560,000
Uganda	1,000,000	6.7	520,000	110,000	91,000	1,000,000
Zambia	1,100,000	15.2	560,000	95,000	56,000	600,000
Zimbabwe	1,300,000	15.3	680,000	120,000	140,000	1,000,000
Total sub-Saharan Africa	22,000,000	5.0	12,000,000	1,800,000	1,500,000	11,600,000

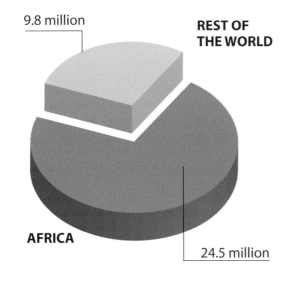

9.8 million

REST OF THE WORLD

AFRICA

24.5 million

Figure 3.9 The global HIV/AIDS epidemic ➔

Case Study: Malawi

In Malawi, devastating food shortages have resulted as a consequence of high rates of HIV/AIDS. It is estimated that by 2020, Malawi's agricultural workforce will be 14% smaller than it would have been without HIV/AIDS. In other countries, such as Mozambique, Botswana, Namibia and Zimbabwe, the reduction is likely to be over 20%.

In 2008, Toby Solomon, the Commissioner for the Nsanje district in Malawi, summed up the devastation caused by HIV/AIDS on agricultural production: 'Our fields are idle because there is nobody to work them. We don't have machinery for farming, we only have manpower – if we are sick, or spend our time looking after family members who are sick, we have no time to spend working in the fields.'

Malaria

Malaria thrives in hot temperatures that enable the parasite that causes the disease to mature more quickly in the bodies of the mosquitoes that carry it. Malaria is Africa's biggest killer and the consequences of malaria for African development are similar to those caused by HIV/AIDS. It is estimated that malaria accounts for economic losses amongst African countries totalling $12 billion per year. Malaria is also responsible for slowing economic growth by around 1.3% per annum. The World Health Organisation (WHO) estimates that malaria accounts for 25–40% of outpatient visits and 20–50% of hospital admissions in African countries where the disease is found. This places a huge burden on health services. In Ghana, malaria accounts for about 30% of all hospital resources. Ghana spent approximately $760 million on malaria treatment in 2006 alone.

When insecticide-treated malaria nets are used properly by three-quarters of the people in a community, malaria transmission is cut by 50%, child deaths are cut by 20% and the mosquito population drops by as much as 90%. It is estimated, however, that fewer than 5% of children in sub-Saharan Africa currently sleep under any type of insecticide-treated net.

The illness means that millions of people in Africa cannot work to their full potential with many others being unable to work at all. Malaria causes fever, chills, muscle ache and a range of 'flu-like symptoms. Kidney failure, brain disease and severe anaemia can develop. Babies born to infected women have low birth weights which decreases their chances of survival.

Amongst the young in Sudan, malaria means fewer days in school, poor attainment and high dropout rates from school. Studies have shown that up to 50% of medically linked absence from school in the sub-Saharan region is due to malaria.

Farming methods

Poor farming practices such as deforestation, overcropping and overgrazing are exhausting the land in many African countries. Increasingly, fertile farmland is under threat from erosion, salination or desertification. Added to these problems is poor irrigation and water management. These combined factors result in limiting agricultural yields.

Wood is the major fuel for many rural Africans, and large numbers of trees are cut down to provide fuel and shelter every year. Land is also cleared of trees using slash and burn to replace agricultural land that has failed due to overuse. Trees are not replanted, which results in deforestation, which leads in turn to desertification with soil being blown away or washed away during the rainy season.

Position of women and land tenure

Figure 3.10 →

Women in Africa account for 70% of food production and 80–90% of food processing, storage and transport. However, discrimination and violence against women is a major problem and this limits the ability of African countries to reduce poverty. The Department for International Development (DFID) considers that gender equality is at the heart of development and is essential in achieving the Millennium Development Goals (MDGs) (see pages 144–145). Land rights tend to be held by men, and women have access mainly through a male relative, usually a father or husband. Even then, women are routinely obliged to hand over the proceeds of any farm sales to a male and have little say over how those earnings are used. Moreover, such limited access is very tenuous and can be quickly lost. One study showed that in Zambia more than one-third of widows lost access to family land when their husbands died. 'It is this dependency on men that leaves many African women vulnerable', Ms Joan Kagwanja, from the UN Economic Commission for Africa, told *Africa Renewal* magazine.

Case Study: Ghana

In Ghana, women lack full land rights but constitute 52% of the agricultural labour force and produce 70% of subsistence crops. They represent 90% of the labour force involved in the marketing of farm produce. There is a growing scarcity of land which further affects their limited rights to land.

Women are often given poor or marginal land. Land clearing is done by men which gives them the control over how the land is used. In marriage a wife's duty is to work her husband's farm and she has no opportunity to farm for herself and decide what should be grown. If there is a divorce, the woman loses the land she has farmed because customary law does not recognise marital property. There is little incentive, therefore, in many cases for the woman to fully develop the land to its full potential because she could easily lose it all.

Education

Figure 3.11 Children in an African school ➜

As can be seen from Figure 3.12, in many African countries enrolment levels for primary school are low for boys as well as girls. Without adequate education a country's ability to prosper is severely limited. From education springs all possibilities. For many African children the prospect of undertaking any work other than unskilled labour is very slim. As we have seen, debt owed by countries has meant that free education has ended for thousands of children, further adding to the problem of achieving even the most basic level of education. Without adequate education, where do the doctors, teachers, engineers, scientists, skilled workers and others needed to assist development come from?

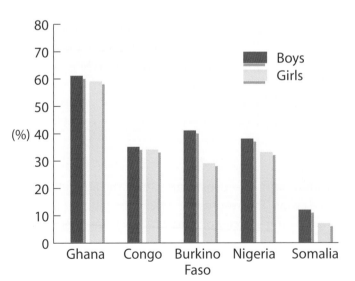

Figure 3.12 Percentage net primary school enrolment in selected African countries ➜

Activities

1 What is the extent of the HIV/AIDS problem in Africa?

2 What are the consequences of HIV/AIDS for development in Africa?

3 What effects does malaria have on the economies of African countries?

Farming methods, education and the role of women

1 How do bad farming methods lead to poor food production?

2 Describe the situation in Ghana for women in terms of farming and land rights.

3 What conclusions can be drawn from Figure 3.12?

4 What are the consequences for African people with low levels of education?

Essay questions

1 To what extent do social and economic factors hinder development in African countries? (15)

2 Assess the importance of debt, HIV/AIDS and bad governance on Africa's development. (15)

3 'Political factors such as bad governance, corruption and armed conflict are the main obstacles in the way of successful development in Africa.' Discuss. (15)

*In each case, refer to specific African countries in your answers.

Responses to development issues in Africa

International organisations, Non Governmental Organisations (NGOs), individual countries and groupings of countries all have a part to play in addressing the issues faced by many African countries. There is no single silver bullet that can solve the complicated problems facing African people. Aid and support can come in many forms and what might be appropriate in one situation may not be suitable in another. At times, immediate short-term emergency aid is essential; while at other times a prolonged programme of long-term support and aid is required.

Different types of aid

Multilateral aid

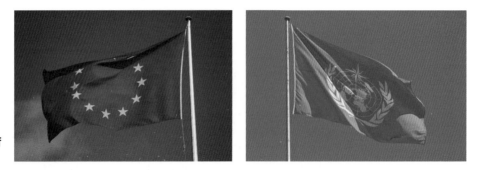

Figure 3.13 The flags of the EU and the UN →

This is aid provided by multi-national organisations such as the United Nations, the European Union or the African Union. There is the advantage that aid is not usually tied and these organisations can operate on a large scale because of their economic power.

Bilateral aid

GHANA

Figure 3.14 Aid can be given directly from one country to another →

This is government-to-government assistance where one country gives aid directly to another. The aid is usually long term and part of a programme of development. It can take the form of emergency assistance at times when disaster strikes. Increasingly, aid comes without strings attached, though much assistance still comes in the form of tied aid (see pages 141–142).

Non Governmental Organisation (NGO) aid

Figure 3.15 Christian Aid and Save the Children →

This is provided by voluntary organisations such as Save the Children, ActionAid, Oxfam, Christian Aid and SCIAF (Scottish Catholic International Aid Fund). Often NGOs will target particular groups, such as children, or will provide specialist services. They are motivated by humanitarian concern and have no political ties.

Food aid

Figure 3.16 Food aid →

Food aid is essential when a disaster strikes such as famine in Ethiopia or, as was recently the case, in southern Africa. It offers an immediate solution, providing unparalleled short-term relief. However, if food aid continues beyond an immediate crisis there can be a host of negative effects; therefore it is essential to balance short-term and long-term needs.

Some problems associated with food aid

- If it is not tightly controlled by the donor, food aid can be misdirected by corrupt governments for their own uses, as happened recently in Sudan.
- It can be a cheap way for developed countries to dump surpluses.
- Speed of delivery can be slow and fail to reach starving people in time.
- If food aid continues after the crisis has passed, local farmers are forced to compete with free food supplies. Farming collapses or recipient governments are less motivated to invest in developing agriculture.
- Food aid is a short-term solution only, otherwise recipients can become aid dependent and long-term causes of food shortages go unaddressed.

Tied aid

Tied aid refers to aid given to a country but with conditions attached. Aid is conditional on the recipient country purchasing goods and services from the donor country. Tied aid has been a target of fierce criticism. It is estimated that tying aid can increase the prices of goods and services by up to 25%.

Figure 3.17 ActionAid →

The NGO ActionAid make the following criticisms of tied aid:

- Spending on goods and services takes place in the donor country not in the recipient country.
- It favours companies in the donor country rather than the recipient country.
- It can increase the costs of aid programmes because the best price is ignored in favour of buying from the donor country.
- It excludes and discourages companies and businesses in the recipient country from participating so local people do not benefit.
- It results in an over-reliance on knowledge, technology and spare parts from the donor country. Self-reliance is discouraged, leading to aid dependency.

The United Nations (UN) has identified that a large majority of its members continue to tie aid. Njoki Njoroge, director of a coalition of over 200 NGOs, explained, 'The USA makes sure that 80 cents in every dollar is returned to the home country (USA).' She cites an example of the USA insisting that expensive American tractors and other moving equipment had to be bought as part of a deal to improve the infrastructure in African countries.

Case Study: An example of tied aid – Eritrea

It was discovered that it would be significantly cheaper for Eritrea, a country in north-east Africa, to rebuild its network of railways using local experts and resources, rather than be forced to pay for foreign consultants, experts and materials. This could not be done because the donor had imposed the condition that all expertise and equipment had to be purchased from its organisations and companies.

Changing perspectives towards tied aid

In 2004, four nations provided more than 90% of their aid untied. Norway, Denmark and the Netherlands have all but abandoned tied aid, while the United Kingdom completely untied all its aid as of April 2001. The European Union (EU) also announced that it would support the OECD agreement, but only in relation to the world's 48 least developed countries.

The benefits of untying aid

- Competitive tendering would be encouraged, attracting bids from local companies.
- It would assist the development of the private sector in recipient countries, thereby creating more jobs.
- Local ownership would be encouraged.
- The value of aid would be worth more to the recipient.
- Dependency on outside support would be reduced, so self-sufficiency would be more likely.

What is good aid?

Good aid is targeted at the people most in need and is not tied. It involves local people who are consulted about possible solutions. It is monitored to ensure that it is delivering what was intended and goes hand in hand with improving good governance in the recipient country. Ultimately, good aid should address the issues that hamper development so that in the future, the recipient country becomes self-sufficient and capable of dealing with the social and economic hurdles that get in the way of development.

Multilateral responses to development issues

The African Union (AU)

In 1999 the African Union (AU) was established. The AU seeks to create a strong and united Africa, with particular attention paid to the needs of women and young people. Peace and security are viewed as essential elements in creating development and a united Africa. However, many have challenged its success in meeting its aims.

Figure 3.18 The logo of the African Union ➜

Aims of the AU

- To eliminate the remaining problems left by colonialism.

- To seek to unite African states in a common cause, creating solidarity amongst African countries.

- To accelerate economic development by co-ordinating and intensifying co-operation.

- To protect individual African states and their right to run their own affairs.

- To promote and encourage international co-operation, especially within the United Nations.

- To promote and defend African concerns on a variety of issues relevant to African people.

To what extent has the AU made progress?

There have been a number of initiatives in the short life of the AU. A common position, for example, was taken on addressing the debt crisis. In 2000 the Solemn Declaration laid down the principles for the promotion of democracy and good governance. Perhaps the most significant development has been the creation of the Peace and Security Council, designed to address regional conflicts in Africa which are the causes of so much poverty and suffering. Africa is therefore aiming to take responsibility for addressing its own security problems rather than relying on outside intervention which has often been inadequate or unsuccessful. For example, the outside world stood by as millions were killed during the Rwandan civil war. Now, the AU has declared that within 10 days an African Standby Force can be sent to intervene in a crisis which has emerged.

Can the AU meet its aims?

Presently, the AU faces major hurdles. It is still a comparatively new organisation and it is still finding its way. An AU official summed up this problem to a journalist in 2005 when he compared the AU to a house under construction with no roof yet. 'People are asking us for protection from the rain and we are not ready yet.' Perhaps a more fundamental problem is finance. Will the AU ever be able to finance the initiatives it seeks to realise? So far, the record is not encouraging. In addition, the AU has proved reluctant to become involved in one of the major challenges to its aims in the shape of Robert Mugabe's violent oppression and economic destruction of Zimbabwe.

There have also been complaints that the administration of the AU is overly complex and does not allow for speedy decision-making. Moreover, it is not yet clear where the AU will find the resources, both human and financial, to address the issues facing Africa. Without significant support and finance from the international community, a question mark must hang over the ability of the AU to realise its aims.

The United Nations (UN)

The United Nations (UN) plays a significant role in attempting to deal with development issues in Africa. One of the main aims of the UN is to co-operate in order to promote economic and social progress throughout the world and it is this aim that guides the work of the Specialised Agencies through which aid and assistance is channelled. The UN Declaration of Human Rights describes the rights that the citizens of all members should enjoy.

Millennium Development Goals (MDGs)

In September 2000 at the United Nations Millennium Summit, nearly 190 countries signed up to a range of goals and targets designed to reduce world poverty and hunger and improve life for people in developing countries. The goals were practical in nature and designed to encourage the international community to stop talking about making a difference and join together to start taking action.

Eight precise targets were also drawn up which the countries involved had to aim to meet in a specified time. Almost all the targets are to be achieved by 2015. While some progress is being made, in some of the affected developing countries progress is too slow, inconsistent and in some cases non-existent. In 2007, there were still more people living in poverty in sub-Saharan Africa than there were in 1990.

The Millennium Development Goals (MDGs) are undoubtedly designed to address the major problems facing many African countries and the setting of a time limit to achieve the goals means that those involved and those benefiting from assistance have a clear goal to be reached. However, when we examine the targets designed to achieve the goals, some say that the objectives set are too modest and will certainly not solve the problems of countries in Africa, though they will without question improve the situation. The targets to address extreme poverty and hunger state that by 2015 the number of people living on less than $1 a day and the proportion of people suffering from hunger will be halved. Without doubt this would mean progress, but what kind of progress? However, other targets are more ambitious such as ensuring that by 2015 all children will be able to complete a full course in primary education. Likewise by 2015 the target is to reduce the under-5 mortality rate by two-thirds.

Fact File

The Eight MDGs

1 Eradicate extreme poverty and hunger.
2 Achieve universal primary education.
3 Promote gender equality and empower women.
4 Reduce child mortality.
5 Improve maternal health.
6 Combat HIV and AIDS, malaria and other diseases.
7 Ensure environmental sustainability.
8 Develop a global partnership for development.

The UK government has adopted the MDGs and through the Department for International Development (see pages 146–149) has made the goals the main focus of its work.

A critical view of the MDGs

In 2009, the UN published a report on the progress of the MDGs. The following quote highlights what had happened up to that point: 'Despite many successes, overall progress has been too slow for most of the targets to be met by 2015.'

In September 2009 the UN further commented that 'poverty-fighting commitments are more important than ever in a world facing economic, food and climate crises. With regard to the MDGs it was stated that although development assistance rose to record levels in 2008, international governments were falling short overall by $35 billion per year on the 2005 pledge made by the G8 countries and by $20 billion a year on aid to Africa. Few countries in Sub-Saharan Africa had made any significant progress towards achieving the MDGs.' The world economic crisis which began in 2008 has meant that some developed countries have reduced the amount of money they spend on overseas aid. The United Kingdom has not done this.

The work of the Department for International Development (DFID)

Figure 3.19 Douglas Alexander, former Secretary of State for International Development →

DFID is the department which organises, plans and delivers all development assistance managed by the British government. The department is led by a Cabinet minister and in 2009 this was Douglas Alexander. DFID is committed to long-term projects to assist development and tackle the underlying causes of poverty. In addition, DFID responds to short-term emergencies and food shortages. All DFID's development work is linked to the UN's eight MDGs which have a 2015 deadline. DFID aid is not tied.

In 2007–08 DFID spent £5.3 billion on aid to poorer countries. In 2010–11 DFID's budget was increased to £7.9 billion and the new Conservative Government has honoured the previous Labour Government's pledge to increase aid to the equivalent of 0.7% of the UK's gross national income by 2013. The figure allocated in 2007–08 was 0.36%. Aid spending on Africa is set to more than double from £1.3 billion in 2004 to over £3 billion by 2010.

How does DFID decide who gets aid?

More and more DFID aid money is given to 'fragile states'. These are countries like Sudan, Ethiopia and the Democratic Republic of Congo, where people often cannot rely on getting access to basic services such as water, education and justice. In many fragile states, human rights are denied. Nearly a third of the world's poorest people live in fragile states.

The money DFID gives to governments comes with conditions. DFID assesses whether those in power are committed to tackling poverty, upholding human rights and managing public money wisely. They must also be determined to tackle corruption and be committed to good governance.

> ## Fact File
>
> ### DFID aid
>
> - The UK has become the largest contributor to the International Development Association (IDA), which provides credits and grants to around 80 of the poorest countries in the world.
> - DFID has allocated £2.134 billion for the period 2008–09 to 2010–11.
> - During the period 2001–07, DFID has provided through the IDA:
>   - over 10,000 new or updated classrooms, training for 45,000 teachers and 10,000 new teachers
>   - 770,000 insecticide-treated nets to prevent malaria
>   - 120 new or re-equipped hospitals
>   - improved water or sanitation services for over 1.5 million people
>   - basic care for 80,000 orphans.
> - In Zimbabwe better access to water and sanitation was provided, plus food and essential health care to 1.5 million people.
> - In the Democratic Republic of Congo, work was undertaken to update 600 classrooms and 750,000 children were provided with school kits in 2007. An education programme will help 1 million extra children enrol into school over the next 5 years.
> - In southern Sudan over 1200 teachers have been trained, ten new schools built and 2000 children have been assisted in returning to school.
>
> Source: dfid.gov.uk

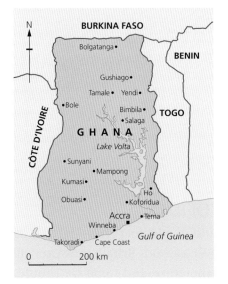

Figure 3.20 Ghana ➜

Case Study: Bringing water to Ghana's cocoa workers

The case study of Ghana is typical of the types of aid given by DFID throughout Africa.

Tens of thousands of cocoa farmers have been given access to fresh water by a DFID joint scheme involving Cadbury Schweppes, the NGO WaterAid and the Ghanaian co-operative Kuapa Kokoo which markets its cocoa under the Fairtrade banner. Up to March 2005, 260 wells had been drilled in villages which give year-round access to clean drinking water.

Fresh drinking water has brought a number of benefits: people now no longer have to queue for hours for water; people no longer suffer from water-borne diseases; village children have more time to attend school because they no longer have to spend a quarter of their waking hours fetching water for their families. However, this is only a small-scale project and much more needs to be done.

Fresh drinking water is a key need for all African people. DFID funding to improve water and sanitation in Africa doubled between 2005 and 2008 from £47.5 million to £95 million.

Figure 3.21 DFID has provided fresh water to the cocoa workers of Ghana →

Education projects

- A grant of £1,140,000 to School for Life to implement the Literacy for Life Change project. The project is expected to run until December 2011.
- Literacy for Life Change is aimed at improving access to basic education in four districts in northern Ghana. Around 12,000 more children (half of them girls) will be provided with basic literacy and numeracy skills.
- Support of £100 million over 10 years (2006 to 2015) to implement the Education Strategic Plan (ESP), which offers free basic education for all of Ghana's children.

How successful is DFID?

The UN recommends, and its members have agreed, that 0.7% of GNI should be allocated to overseas aid. Britain, however, allocated only 0.36% in 2007–08. Britain could, therefore, and some say should, give more. Tony Blair committed Britain to reaching the goal of 0.7% in the future, but while at the moment being amongst the richest countries in the world, Britain is around the middle in terms of the contributions it gives. Denmark, for example, devotes almost 1.2% of GNI to overseas aid.

Concerns have been expressed that former colonies are given preference when it comes to deciding which countries in Africa should receive aid. In addition it is claimed that aid is used to control the internal affairs of African countries. Necessarily, any government has to be selective when deciding which countries will receive aid, meaning that however good the intentions are, many countries will not be helped.

Some have expressed concerns that as a consequence of the recent economic downturn, which has resulted in high unemployment and huge national debt, the UK government may be unable to continue to meet the goals that have been set for DFID.

Activities

Aid

1 What are the differences between multilateral and bilateral aid?

2 What are the shortcomings of tied aid?

3 What progress has been made in untying aid?

4 Outline the advantages and disadvantages of food aid.

5 Define what constitutes good aid.

The African Union (AU)

1 What are the aims of the AU?

2 Give examples of progress made by the AU.

3 Why might the AU not manage to meet its aims?

4 Outline the weaknesses of the AU.

Millennium Development Goals (MDGs)

1 What are the strengths and weaknesses of the MDGs?

The Department for International Development (DFID)

1 What are the aims of DFID?

2 Study the DFID case study on page 148 and give examples of how the projects being undertaken link to the MDGs.

3 How will DFID aid to Ghana help development?

4 What criticisms could be made about DFID aid?

The work of the UN, NGOs and the EU

The work of the United Nations (UN) Specialised Agencies

The Four Specialised Agencies we will examine in depth are:

1 The United Nations Children's Fund (UNICEF).
   This agency focuses on the needs of children and their mothers. Emergency aid, medical programmes, education programmes and promoting children's rights are all areas UNICEF is involved with.

2 The Food and Agricultural Organisation (FAO).
   The FAO focuses on developing agriculture, raising levels of nutrition and improving conditions for rural dwellers.

3 The World Food Programme (WFP).
   This agency focuses on combating hunger and encouraging long-term food security.

4 The World Health Organisation (WHO).
   The WHO focuses on meeting medical needs and promoting good health. Research, training, mass immunisation campaigns, AIDS awareness and developing health services all feature in WHO programmes.

UNICEF

Figure 3.22 The logo of UNICEF ➜

Fact File

UNICEF's priorities and work

- Child protection – building a protective environment.
- Girls' education – providing high-quality basic education.
- Immunisation – reaching every child with life-saving vaccines.
- HIV/AIDS – preventing parent to child transmission; helping those orphaned.
- Helping communities and families.
- Emergency assistance for countries in crisis.

- Providing good-quality lessons in schools.
- Gender equality.
- Preventive health care.
- Promoting breastfeeding, a healthy diet and addressing nutritional deficiencies.
- Working for children's rights.
- Improving sanitation, water supplies and hygiene.

A combination of some or all of the work outlined in the Fact File will be evident in any African country which has been targeted. UNICEF is involved in helping women and children in 45 sub-Saharan African countries, and the assistance and aid offered is acknowledged to be of a high quality. Millions of children and their mothers in Africa have directly benefited from the work of UNICEF. However, the massive scale of the problems encountered can confound even the best efforts of those involved.

Case Study: Uganda

In 2007 UNICEF, other United Nations agencies and the Ugandan government launched a campaign to improve primary school enrolment in the north of the country. The project concluded in 2009.

The 'Go to School, Back to School, Stay in School' campaign was launched in the district of Kotido, and aimed to benefit 1.3 million children. Fewer than 50% of the children in the area entered primary school and of those who did enrol 50% or fewer completed their schooling. The campaign initially targeted 450,000 children returning home from displacement camps, as well as 4500 teachers in 650 schools.

UNICEF assisted the campaign by providing educational materials such as writing tools, mathematical sets and school bags, hygiene supplies such as sanitary cloths and soap plus sports equipment such as football and volleyball kits. UNICEF is also providing teacher-training materials for use by primary school teachers.

Case Study: Malawi

In 2006 UNICEF launched a $13 million appeal but received only $11,582,403 in contributions or pledges. The appeal focused on helping children with HIV/AIDS and malnutrition, giving food assistance and dealing with 400,000 orphans.

Despite these initiatives, the situation in late 2006 for children in Malawi was still very bad as a result of extreme poverty, bad weather conditions, bad harvests, a high rate of HIV/AIDS and an outbreak of cholera. About 40% of the population needed food assistance, of whom 1 million were children under the age of 5 or pregnant women.

FAO

Figure 3.23 The logo of the FAO →

Fact File

The FAO's priorities and work

- Achieving food security for all.
- Raising levels of nutrition.
- Improving agricultural productivity.
- Improving the lives of rural populations.
- Providing research and advice.
- Mobilising action to meet the needs of specific countries.
- Supplying tools, legal advice and information.
- Acting as a neutral forum where representatives from developing countries can meet to discuss issues of common concern and attempt to find solutions to the problems of food insecurity.

The FAO works to raise awareness amongst rural communities as to how best to manage land and water supplies and raise food production. It undertakes many research projects and puts the results of these within the reach of those who most need it. For example, the FAO website receives 1 million hits a month from individuals and organisations wishing to access reports and technical documents. By disseminating knowledge, sharing expertise and becoming involved in a variety of projects, the FAO has become a leading force in the war against hunger.

Case Study: Africover Project

Between 1997 and 2001, the FAO created a huge database containing information on roads, climate, drought, natural resources and a host of other indicators. By using a high-resolution satellite, Africa is continuously scanned reporting on weather patterns, projected crop yields and so forth, allowing comparisons with previous years to be made. The gathered data allow African governments, NGOs, the UN Specialised Agencies and other aid providers the opportunity to forward plan and take account of potential disasters such as drought or famine. All these interested groups are alerted on a daily basis and they in turn confer with the African countries' governments on what action might be needed.

The Africover Project has developed a combined approach to addressing the problems of food insecurity in Africa. The FAO has worked in partnership with African governments providing training in the use of the technology associated with the Africover Project in addition to training in the methodologies required to interpret and develop the databases created by the satellite monitoring of Africa.

FAO projects
- Providing technical support for farmers.
- Emergency eradication of African Swine Fever.
- Undertaking an agricultural census.
- Strengthening the National Food Control system.
- Developing fisheries in communities.
- Promoting vegetable and fruit tree production.
- Rabbit breeding.
- Supporting pig breeders.
- Developing bee keeping.
- Developing technologies to establish a fish-smoking industry.
- Providing life jackets for fishermen to ensure continued fishing during the heavy rain season.
- Forestry improvement.
- Controlling the use of pesticides to the benefit of farmers.
- Advice, guidance and evaluation of projects.

Such projects undertaken by the FAO are often long term in nature and do not seek to provide a quick solution to an immediate problem. Instead, they focus on long-term solutions to food insecurity by taking into account the particular circumstances of each country. Such aid allows African people to become involved and responsible for their own development, rather than passively relying on handouts. By empowering people to take responsibility for their food production and economic development they become less reliant on outside assistance and have a framework from which they can progress.

The World Food Programme (WFP)

Figure 3.24 The logo of the World Food Programme ➜

WFP is the world's largest humanitarian agency, fighting hunger worldwide. Each year, on average, WFP feeds more than 90 million people in more than 70 countries. In recent years, the number of hungry people in the world has grown to almost one billion, which means that one person in seven does not get enough food to be healthy and lead an active life. Of those hungry people, 265 million live in sub-Saharan Africa. WFP is on the frontline, using food assistance to help break the cycle of hunger at its roots.

Fact File

The scale of the hunger problem

- Ten million people a year die of hunger and hunger-related diseases.
- One in three of the world's hungry live in sub-Saharan Africa.
- During the period 1970–97, the number of hungry people in the world dropped from 959 million to 791 million; however, by 2002 the number had risen to 852 million and is increasing at a rate of almost 4 million each year.
- In the 1990s global poverty dropped by 20%, but world hunger increased by 18 million people.
- Hunger kills more people in Africa than AIDS, malaria and TB combined.
- Children suffering from hunger are much more likely to die if they contract a common disease.
- Undernourished children lose their curiosity and motivation and millions do not carry on with their education as a consequence.
- Every 5 seconds a child dies of hunger.
- For a cost of 19 cents, a child can be fed in school for a day in Africa.
- Women are much more affected by hunger than men. Seven out of ten of the world's hungry are women and girls.

Case Study: Burkina Faso

In 2009 the WFP announced that its food voucher programme had been expanded in Burkina Faso and that 180,000 people had benefitted in the country's two biggest cities. The project is designed to improve people's access to food, while helping to boost the local economy. Food is usually available in urban markets, but many poor people cannot afford to buy it. By distributing vouchers, instead of food, people escape hunger by buying food in the local markets which benefits the economy. Families receive vouchers worth $3 that can be cashed in for maize, cooking oil, salt, sugar and soap. Rising prices in Burkina Faso had put some staple foods beyond the reach of many poor city dwellers. This is what prompted the WFP to launch its first ever emergency food voucher programme in Africa. The scheme has been so successful that it may be extended to other countries.

Figure 3.25 Burkina Faso ➜

Providing free school meals

Figure 3.26 ➜

The WFP is the largest provider of free school meals. In many African countries the WFP promotes education for girls and part of this initiative involves giving a month's free food rations to the parents of girls enrolled in

Case Study: Kenya

In 2008, protests in Kenya turned into prolonged ethnic violence. The WFP responded swiftly to deliver assistance to 186,000 displaced people. Around 160,000 people living in the slums of Nairobi also received food aid. In 2009 the WFP continued to assist around 200,000 people who were affected by violence and helped displaced farmers resettle on their land.

From 2009 onwards the WFP plans to feed an annual average of 650,000 children through its school meals programme. This programme is due to run over 5 years.

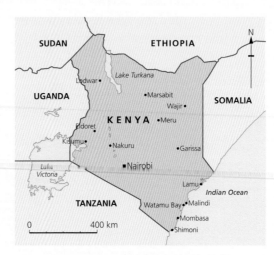

Figure 3.27 Kenya →

school. This has resulted in an increase in enrolment of girls of up to 300% in some areas. It has been demonstrated that where African women have been educated in school, there is a 50% drop in child malnutrition.

A UNESCO (United Nations Educational, Scientific and Cultural Organisation) survey has shown that in countries with an adult literacy rate of 40%, per capita GNI averaged $210 while in countries with at least an 80% rate, GNI was $1000, thus illustrating the importance of education as part of any development programme.

In Niger the school meals programme has increased education rates for girls, especially in rural areas. The proportion of girls enrolled in school rose from 36% in 2000 to 43% in 2006. Education results in students' health improving and enhances the ability of children to look to the future. Educated parents are more likely to send their children to school.

Problems in Somalia: WFP stolen food 2009

Figure 3.28 →

Jonathan Rugman, a Channel 4 journalist, reported in June 2009 that at a time when millions of people were starving in Somalia, thousands of sacks of food bearing the WFP logo, and not meant for sale, were being sold in markets. The UN launched an inquiry into the fraud.

One of the UN's largest international relief efforts was investigated after it emerged that thousands of sacks of food aid were being diverted from starving refugees and openly sold for profit.

When Jonathan Rugman interviewed one market trader he was told, 'We buy food aid from WFP staff directly or from people they employ. They take us to the warehouses used by the WFP and let us load our lorries. The goods are freely available and you can buy as much as you like, but we usually buy no more than 500 to 1000 sacks at a time. Just a tonne or half a tonne a day can be shifted more discreetly.'

Despite these accusations, the WFP's Somalia Director was quoted as saying 'There is no big corruption going on. Relative to the environment, we are doing a very good job. And the donors know it.'

The UN: an assessment

The UN has an excellent track record of providing assistance to developing countries in Africa. However, much more could be done. The UN and all its agencies spend about $10 billion each year, which seems a large sum until one considers that this works out at $1.70 for each of the world's inhabitants which is a tiny fraction of what governments spend on military budgets. For over a decade, the UN has been forced to cut back on key programmes to developing countries because of financial crises, caused largely by member states not paying their contributions to the UN. In addition, many members have cut contributions to voluntary funds.

The UN can be overly bureaucratic in its decision-making and also undemocratic, which can result in it being slow to act in times of crises. The UN was criticised for being too slow to act in Ethiopia and Sudan when millions were facing famine there. Moreover, during the famine in Sudan in the 1990s, aid was delayed until the Islamic Government admitted that it was suffering famine. The example of Somalia in 2009 highlighted that corrupt practices on the ground can limit the good intentions of the UN. Indeed, the problems of bad governance and corruption in many African countries limit the impact that UN aid and support can deliver.

Activities
United Nations Children's Fund (UNICEF)

1   What are the main aims of UNICEF?

2   How does UNICEF try to achieve these aims?

3   Assess the strengths and weaknesses of UNICEF aid projects in Uganda and Malawi.

The Food and Agricultural Organisation (FAO)

1   Outline the aims and work undertaken by the FAO.

2   What is the Africover project?

3   How can it help in the war against hunger?

The World Food Programme (WFP)

1   What are the aims of the WFP?

2   What are some of the problems associated with hunger?

3   Explain how the WFP operates in Burkina Faso and Kenya.

4   What are the benefits of providing free school meals?

Essay questions

1   To what extent can the UN assist development in Africa? (15)

2   Assess the influence of the UN on development in Africa. (15)

3   Critically examine the view that UNICEF is the most important UN Specialised Agency in assisting African development. (15)

 *Refer to specific African countries in your answers.

The European Union (EU)

Aid provided by the EU is multilateral and is financed through the European Development Fund. Up until 2000, aid to African, Caribbean and Pacific (ACP) states was delivered through the mechanism of the Lome Convention. Today, the Cotonou Agreement, signed in June 2000 in

Cotonou, the capital city of the African country Benin, has replaced the Lome Convention.

What is the Cotonou Agreement?

The Cotonou Agreement is a 20-year programme for delivering aid to ACP countries. For the first 5-year period, 13.5 billion euros was allocated for aid. There will be reviews every 5 years until the 20-year period is up, but annual reviews can be undertaken if necessary. During the first 5 years, the EU supported ACP governments to create a balanced economy, expand the private sector and improve social services in the countries covered by the agreement. Another objective is to integrate ACP states into the global economy.

The Five Pillars

The Cotonou Agreement is based on five interlinked pillars:

1 a comprehensive political dimension
2 participatory approaches
3 a strengthened focus on poverty reduction
4 a new framework for economic and trade co-operation
5 a reform of financial co-operation.

Criticisms of the Cotonou Agreement

A number of NGOs and even the British government have concerns about aspects of the Cotonou Agreement. The issue of 'reciprocity' is the cause of much criticism. Simply stated, reciprocity means that if, for example, the EU undertakes to remove import tariffs on goods coming from an ACP country, then that country should respond in kind by cutting a tariff on EU goods being exported to that country. In other words, the EU expects a level playing field in matters of trade.

Critics point out that this will force open the markets of some of the poorest countries in the world, allowing EU companies to flood these countries with their goods at the expense of local producers. Some have said that the agreement is a way for Europe to further its commercial interests. The United Nations Commission for Africa has expressed its concern by warning that sub-Saharan Africa's low- and medium-technology industries could face having to cut half of their unskilled labour if existing protections were cut.

Case Study: Mozambique

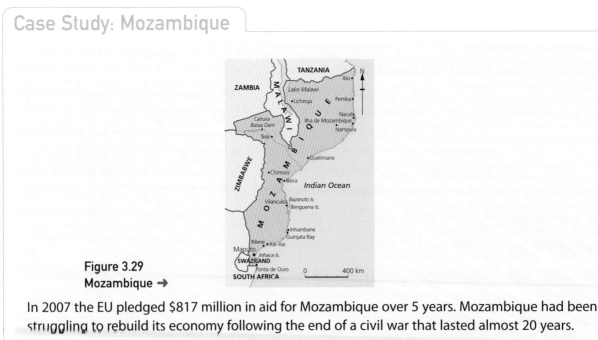

Figure 3.29
Mozambique →

In 2007 the EU pledged $817 million in aid for Mozambique over 5 years. Mozambique had been struggling to rebuild its economy following the end of a civil war that lasted almost 20 years.

The country has also experienced devastating droughts as well as floods in recent years, which have damaged agricultural production and forced its people to rely on food aid and other humanitarian relief.

The worst of the droughts in 2007 occurred in the densely populated southern part of Mozambique. In contrast, the northern areas of the country were dealing with the aftermath of a series of flash floods caused by unusually heavy rainfall.

The floods killed people and destroyed livestock and crops in four provinces. Mozambique, whose 14.3 million people are among the poorest in the world, is one of the top recipients of EU aid.

Aid to east Africa

In 2009 the EU pledged a total of 54 million euros in humanitarian aid to vulnerable people in Ethiopia, Eritrea, Kenya, Somalia and Uganda. Of this, 6 million euros will be allocated for health, food, water and sanitation projects to target the most vulnerable people in Ethiopia.

Somalia will get 13 million euros to be used to assist victims of climatic hazards. Aid will focus on health and nutrition, providing water and sanitation, and securing food supplies for thousands of displaced people and other vulnerable communities.

Three million euros has been allocated to address the immediate needs of the most vulnerable people in Eritrea while 22 million euros worth of food assistance will be given to Ethiopia, Somalia, Kenya and Uganda through food aid.

Somalia, Ethiopia, Kenya and Uganda will also receive 10 million euros in the form of a drought response fund.

Criticism of EU aid

The well-respected think tank Open Europe has criticised the EU's aid programme for being slow, inefficient and poorly targeted.

In their recent report, the think tank stated that EU member states should channel all their aid through their own national programmes, leaving the EU with no more than a co-ordinating role. It also says that EU aid comes with too many political strings attached.

The European Commission wants EU members to channel more of their aid through the EU, but Open Europe says 'it makes no sense'.

It also argues that:

- Only a third of EU aid goes to the poorest countries.

- A fifth of EU aid arrives more than 1 year late.

- The EU spends up to 8.7% of aid money on administration, compared to 5% in the case of the UK's Department for International Development (DFID).

- There are numerous examples of aid being mis-spent.

- The EU links aid to other objectives such as migration control and the removal of trade barriers.

The report says that the proportion of EU aid going to the poorest countries has halved since the start of the 1990s to 32%.

Source: bbc.co.uk/news

Activities

1 In what ways does the Cotonou Agreement hope to assist development in Africa? What major criticisms have been made of the Cotonou Agreement?

2 How might EU aid assist Mozambique?

3 How might EU aid help in east Africa?

4 Identify any shortcomings you can see of the aid which is being provided by the EU.

The work of Non Governmental Organisations (NGOs)

NGOs raise money from voluntary and private sources to fund projects in developing countries. They are free from government interference and can determine for themselves what their aims and policies are. They provide emergency relief at times of crisis and are most obviously in the public eye at these times when they are involved in high-profile fundraising, for example during the famines in Ethiopia and Sudan.

NGOs work in partnership with other bodies providing short-term and long-term aid. There are literally hundreds of NGOs. Some provide specifically targeted aid to groups such as Save the Children and others act on a broader scale such as Oxfam. By focusing on the work of three NGOs, a fuller picture of the role and work of NGOs generally will unfold.

Christian Aid

Christian Aid channels its funds into local community groups to help people directly. No money is given to governments. It does not send goods overseas, preferring to give money directly to communities to enable them to purchase local commodities, thus benefiting the economy of the country involved. Volunteers are not sent overseas, but instead local people are employed.

Figure 3.30 The logo of Christian Aid →

Fact File

Christian Aid

- The organisation is inspired by Christian values.
- Aid is given on the basis of need not religion.
- They campaign against injustice and poverty.
- They are interested in long-term solutions to the causes of global poverty.
- They work with partners in the countries to which they give aid at grassroots level, supporting over 500 local organisations.
- Over £30 million each year is given to partners.
- They work in alliance with other organisations such as Make Poverty History, the Trade and Justice Movement, the Disasters Emergency Committee etc.
- Christian Aid is involved in research and producing briefing papers which are designed to draw attention to issues and suggest ways of tackling these issues.
- Christian Aid is not involved in missionary work.

Where does the money go?

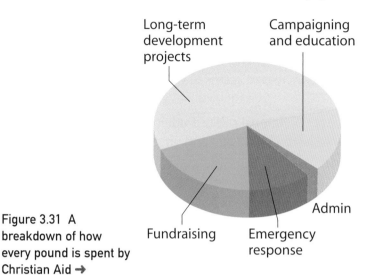

Figure 3.31 A breakdown of how every pound is spent by Christian Aid ➜

- Long-term development projects
- Campaigning and education
- Fundraising
- Emergency response
- Admin

Case Study: Zimbabwe cholera outbreak, 2009

Zimbabwe was incapable of dealing with the cholera epidemic which at its peak saw around 3800 new infections each week. Medical services were wholly inadequate and President Mugabe even denied there was an outbreak on the scale reported by independent organisations.

By early June 2009, 100,000 cases had been reported with more than 4200 deaths. The responses of NGOs working across Zimbabwe, including Christian Aid, were crucial. By early April through the hard work of the NGOs, the number of new cases emerging each week had been reduced to 2000.

Donations to Christian Aid's Zimbabwe appeal meant that £50,000 could be given to the Zimbabwe Project Trust to be spent in two of the worst affected areas. Here they supplied emergency sanitary packs containing soap, disinfectant and cans for storing clean water. As long as sewage and water works remain broken, cholera, a water-borne disease, will continue to pose a risk. Christian Aid believed, therefore, that it was essential to continue to raise awareness within local communities about how to avoid infection if the epidemic was to be stopped. Christian Aid continued its appeal in order to reduce future risks of an outbreak of cholera.

Figure 3.32 Cholera outbreak ➜

Case Study: Ethiopia

A Christian-Aid-sponsored water sanitation project has brought clean water and greater security to the women of Ethiopia. The project has given people in towns and villages access to a clean water supply, food security and sanitary conditions. It has increased access to water in the areas it covered from 3.8% to 70%.

For the women of Ethiopia, the project has brought additional safety. Traditionally, women in rural Ethiopia have had to walk up to 12 hours a day to fetch clean water and on these trips they were exposed to a high risk of rape and abduction.

Nunu Tesfaye, 40, from one of the Ethiopian villages helped, says: 'Most of the time it was younger girls collecting water who would be raped; they were afraid to go, but their family would force them. Now, because of this project, many sisters and mothers can stay at home and wash their children.' Nunu is thankful for the extra safety for women in her community.

Save the Children

Save the Children is an NGO that focuses on the needs of children. The organisation works in a practical way to address these needs. Save the Children is involved in helping children in 21 African countries and works both by delivering emergency relief and by funding long-term aid projects. It works collaboratively with other organisations and African governments; when a crisis occurs, they undertake an analysis to ensure that they are not duplicating the work already being done by other organisations and agencies.

Save the Children targets the most vulnerable groups such as female-headed families and assists with projects to grow food and access safe water. They also supply seeds and tools, help improve crop yields and train local people in soil conservation and irrigation techniques.

Figure 3.33 The logo of Save the Children ➜

Where does the money go?

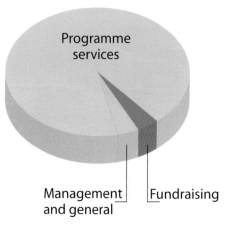

Figure 3.34 How Save the Children spend the money they raise ➜

Programme services

Management and general

Fundraising

Case Study: Sudan

By focusing in detail on the work of Save the Children in one country, Sudan, we can get a comprehensive picture of the work undertaken by this NGO throughout Africa.

In March 2004, the government of Sudan gave permission for Save the Children to work in the Darfur region to address the urgent needs of children and families displaced by years of conflict. Within a month, hundreds of thousands of children and their parents had received food, water and basic health care including emergency obstetrical care for women.

As Save the Children was completing its fifth successful year in West Darfur, they received a letter from the Sudanese government asking them to suspend operations. They were among thirteen international aid organisations to have their permission to deliver aid withdrawn. At a stroke, years of successful work came to an end because of a political decision.

Figure 3.35 The Darfur region of Sudan ➔

Until the suspension of work in West Darfur, Save the Children was reaching displaced children and women in camps and the surrounding conflict-affected communities every month, providing protection for the most vulnerable. Save the Children had:

- Distributed tons of food to children and adults and developed programmes for severely malnourished children.
- Built and repaired water yards, pumps, pipelines and latrines, promoting sanitation and good hygiene to thousands of people every month.
- Developed health care facilities offering outpatient treatment, vaccinations and reproductive health services, plus trained staff.
- Supported emergency education programmes in which 42 schools were set up or renovated, giving thousands of children access to education with a regular routine and a supportive atmosphere.
- Co-ordinated and managed four camps.

Save the Children has been in South Sudan for over ten years and work there still continues, despite the organisation being forced to leave Darfur. The challenges children face are enormous. Ongoing conflict means many live with the ever-present threat of violence, plus a high possibility of

Case Study: Sudan

exploitation and abuse. There are also food and water shortages and very poor standards of health care and education. As a result, Sudan has one of the lowest life expectancies in the world, and one of the highest infant mortality rates. Life expectancy at birth is only 56.5 years and only 61% of the population is literate.

Source: adapted from savethechildren.org

How successful are NGOs?

How does one define success? The issues affecting Africa's development are immense and dwarf the resources of all NGOs, let alone one particular NGO. What is true, however, is that at their best, NGOs can make a striking and important contribution to improving the lives and futures of many African people. The examples in the preceding case studies show how lives have been changed for the better.

Needless to say, NGOs have their shortcomings. One growing concern is the so-called 'compassion fatigue' felt by the public as it is asked to donate to yet another important cause. Some NGOs are accused of spending too much on administration, which can put people off donating. Other NGOs are well meaning, but lack expertise and fall short of the standards expected of an aid organisation. In comparison to the UN and international governments, individual NGOs operate on a small scale and consequently their impact is necessarily limited.

There are numerous examples of superb work being done by various organisations, but their impact in addressing the multiple causes that impede development is on a small scale. In addition, many NGOs target particular groups, such as Save the Children, so their success can only be measured within the narrow framework in which they work. NGOs are one part of the jigsaw that is the possible solution to addressing the issues surrounding Africa's development. It is a matter of judgement as to how effective they are as part of the larger picture.

Criticisms of NGOs by an African analyst

'Some NGOs, like Oxfam, genuinely contribute to development. However, others are sometimes ideologically biased or religiously committed and promote their particular views. Many NGOs promote Western values such as women's liberation, human rights, civil rights, the protection of minorities, freedom and equality. Not everyone finds these liberal values acceptable and they may clash with traditional views.

NGOs are self-appointed and answer only to themselves. They are unelected and cannot be voted out. They frequently attempt to tell those who are elected democratically, and those who voted them into office, how to organise their countries.

NGOs in places like Sudan, Somalia and Zimbabwe have become the preferred agencies for delivering Western aid. According to the Red Cross, more money goes through NGOs than through the World Bank. Their power over food, medicines and funds create the power of an alternative government and sometimes corruption takes place.'

Source: modernghana.com

Activities

1 How do NGOs get their money?

2 What do NGOs try to do?

3 Outline the aims of Christian Aid.

4 Comment on the appropriateness of the aid given to Uganda and Ethiopia.

5 Outline the aims of Save the Children.

6 What has Save the Children done in Sudan?

7 What challenges does Save the Children face in Sudan?

8 'There are limitations to what NGOs can do to assist development in Africa.' Provide arguments to support this view.

Essay questions

1 To what extent can NGOs assist development in Africa? (15)

2 Discuss the view that 'NGOs do little to assist development in Africa compared to the work done by the UN.' (15)

*Refer to specific African countries in your answers.

Is aid the way forward to assist Africa's development?

The limits and shortcomings of aid

The Organisation for Economic Co-operation and Development's Development Assistance Committee (DAC) released a report in February 2009. According to the DAC, international development 'comes in too many small slices from too many donors … creates high transaction costs and … makes it difficult for partner countries to effectively manage their own development'. The Zambian economist and former New York-based investment banker Dambisa Moyo and Canadian professor of economics Elizabeth Caucutt claim that development assistance is responsible for underdevelopment.

Dambisa Moyo said in an interview that 'it's largely aid that has held Africa back. With aid you get the corruption – historically, leaders have stolen the money without penalty and you get the dependency, which kills entrepreneurship.'

Elizabeth Caucutt said of aid, 'It also disenfranchises African citizens, because the government is beholden to foreign donors and not accountable to its people.' She concluded with the analysis, 'The case for foreign aid ... is weak.'

Source: Adapted from ipsnews.net

Two opposing UK views on aid to Africa

Aid is not the answer

Richard Dowden, Director of the Royal African Society, argues a radical view claiming that aid is not the answer to Africa's problems. He concedes that humanitarian relief will always be needed when a disaster hits a country; however, he questions the view that aid can transform societies. At best, he argues, aid can only accelerate a process that is already under way. He explains that nearly a trillion dollars has been spent on aid to Africa since the 1960s but the situation now for African people is worse than ever. Much aid was spent without consultation with local people and what are left are abandoned and useless projects.

Africa is a continent in which countries were created artificially by colonial powers and have not produced effective governments. This means that aid providers have had to work alongside bad governance, making it impossible to deliver the development needed. He highlights the fact that South Africa and Botswana have well-run governments and do not need aid. On the other hand where governments have collapsed, such as in Somalia, it is impossible to put development aid into action effectively. Those in the middle, he explains, such as Mozambique, have become aid-dependent and have had their self-reliance undermined. Dowden maintains that only Africans can bring change to Africa.

Dowden argues that good governance is the essential component to facilitate development. Only by African governments raising appropriate taxes and spending them wisely can development take place. Short-term aid to assist countries moving in this direction may be appropriate, but otherwise aid will be wasted. The people themselves must undertake development.

The role of international governments is a vital one by creating fairer trade systems, ending unfair subsidies to their farmers, lowering tariffs and trade barriers to allow Africa to trade more processed goods. Furthermore, the developed world should stop the brain drain from Africa by ceasing to lure talented and highly educated Africans to lucrative work in Europe and America. The British government in particular should take action to stop arms trading with African countries, thus creating more stability. Finally, action needs to be taken to stop money laundering by corrupt African leaders who frequently use British banks for their purposes.

Aid needs to be doubled

Max Lawson is Policy Advisor for the internationally known and respected NGO, Oxfam. He argues that aid to Africa 'must be doubled'. If aid were to be stopped, he argues, the millions of Africans caught up in conflict or natural disasters would suffer unimaginably. He maintains that aid is like a life support system which if cut off would result in widespread deaths.

He makes a strong case that long-term development aid can play a crucial role in assisting developing countries work their way out of poverty. Education gives children a chance of a life they otherwise would not have and in many African countries children are attending schools thanks to international aid projects. Road building projects have allowed Ethiopian farmers, for example, to reach markets to sell their crops more easily. Children can get to school and more people can travel to receive medical assistance. Many African countries have been devastated by war and international aid is helping to rebuild these countries. Assistance has been given to help with reconciliation and building peaceful societies.

Aid is not the only answer to Africa's problems, argues Max Lawson. He wants to see unfair terms of trade with African countries ending. However, he maintains that it is not the 'either or' situation that Richard Dowden's analysis maintains. Aid has a part to play and must be improved where it is not achieving its aims. More needs to be done to empower ordinary people and fight government corruption. Democracy is spreading in Africa and aid can strengthen this process. Max Lawson believes that we provide too little aid to Africa and the current £13 billion a year given by rich countries needs to be doubled in concert with ending debt and changing the rules of world trade.

Overview

No one agency or government can solve the problems confronting many African countries. The social, economic and political factors which explain Africa's development issues are complicated and cannot be addressed satisfactorily by short-term solutions.

Huge levels of international debt, corrupt or inefficient governments, trade that favours developed nations, not to mention the power of international corporations, the devastation caused by HIV/AIDS and desperate poverty, must all be tackled. This will require an effort of will and commitment by governments unparalleled in scope. Currently, admirable work is being undertaken by a variety of providers, but each has its limits and shortcomings.

Klaus Schilder, an expert in development policy at the humanitarian organisation Terre des Hommes, is sceptical about criticisms of aid which suggest it does not help African countries. In an interview he said that development aid for Africa was necessary but must be part of a 'world structural policy, which includes a fair trade policy, good governance, the building of democratic institutions and long-term investments.'

Activities

1 What are the limitations of aid?

2 a) Provide arguments for and against the view that aid is the best way to assist African countries to develop.

   b) Overall, which view do you support? Give detailed reasons to support your view.

Essay questions

1 To what extent can aid assist African countries to develop? (15)

2 'Trade and good governance are the way forward for African countries, rather than aid.' Discuss. (15)

3 Critically examine the view that without good governance and an end to corruption, aid can do little to assist long-term development in Africa. (15)

*Refer to specific African countries in your answers.

4 The People's Republic of China

Background

Geography

The People's Republic of China is the third largest country in the world, in terms of land mass, after Russia and Canada. It covers an area of 9,596,962 km² (about 3.7 million square miles). It stretches 5500 km (3400 miles) from north to south and 5000 km (3100 miles) from east to west. China has land borders with fourteen other countries: North Korea, Russia, Mongolia, Kazakhstan, Kyrgyzstan, Tajikistan, Afghanistan, Pakistan, India, Nepal, Bhutan, Myanmar, Laos and Vietnam.

The sheer size and diversity of China's landscape and terrain has, in many respects, influenced its development. The high areas of the landscape are in the west and the low areas are in the east. Mountains account for about one-third of China's total land mass, the tallest being Mount Everest, which is also the tallest mountain in the world.

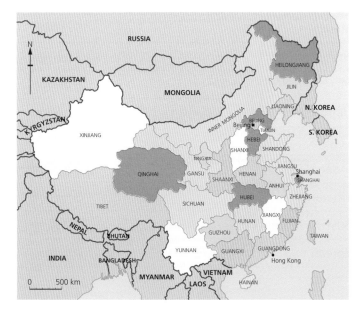

Figure 4.1 China ➜

As a consequence of its vast size, China experiences a variety of climates; from deserts in the north-west, to hot tropical rainforest in the south-west. From hot, humid summers in the south and on the east coast, to cold, dry winters in the north-east. There are also thousands of rivers throughout China, the two most important being the Yangtze (Chang Jiang) and the Yellow River (Huang He). The Yangtze is the world's third largest river.

Most of the recent economic development in China has taken place in the eastern coastal provinces at the expense of the rural interior which has been left more underdeveloped. This inequality is noticeable when moving from the east coast cities, where skyscrapers and white-tiled buildings are commonplace, to the more rural west, which gets noticeably poorer with subsistence farming and high illiteracy.

People and culture

The People's Republic of China has a population of 1.3 billion. This is one-fifth of the world's population and more than any other single country on Earth. Around one-third of these people live in urban areas or cities with the rest living in more rural areas. There are several ethnic groups in China. The largest of these is the Han Chinese, who make up about 91.5% of the total population. Table 4.1 shows how the Chinese population is broken down by ethnic group.

Table 4.1 **China's ethnic groups**

Ethnic group	Number of people
Han	1200 million
Zhuang	16 million
Manchu	10 million
Hui	9 million
Miao	8 million
Uighur	7 million
Yi	7 million
Mongol	5 million
Tibetan	5 million
Buyi	3 million
Korean	2 million

China's flag

The large golden star on China's flag represents the leadership of the Communist Party of China, while the four smaller stars represent the four social classes of people in China: workers, peasants, petty bourgeoisie and patriotic capitalists.

Figure 4.2 The flag of China ➡

The flag's red colour symbolises the Communist Revolution and is also the traditional colour of the people, while the gold represents the yellow race of the Chinese nation.

Government and economy

China has a culture that stretches back over a period of almost 4000 years, making it one of the world's oldest civilisations, but it is only recently that it has become what some call a 'modern' nation. Since the 1980s, China has changed faster than any other country in the world.

China's emperor was overthrown in 1912 when China became a republic. Then in 1949, following a civil war with the Chinese nationalists, the communist government began its rule.

Today China is an authoritarian state ruled by this very powerful communist central government. However, with its massive labour force and its abundance of natural resources (compared to other countries), economic change has been inevitable. This has forced the communist government to relax some restrictions and allow more economic and personal freedoms, but it has come at the expense of the environment.

Since the early 1980s private enterprise has been allowed to flourish. Now China is the world's top exporter and is attracting record amounts of foreign investment while it is investing billions of dollars abroad in other countries. China is also a member of the World Trade Organisation and so benefits from access to foreign markets. However, it must also open itself to competition from foreign markets.

Some people are concerned that the reduction of state-run companies in favour of private enterprise has brought with it serious social costs such as unemployment and instability. In addition, China's massive growth has increased its need for energy. China is the second largest consumer of oil and the largest consumer of coal on the planet. While it spends billions of pounds in pursuit of foreign energy supplies, it has invested much in hydro-power, including the $25 billion Three Gorges Dam project.

Today many leading academics say that the twenty-first century will be 'China's century'. With 1.3 billion people living cramped together on 30%

of the land, the old and the new are forced to co-exist side by side: the old traditional way of life of farming, with communal values and a strong attachment to the family unit, alongside the newly emerging, Western-influenced culture with a zeal for consumerism and innovation driven by new technology in a modern digital age.

Progress with challenge

Chinese President Hu Jintao has said that 'challenge and opportunity always come together'. China today faces many challenges. While the Communist Party has allowed economic liberalism to take hold, it appears to have no intention of allowing China to head towards democracy. The economic reins may have been loosened but the political reins are being held as tightly as ever.

Mr Hu went on to say that the progress of the last 30 years confirms his belief that there is no need to change the way China is governed. 'The path of socialism with Chinese characteristics, led by the party, its policies and its theories, is correct', he said.

The breakneck speed of this economic development has thrown up many social, environmental and demographic issues. These include corruption at national and local level, a rising gap between the rich and the poor, inadequate health care and educational provision, and rising unemployment, especially in rural areas, partly brought about by the changes in the use of traditional agricultural land for industrial use and the subsequent increase in pollution.

Fact File

Official name: People's Republic of China

Form of government: Communist state

Capital: Beijing

Largest city: Shanghai

Population: 1,338,612,968

Major language: Mandarin

Major religions: Buddhism, Christianity, Islam, Taoism

Currency: Yuan (or renminbi)

Area: 9,596,962 km^2 (about 3.7 million square miles)

Major mountain range: Himalaya

Major rivers: Yangtze, Yellow

Life expectancy: 71 years (men), 75 years (women) (UN)

Main exports: Manufactured goods, including textiles, garments, electronics, arms

GNI per capita: US $2360 (World Bank, 2007)

China is 8 hours ahead of Britain (7 hours during British Summer Time).

Timeline

1949: 1 October, Mao Zedong founds the People's Republic of China.

1958: Mao launches the 'Great Leap Forward', a 5-year economic plan. Farming is collectivised and labour-intensive industry is introduced. Disruption to agriculture is blamed for the deaths by starvation of millions of people following poor harvests.

1966–76: 'Cultural Revolution', Mao's 10-year political and ideological campaign aimed at reviving revolutionary spirit, produces massive social, economic and political upheaval.

1976: Mao dies.

1977: Deng Xiaoping takes over and China undertakes far-reaching economic reforms.

1979: Government imposes a one-child policy in an effort to curb population growth.

1986–90: China's 'open-door policy' opens the country to foreign investment and encourages development of a market economy and private sector.

1989: Troops open fire on demonstrators who have camped for weeks in Tiananmen Square.

1993: Work on the Three Gorges Dam begins.

1997: Deng Xiaoping dies aged 92. Hong Kong reverts to Chinese control.

2001: China joins the World Trade Organisation.

2002: November – Hu Jintao is named head of the ruling Communist Party.

2003: Hu Jintao is named President.

2007: July – China's food and drug agency chief is executed for taking bribes.

2008: May – A massive earthquake hits Sichuan province, killing tens of thousands.

2008: August – Beijing hosts Olympic Games.

2008: September – Nearly 53,000 Chinese children fall ill after drinking tainted milk.

2009: July – Scores of people are killed and hundreds injured in the worst ethnic violence in decades as a protest in the restive Xinjiang region turns violent.

2009: October – China stages mass celebrations to mark 60 years since the Communist Party came to power.

Six men are sentenced to death for involvement in ethnic violence in Xinjiang.

2009: December – China executes Briton Akmal Shaikh for drug dealing, despite pleas for clemency from the British government.

2010: China overtakes Germany to become the world's biggest exporter.

Source: BBC

Activities

1 Create a fact file on China to include: population, size, nationalities, government, religions and economy.

2 Outline the challenges that face China today.

China's economy

Economic reforms

The past 30 years have witnessed a lightning transformation of China as it has reformed and opened its economy. The rolling back of state ideological interference in economic policy in favour of a more pragmatic market-oriented view has allowed individual initiative to thrive and led to the emergence of many entrepreneurs. The overall result is that China is now the second largest economy in the world and has seen massive reductions in poverty levels. Over 400 million fewer people were living in extreme poverty in 2001 than in the previous 20 years (this is more than the combined populations of the USA and the UK). China also now has the fastest increases in income levels ever seen.

Historically

Throughout the 1980s China combined central planning with market-oriented reforms and in so doing witnessed an increase in productivity, living standards and technological quality. Agricultural reforms led to the commune system being replaced by a household-based system that allowed rural farmers more freedom and greater decision-making, especially about what crops to grow. As a result total food production rose. Village enterprises began to spring up in rural areas while state enterprises were privatised on a large scale alongside competition in the marketplace with limited foreign direct investment and imports. As a result rural incomes doubled and China became self-sufficient in grain production. In the 1990s Deng Xiaoping kept up the pace of economic market reforms, announcing that he wanted to create a 'socialist market economy'.

Modern China

In the first decade of the twenty-first century the Chinese State Constitution recognised and laid down legislation to protect private property rights. Also on the agenda at this time was the aim of building a 'harmonious society' through a commitment to reduce unemployment, to address inequalities of income distribution between urban and rural areas and to sustain economic growth while protecting the environment.

Sustained massive investments in infrastructure and technology over the last 20 years have created a transport network second to none. Getting around in China's major cities has been made easier by a network of subways while modern high-speed trains whizz between them. In the last 10 years China has built enough roads to go around the globe sixteen times.

China now has the highest number of students in higher and further education in the world, around 30 million students in technical colleges and universities. In addition, more and more Chinese students educated abroad are returning home to work and start new businesses. Together, all this accounts for large-scale investment in the future of China's rapid development.

Trade

In the UK we are more likely to clothe ourselves, furnish our homes, watch television, listen to music, play games with our children and even decorate our Christmas trees with goods manufactured in China than in any other country. A staggering 46% of the UK's total imports are from China. In 2007 the UK imported £18,795 million worth of goods from China. In contrast, we only exported £3781 million worth of goods back to China

China's Foreign Minister has been quoted as saying, 'China is now the factory of the world. Developed countries have transferred a lot of manufacturing to China. What many Western consumers wear, live in, even eat is made in China'. China makes 25% of the world's washing machines, 50% of the world's cameras and 90% of the world's toys.

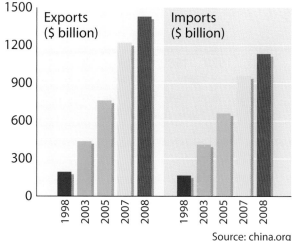

Figure 4.3 China's trade with the world →

Source: china.org

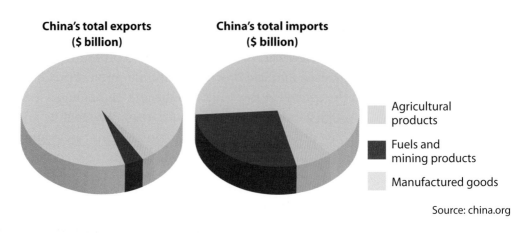

China's total exports ($ billion)

China's total imports ($ billion)

Agricultural products

Fuels and mining products

Manufactured goods

Source: china.org

Figure 4.4 Comparing China's total exports and imports by main commodity group (%), 2009 →

Agriculture

China has more people to feed than any other country on the planet and its population has been increasing by around 12 million people every year. Therefore, agricultural production for its own consumption is very important to the country. In 2009 China spent £65 billion on agriculture and it remains the largest producer and consumer of agricultural products in the world. Surprisingly, only 10% of China's land is suitable for agricultural use and agriculture is only responsible for 13% of China's GDP.

Despite increases in the production and consumption of agricultural products, rural farmers, around 300 million of them, have seen their incomes fall behind those involved in other sectors of the economy, especially those in the coastal cities. This has created an income gap between the cities and the countryside. There are around 750 million people in rural China, more than the combined total populations of the USA and the EU, and their average income is one-third that of urban workers.

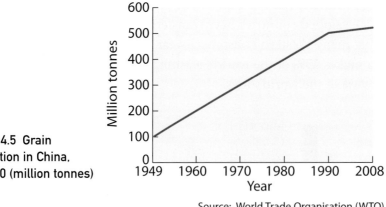

Figure 4.5 Grain production in China, 1949–80 (million tonnes) →

Source: World Trade Organisation (WTO)

Industry

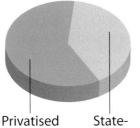

Figure 4.6 Privatised versus state-owned industry sector as a percentage of GDP →

Privatised   State-owned

Source: BBC

Around 46% of China's GDP comes from its industrial and construction sector with around 60% being privatised.

Unemployment

One problem facing the authorities in China today is the growing rate of unemployment. In 2009, of the 130 million migrant workers who moved to the cities in search of employment, just over 20 million had to return home because they could not find work. This is around four times the population of Scotland. When added to the already large number of rural unemployed, some economists put the total number of rural unemployed at up to 40 million, twice the population of Australia. But unemployment is not restricted to rural areas. In the same year urban unemployment stood at 9 million people.

In 2010 the estimated work force of China was just over 808 million people, with 43% being employed in agriculture, 32% in services and 25% in industry.

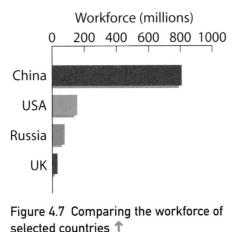

Figure 4.7 Comparing the workforce of selected countries ↑

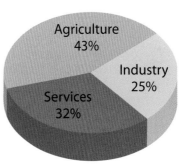

Figure 4.8 The percentages of people employed in the various sectors in China ↑

Source: China.org

Mobile phones

China has the world's largest mobile phone market. More people use a mobile phone in China every day than in any other country. In 2008, 94 million more people got a mobile phone in China, taking the total number of users to 641 million. This is equivalent to 48 phones per 100 people. The total number of handsets in the world is approximately 1.2 billion.

Internet use

China is now the biggest user of the Internet in the world, with the number of people connected to the Internet rapidly rising every year. In 2009 China had 338 million users, more than the combined populations of the USA and Canada. Although this figure is huge, it only represents 26% of the population connected to the Internet, compared to 74% in the USA and 26% in the rest of the world.

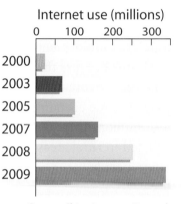

Figure 4.9 Internet use in China (millions) →

Source: China Internet Network
Information Centre

Retail sales

Government measures to stimulate the economy, such as subsidies and tax breaks for home appliances and cars, have been responsible for ensuring that retail sales grew in 2009 despite a global economic downturn. These retail sales, along with increases in investment and exports, have been mainly responsible for China's meteoric economic growth. In a 4-year period between 2005 and 2009 retail sales in China more than doubled.

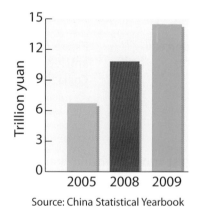

Figure 4.10 China's retail sales →

Source: China Statistical Yearbook

China overtakes the US in car manufacture

In 2008 the ascendancy of China as a world leader in car manufacture was reinforced when it overtook the USA. In that year China manufactured 9.3 million cars, while the USA built 8.7 million. Since 2005, domestic car

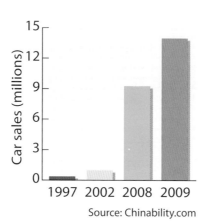

Figure 4.11 China's car production (millions) →

Source: Chinability.com

production in the USA has fallen by nearly 50% while in 2009 sales of new cars in China rocketed by 46% to nearly 14 million, making China the world's largest car market. China produces most of its cars for domestic sale and the local car market has benefited from the country's booming economy and the soaring disposable incomes of its consumers.

The 5-Year Plan

The 5-Year Plan for National Economic and Social Development, or the 5-Year Plan as it is more commonly known, sets out national key construction projects, identifies the direction of future development and sets targets. The 5-year plan for 2006–10 is called the 11th 5-Year Development Guidelines.

Special Economic Zones (SEZs)

Special Economic Zones in China are designated areas within which 'special' economic regulations are in force that are different from those in the rest of the country. Essentially the word 'special' refers to the measures that can attract foreign direct investment (FDI). For example, organisations and companies doing business in SEZs receive tax incentives and the opportunity to pay lower tariffs. They can acquire land fairly cheaply, pay lower wages than in other countries and do not have to pay duties on imported raw materials.

The Chinese government has set up four SEZs in two provinces: the cities of Shenzhen, Zhuhai and Shantou in Guangdong Province and the city of Xiamen in Fujian Province. In addition, China has even declared the whole province of Hainan to be an SEZ, which is quite unique, as all other SEZs are cities. All SEZs are on the southern coast of China with direct access to the sea.

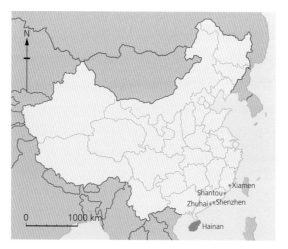

Figure 4.12 The Special Economic Zones →

One of their 'special' characteristics is the fact that they contribute to China's development and expansion by opening the door to FDI and providing much-needed employment. For example, in the case of Shenzhen and Zhuhai, they both have stronger economic links with foreign investors than with China's interior areas.

Foreign Direct Investment

FDI relates to the level of foreign ownership of productive assets, such as factories and machines within a country. In 2009, China had attracted over $90 billion in FDI and had allowed almost 25,000 foreign company projects.

Fact File

The companies which have invested in China are:

- Coca-Cola
- Gap
- Wal-Mart
- Dell
- Volkswagen
- McDonalds
- Kentucky Fried Chicken.

Activities

1 Describe the economic reforms witnessed in China over the last 30 years.
2 Describe the changes in China's exports and imports between 1998 and 2008.
3 Why is agricultural production so important to China?
4 What percentage of China's industrial and construction sector is state-owned?
5 What is China's estimated workforce total and in what sectors are China's workforce employed?
6 What happened to China's retail sale growth rate between 2005 and 2009?
7 Describe changes in car manufacturing in China compared with the USA.
8 What is meant by the 5-Year Plan in China?
9 What are Special Economic Zones and why are they so special?
10 What is meant by foreign direct investment?

Social and economic inequalities in China

China's dramatic growth in wealth has transformed the lives of billions of Chinese citizens. However, it has created significant inequalities in education, health and housing provision. In 1984 China was one of the world's most equal places. Today China is the world's most unequal.

In 2003 China had no billionaires, but by 2010 China was second behind the USA for the country with the most billionaires. In 2010 it had 160 billionaires, up from 130 in 2009.

Another 900,000 people have a personal fortune of more than $1.5 million and 102 women are among China's 1000 richest people. In fact, Chinese women make up more than half of the world's richest self-made women. In 2006 paper-recycling tycoon Zhang Yin became the first woman to top the list of China's richest people. She is now the richest self-made woman in the world, ahead of TV celebrity Oprah Winfrey and Harry Potter author J. K. Rowling.

Figure 4.13 Paper-recycling tycoon, Zhang Yin ↑

Figure 4.14 Xu Jiayin, Chairman of property company Evergrande, is worth more than $6 billion, making him one of China's rich elite ↑

Rising inequality

While the number of billionaires increases, the numbers of those living on less than $1 a day also increases. In 2009 it reached as much as 200 million; that is 40 times the total population of Scotland.

Although reforms have brought benefits to almost everyone, not everyone has benefitted equally. The opportunities to get rich in a western province like Gansu are very different to those of a coastal region like Fujan. A deep divide is growing ever deeper and ever wider as coastal provinces boom, central areas start to develop more and rural provinces that are still largely state-run economies are used as a source of cheap labour for the urban coastal manufacturing and Special Economic Zones.

Impoverished migrant workers who leave their villages and farms and flock to the cities in search of work are largely responsible for creating China's new-found economic wealth. However, their children do not have the right to a free education when they move. They can attend special schools in most cities but while they receive some financial support from city governments, they have to pay school fees.

Urban middle class

Trying to define an urban middle class in China is a very difficult thing to do. In the 1950s the urban middle class aspired to own a bicycle; in 2010 it was a car. The China State Information Centre starts by saying that anyone with an annual income of between $7,300 and $73,000 is considered to be middle class. Others would say that around 10% of the population (130 million people and growing) is middle class; these people enjoy newer freedom and an appetite for more and own a car, a new apartment and the latest gadgets. The other 90% of the population can only aspire to this.

Others say that China has two classes. First there is the 'Consuming China', of which there are around 10 million people mostly living in the more metropolitan areas of Beijing, Shanghai and Guangzhou. Then there is the 'Surviving China', meaning everyone else. What is clear is that while economic reforms have lifted millions out of poverty, they have created an underclass.

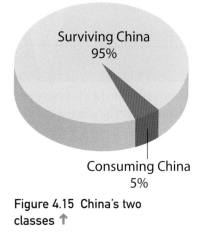

Figure 4.15 China's two classes ↑

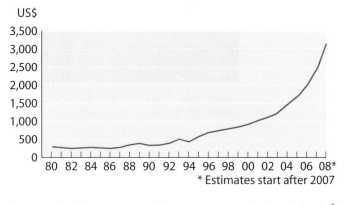

* Estimates start after 2007

Figure 4.16 Average annual income per capita, 1980–2008 ↑

Source: International Monetary Fund, World Economic Outlook Database, October 2008

Figure 4.16 shows a 150% increase in the average annual income per capita in 10 years from 1998 to 2008.

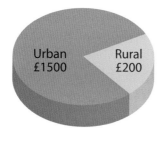

Figure 4.17 Average annual income by area, 2008 →

The richest one-fifth of China's population earn 50% of the total income, with the poorest one-fifth earning only 4.7%.

Figure 4.17 shows that wages in the cities are much higher than wages in rural areas. A major reason for this inequality between rural and urban areas is that urban coastal areas have had a growth advantage.

The top two industries with the highest paying salaries and the fastest growth in China are the financial industry and the IT industry. In 2003, the average salary for the financial industry was £14,500, compared to £39,600 in 2008. The average salary in this category increased by around 25%. In 2003, the average salary for the IT industry was £20,500, compared to £36,300 in 2008. The average salary in this category increased by 12%. The fastest growing sector is the security sector in the financial industry. In 2003, the average salary was £27,300, compared to £110,300 in 2008.

According to China's Agriculture Ministry, in 2008 the average city worker earned almost eight times more than a worker in the country. The average income gap is estimated at £1300. In 2008 the average income for a worker in rural China was around £200, while those in the cities earned £1500. Wages in big cities like Shanghai and Beijing are even higher. One of the major causes for the income inequality is the low price of agricultural products such as rice, vegetables and fruits.

However, much of China's economic development has been export-led and financed by foreign direct investment (FDI). In addition to Special Economic Zones (SEZs), China has also established fifteen Free Trade Zones (FTZs), all in coastal areas, most near to cities with access to the sea. Moreover, China also created fifteen Export Processing Zones (EPZs), again in coastal areas. Altogether these SEZs, FTZs and EPZs attract foreign companies who often pay higher wages than local companies and especially inland local companies. This causes wage differences between rural and coastal areas to rise.

Activities

1 In your own words explain what is meant by China's urban middle class.

2 Explain the main reasons for rising inequality in China today.

3 Explain what is meant by China's two classes.

Education

In China the education system is run by the state through a Ministry of Education. Chinese Education Law lays down that all citizens are entitled to

9 years of free compulsory education – 6 years of primary school and 3 years of middle school. In addition, pupils – or students as they are called in the People's Republic of China – can then either opt to attend further study at high school followed by college or they can opt to go to vocational schools to learn the skills necessary to gain employment in jobs such as technicians.

China's economic growth rates over the last 10 years have remained steady at around 9%, lifting millions out of poverty. This reduction in poverty has led to higher standards of living for many Chinese citizens and a subsequent improvement in both the quality of and access to basic education. Good progress has also been made in increasing enrolment in both the primary and secondary sectors and in increasing adult literacy levels.

However, there remain significant areas of extreme poverty in the rural and western regions of China, leading to severe inequality in terms of access to education services. The high enrolment rates hide the inequalities between the regions. Evidence from the World Bank shows that three main groups of people are not experiencing these high levels of access and quality of education: the rural poor, girls and migrants are clearly disadvantaged in terms of access to education because of poverty.

Literacy rates

Before 1949 the literacy rate in China was 20%. In 2010 the literacy rate was 93%, with that for males at 96% and females at 90%.

Inequalities in education between rural and urban students

The policy of free 9-year compulsory education currently benefits urban children and the government is extending it to include at least 150 million rural children.

The result is that all urban students now receive free tuition and students from low-income families receive free textbooks and subsidised boarding fees. Education departments have been given responsibility for education funds and anyone who misuses these can be punished.

Much effort is now being made to ensure that children of rural migrant workers receive proper schooling in urban cities. Most migrant schoolchildren attend state-run public schools with no tuition fees and for those who attend private schools, subsidies are also available. This is accompanied by more support for compulsory education in rural areas, including priority in funding, reinforcement and renovation of school buildings, the opening of more boarding schools, an increase in subsidies to poor students and an improvement in working conditions for rural teachers.

Today, despite Chinese Education Law insisting that all citizens are entitled to 9 years of free compulsory education, regulations concerning the children of a floating population can be neglected. A recent survey found that while 100% of children of local Beijing residents were enrolled in primary and secondary schools, only 40% of migrant children were. Also, 81% of children of migrants from Henan and 35% from Zhejiang were not enrolled in school.

Figure 4.18 Students at a Chinese school →

Nevertheless, in recent years, a number of 'migrant children schools' have been established to meet the educational needs of migrant children in some areas. These are schools established by migrant communities without financial support from the state and most are run illegally because they are unable to obtain official approval.

Fact File

Education

- Chinese citizens must attend school for 9 years.
- Chinese youths between the ages of 15 and 24 have a 99% literacy rate.
- Though China's primary and secondary schools are lacking in supplies and modern structures, they have created a special fund that will allow them to match the standards of well-developed countries.
- Private schools were not allowed until the 1980s.
- Local governments and businesses keep an eye on secondary education. High schools and upper middle schools are run by state and local governments as well as local business leaders.
- After-school education is an important aspect of the Chinese education system, and it is watched over by the Communist Youth League, Committee for Women's and Children's Work, and various departments in charge of education, technology, culture and more.

Source: adapted from teachingtips.com

Health care

Just how does a country with the largest population on the planet organise its health care provision? Under the old communist-style provision of cradle-to-grave welfare, health care was provided free or almost free through work units and state enterprises that had a strong network of primary care. This primary care was operated in some cases by 'barefoot doctors' – farmers with basic health training who looked after people in villages under rural schemes.

Now, after years of free-market reform, China has a hybrid health care system combining an employer based insurance scheme and state social service supplements. The private sector is now involved and has introduced a 'pay-as-you-go' system, leading to the collapse of the primary care system. But for many people, paying as they go is proving too expensive; they cannot afford to pay anything towards their health care. This means that for millions of the country's less wealthy, prices have become a barrier and basic health care is simply unaffordable.

However, China's Ministry of Health has set itself a target to introduce a universal health care system where people only pay for 20% of treatment by 2020. But while they wait, some people are seeking out and attending the increasing number of cheap, illegal clinics – known as black clinics – that are operating, particularly in the rural areas.

Figure 4.19 One of China's black clinics →

These black clinics have also been appearing on the outskirts of China's cities, often near large construction sites where hundreds of migrant workers are employed. They do provide a cheaper alternative to the main government clinics and hospitals, but there are issues around how hygienic and clean they are. They are unregulated and can be dangerous since the staff may have no formal medical qualifications and it is not clear where they buy their medicine and equipment.

It could be argued that China's health care system is turning into a two-tier system – one for the rich and one for the poor. One government-backed and regulated but expensive; the other illegal, unregulated and dangerous but cheap. Health is now subject to market forces: those with money who can afford the best of care and those without money who either go without treatment or seek help in the black clinics. A recent World Bank report highlighted that one in five of China's poor blamed their poverty on having to pay health care bills.

Case Study: Lee Win

Lee Win is a migrant worker from the province of Hebei who moved to Beijing with her 5-year-old son to look for work. She says that she has often visited black clinics. 'The government keeps telling us that by attending these clinics we are endangering our health but as a migrant worker on a low wage I cannot afford treatment so the black clinics are my only option. If my son became ill I would take him to a proper hospital but as for me, well I wouldn't bother. My friend and his wife say that they would never go near them because they are unhygienic.'

Health care costs

In the past, the major killers in China were pneumonia and tuberculosis, illnesses mainly associated with poverty, but changing lifestyles and prosperity for many of China's people have brought about a dramatic change. The big killers are now cancer, heart disease and strokes, with 80% of people in China dying from these conditions. The wealthier now own cars and therefore cycle less, they can afford richer diets and so eat less healthily with more fatty foods and meat, they also smoke and drink more. In essence they are adopting more of a Western lifestyle with its associated health problems.

The problem for many poor Chinese is that these illnesses are expensive to treat and take many years of treatment. Paying for this kind of treatment can effectively bankrupt whole families. Government social insurance schemes can help with payments. Many millions of rural dwellers are joining rural health schemes whereby a small annual payment is matched by a payment from the state. It does provide some cover, but sometimes not enough. It usually only covers a small part of the total medical bill, so contracting a chronic illness can still lead to bankruptcy.

Case Study: The Chang family

In the province of Sichuan, health care reform has come too late for the Chang family. Living in a rural village, the Changs care for their elderly mother who has a terminal illness.

'Medical bills have left us with no money and so my mother's treatment has stopped. Our family and friends helped raise some money but that has been used up also. Even our son left school to get a job and help contribute. We have now used up all our life savings. Paying for my mother's treatment has left our extended family and our neighbours facing poverty.'

Case Study: Soun Man

Soun Man is 30 years old and comes from Jiangxi Province in southern China. He works as a construction worker in Beijing. He considers himself to be lucky because he has medical insurance based in his home province.

'I'm lucky that my insurance is valid in the city. I'm not covered for minor illnesses, but I can claim 30% of my medical expenses for serious problems,' said Soun. 'If I go to the doctor's here in Beijing, I just have to get a receipt and take it back to my village to get my money back.'

He can afford to go to the city's health centre, which is only a few streets away from the backstreet clinic. It is well maintained and looks new with staff wearing clean, white laboratory coats. The problem is that not everyone can afford to use it.

'Many of my friends do not go to the health centre because either they have no insurance or their insurance is not valid in the city and it costs ten times more than the illegal black clinic. Others have insurance, but they still cannot afford to pay the top-up necessary for all their treatment.'

Healthy China 2020 Programme

China's Ministry of Health is working towards providing basic health care for all its citizens. The Healthy China 2020 Programme will provide a universal national health service and promote equal access to public services in an attempt to copy the NHS in the UK.

At present, health care provision for the tens of millions of rural dwellers is inadequate and the cost of medical care to the urban poor is leading to severe inequality. A World Health Organisation survey measuring the equality of medical treatment placed China 187th out of 191 countries. It found that the poor are not visiting doctors or hospitals because of the cost of treatment while the rich are paying ever-increasing sums. Official Chinese government figures show that between 2007 and 2010, visits to hospitals reduced by 5% while hospital profits increased by 70%.

Obesity

China has recently begun to see increases in levels of obesity. These tend to be confined to urban areas. Around one-third of city residents are overweight through what is known as the Western disease. As Chinese people consume more and want more, they are subject to a more pressurised lifestyle where they take less exercise and have a less healthy diet, preferring fast food like McDonalds and Kentucky Fried Chicken. The government is so concerned with the situation that it is supporting summer weight-loss camps for children and teenagers. They feel the rise in obesity levels is putting unnecessary strain on the health service and costing the economy through an increase in days lost from work.

Figure 4.20 China has seen increasing levels of obesity in recent years ➜

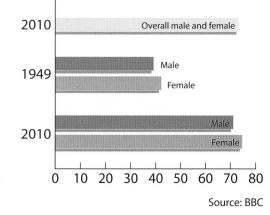

Figure 4.21 Life expectancy in China ➜

Source: BBC

Fact File

Smoking

- Almost 25% of Chinese people smoke: 67% of these are men and 33% are women.

- About one-third of male teenagers smoke and nearly 8% of females.
- One of every three cigarettes consumed worldwide is smoked in China.
- Smoking will kill about one-third of all young Chinese men (under 30 years).
- About 3000 people die every day in China due to smoking.
- There are more than 300 million Chinese smokers – more than the entire US population. They consume an estimated 1.7 trillion cigarettes per year. This equates to 3 million cigarettes every minute.
- China is the world's largest tobacco producer, accounting for about a quarter of global tobacco leaf production.
- China used to be closed to tobacco multinationals but in the last two decades, with the opening up of the Chinese economy, multinationals have been aggressively fighting for a piece of the 'prize' Chinese tobacco market.
- Smoking contributes to four of the five leading causes of death in China today.

Source: BBC

Infant mortality rates

According to UNICEF, infant mortality tops the list of preventable causes of child death in China at 60%. In rural areas, almost twice as many mothers die in childbirth as in urban areas. Also, infant and child mortality is almost three times higher in western than eastern regions, two and a half times higher in rural than urban areas, and two to five times higher in the poorest rural counties than in large cities.

Activities

1 Describe the changes to China's health care provision.
2 What is the Healthy China 2020 Programme?
3 Describe the difficulties some people in China face in accessing adequate health care.

Housing

The growth in private homeownership in China exemplifies how the state has altered its traditional 'cradle to grave' socialist ideology. Not only do people now buy their own homes, they also pay for their own medical insurance and pensions as well. It was only fairly recently that those who worked for a state-owned factory or organisation had all their needs met and this included housing, medical and pension needs. In fact, employers often provided accommodation in apartments they had built.

But today, the government has decided that the way to overcome increasing housing shortages in the crowded cities is to have private developers build large apartment blocks and allow people to own their homes. Instead of paying welfare benefits, the government now gives support towards property purchases. This means that more and more people are having to find their own housing, either living with their families or buying or renting from the private sector. This change is illustrated in the comment of a government minister who said that 'housing is a consumer product, not a welfare product'.

Private developers

Consequently, private developers are now building more and more private apartments. Homeownership is growing fast, especially in larger and more modern cities like Shanghai, where over 50% of houses are now owner-occupied. However, this prosperity is not universal: in some provinces, less than 10% of the population own their own homes.

The main reason for this is that some simply cannot afford it. Homebuyers have to pay a 20% deposit and take out a mortgage for the rest from the bank and despite being able to apply for a low-cost loan from the government to reduce their repayments, this depends on how long they have worked.

Affordable housing

It is estimated that an apartment in China's urban areas costs around eight times the average annual income of a household. In rural China this jumps to 29 times. This means that homeownership is beyond the means of around 60% of China's urban households and 85% of the rural migrants who are flocking into the cities every year.

Young first-time buyers in the property market, especially those born after 1980, are too late to have benefited from the cheap housing once provided by the state. Instead, they have to get what they can in a very competitive housing market where prices are constantly rising. Chinese banks estimate that over 60% of first-time buyers rely on their parents for the deposit to secure a mortgage and help with their repayments.

Compulsory eviction

Every piece of land in China remains under the control of the state and the present legal system permits local officials to compulsorily take over land and evict residents by confiscating homes to make way for urban development projects. These compulsory evictions are a major worry for Chinese residents and have recently led to riots by people afraid of having their homes seized. Bullying tactics have been used by local officials to force people out of their homes, including the use of violence and the cutting off of water and power.

Many thousands of people in China have been forcibly evicted to make way for major projects including the Three Gorges Dam and to get Beijing ready to host the 2008 Olympics. It is claimed they received much less than their homes were worth in compensation. However, in 2010 law changes by the government banned forced evictions and brought in an appeal system for potential evictees. Anyone losing land or property now has to be given at least its market value in compensation.

Case Study: Gao Hong and Yang Xiaoling

Gao Hong and Yang Xiaoling are very happy that they are now homeowners in China.

They have just become the proud owners of an apartment block in a suburb of China's biggest city, Shanghai, that cost them £34,000. However, in a more rural setting it would have cost less than £10,000.

For them and others in China it represents a move into the new property-owning middle class that is emerging in China. Previously they had lived in a small government-provided flat in the city centre. However, the supply of land is controlled by the government and the compulsory sale of the land occupied by their apartment block for private redevelopment meant they were evicted and had to move. This helped them to decide it was time to buy. Now in their new home they pay almost £180 a month – one third of their income – to cover their mortgage. Previously they paid £5 a month rent to the government.

Figure 4.22 →

Urban overcrowding

Despite having the largest population in the world, as a whole country China is not overcrowded. The west and central regions are much less populated than the eastern coastal areas. It is these dense urban regions that suffer from overcrowding. The problem is created because in these cities there just are not enough jobs or living spaces to go around.

Twenty million people live in Beijing and drive 4 million cars. A recent survey conducted by the government found that people's biggest complaints about living in Beijing were to do with the high population density and high traffic volume. Those who live in the central city said Beijing suffers from 'five toos': too many people, too much traffic, too costly housing, too high cost of living and too bad climate.

Most of these complaints are connected with the city's unusually high population density: 14,694 people per km^2 in its urban areas, compared with 8811 for New York, and 4554 for London.

Source: china.org

To reduce traffic congestion and pollution, commuters are encouraged to use bicycles rather than cars. Today 20% of Beijing residents ride bicycles, and the government hopes to raise the figure to 23% by 2015. By that time, public transportation will account for 45% of Beijing's traffic, while private and business cars will account for 22%. Taxis and other vehicles account for the rest.

China was once known as the 'bicycle kingdom'. In 1989, there were more than 4 million bicycles in Beijing and 60% of people used them. Today gas-guzzling, fume-spewing cars in constant traffic jams have taken over.

Figure 4.23 →

Activities

1 How has the provision of housing in China changed over the last few years?

2 Why do some Chinese people find it difficult to get onto the property ladder?

3 What is meant by compulsory eviction?

4 Why is land control causing problems for China's residents?

5 What do you think is meant by Beijing's 'five toos'?

Crime

According to the Regional Security Office (RSO), the overall crime threat in China is low. In fact, China is a very safe place to live. The elderly and women have no fear of visiting the shops day or night, drunks are rarely seen on the streets and gangs of teenagers do not hang around street corners or parks.

Perhaps this is because in China if you get caught for breaking the law you get punished, and punishment in China is no soft option. There are no ASBOs or Community Service Orders or even fines here. This is a country where you can be executed for 68 different crimes.

Despite this, China is seeing a rise in petty and violent crime. Some say this is related to the rising levels of unemployment, especially in the south where many factories have closed. Statistically, the most common type of crime is the theft from tourists of wallets, purses, mobile phones and credit cards.

One growing threat to wealthy citizens is of being kidnapped and ransomed for money. In one year alone it was reported by the Ministry of Public Security that over 4000 people had been kidnapped in China. In 2008 in the province of Guangzhou a wave of kidnappings were reported during the Canton Trade Fair, which had attracted a lot of tourists and wealthy nationals.

Organised crime

The Ministry of Public Security also reports that organised crime is a growing problem in China. This is becoming more noticeable in the rise of traditional criminal activities such as extortion, theft, kidnapping, human smuggling and drug trafficking. However, new-style gangsters are also involved in more serious and violent activities such as loan sharking, human trafficking, gambling and prostitution.

A series of 'Strikehard' campaigns throughout the last decade led to a large number of convictions and executions but failed to prevent rising crime levels. This response has also come in for harsh criticism for being 'too little too late' since it is claimed that the police only arrested the 'little soldiers not the big bosses'. Between 2006 and 2010 a countrywide campaign to crack down on gang crimes was launched, resulting in the police investigating over 1200 gang crime cases and arresting more than 9000 people. Also in 2010 a special task force was set up to tackle rising levels of more violent and unpleasant crimes. Despite this, the UK Home Office comments that the Chinese police are limited in what they can effectively do due to a prevalence of corruption amongst local officials.

Two prominent members of an organised crime gang in China's Hubei Province were executed after their death sentences were approved by the Supreme People's Court. Liu Lieyong was sentenced to death for the crimes of organising and leading an organised criminal gang, murder, extortion, blackmail, illegal possession of arms and gambling. Chen Xiaohui was convicted of participating in an organised criminal gang, murder, intentional injury, inciting disorder, illegal possession of arms, blackmail and gambling.

First European to be executed in China in more than half a century

Akmal Shaikh, a British man, was executed in China in 2009 after being caught with a suitcase containing £250,000 worth of heroin. He was the first European to be executed in China in more than 50 years. A spokesman for the Chinese Embassy in London said that under Chinese law anyone found with 50g of heroin can be executed. Akmal Shaikh was found with 4kg so this was treated as an extremely serious offence.

Source: adapted from *The Guardian*

Execution in China

In China most executions follow the same routine. The prisoner is notified that their execution is imminent by the Chief Prosecutor accompanied by an escort of paramilitary guards.

In some provinces, prisoners condemned to death are taken into a field or yard, made to kneel down and then shot once at short range with a rifle in the back of the head, often in front of a crowd of spectators.

In other provinces execution is by lethal injection, the same process as in the USA, which is considered more humane and discreet. Four straps hold the body in place with legs tied together and arms outstretched. Sensors are then attached to the head and chest along with other clasps to keep both arms outstretched. On one side, the sleeve is rolled up and a syringe inserted and connected to an electric pump. After injection it takes around 30 seconds to 1 minute for the prisoner to die.

Fact File

The death penalty in China

- There are no official figures on the number of executions, though some sources estimate that it was as many as 5000 in 2009.

- Amnesty International claim that there were 1718 executions in 2008.
- In 2009 72% of the world's total executions took place in China.
- Sixty-eight offences can result in execution, including non-violent crimes such as tax fraud and embezzlement.
- Those sentenced to death are usually shot, but some provinces have introduced lethal injections.

Activities

1. Why do you think China might be a relatively safe place to live?
2. Can you think of any reasons why petty and violent crime is rising?
3. What do some wealthy citizens fear?
4. What is meant by organised crime?
5. Explain what is meant by China's 'Strikehard' campaigns and to what extent have the campaigns been a success?
6. How does China deal with its most hardened criminals?

Environment

Hand in hand with China's rapid and substantial industrial and economic expansion is its increasing need for more and more energy and natural resources. This is having a significant impact on the environment not only of China but of its neighbouring countries and the world. Within China itself pollution levels have increased significantly and its natural resources are in danger of being degraded. In fact, China is the planet's largest individual emitter of energy-related carbon dioxide and other greenhouse gases today. However, since China is considered to be a developing nation it is not required by the Kyoto Protocol to reduce its emissions.

Two studies on air quality in cities worldwide, one by the World Health Organisation and the other by the World Bank, found that seven of the world's ten most polluted cities and sixteen of the world's twenty most polluted cities are all in China. They also concluded that these cities are causing air pollution in neighbouring Japan and Korea. Respiratory problems and heart diseases related to air pollution are now the main cause of death in China today.

Having access to clean drinking water is another major problem for around 50% of China's population and most of its major rivers are polluted. It is estimated that around 300 million people drink contaminated water in China every day, with around 90% of all urban water sources being severely polluted.

Another issue is the lack of water. In 2009 northern China, where around 60% of food is produced, experienced a severe drought. Rivers in the north are drying up, a situation also blamed on the overuse of river water and the rising number of dams. Urbanisation is contributing to flooding in cities by reducing drainage. It is feared that agricultural production could fall by up to 23% by 2050 due in part to water shortages.

Figure 4.24 The Three Gorges Dam →

The new Three Gorges Dam is the cause of some controversy among environmentalists inside and outside China. The Yangtze basin is susceptible to flooding in seasonal summer rains. The flooding is made worse by the deep silting up of the river bed. Floods have been the cause of major disasters in China in the past. While critics say that erosion and silting of the Yangtze River are threatening several endangered species, Chinese officials say the dam is helping to prevent any further devastating floods and is generating a large quantity of hydroelectric power, a green source of energy that is already enabling a reduction of coal use.

To combat the effects of pollution and the negative impact on China's economy (it is estimated that uncontrolled pollution costs the Chinese economy 10% of GDP each year), the country is tightening up its environmental legislation. In 2005, China joined the Asia Pacific Partnership on Clean Development, requiring it to reduce pollution and tackle climate change. Also, its last two 5-Year Plans have given priority to pollution and associated environmental issues. Its most recent plan set itself the target of reducing energy consumption related to GDP by 20%, a target which the European Union has until 2020 to achieve.

However, according to the environmental action group Greenpeace, the three top manufacturing firms in China – Huaneng, Datang and Guodian – emitted more greenhouse gases in 2008 than the whole of the UK. This is exacerbated by heavily polluting industries uprooting from cleaner, richer nations and relocating to China in order to reduce production costs. This 'carbon laundering' results in more greenhouse gases being pumped into the atmosphere at China's expense.

As a contrast, when greenhouse gas emissions are considered on a personal scale, the emissions per person in China are a small fraction of those per person in Europe and the USA.

Activities

1 Why is China not required by the Kyoto Protocol to reduce its emissions?

2 What did the WHO and the World Bank conclude about air quality in China?

3 Why are issues about water important to China?

The Chinese political system and protest

Introduction

For over 60 years China has been run by the Chinese Communist Party or CCP. The CCP has ruled China with an iron rod and any opposition or criticism of its total control has been met with brutal force.

Power in China's political system starts at local village and workplace level and expands upwards in a pyramid shape to the top where the most powerful decision-making organisation is the CCP's Standing Committee of the Politburo. Members of the Politburo are unelected by the people and have only made it into the Politburo with the help of important and powerful patrons and by demonstrating total and consistent loyalty to the Communist Party over many years, in most cases for a whole lifetime.

Once a person has become a member of the Politburo, their individual power is derived from the personal relationships and friendships they have built up with their superiors and protégés over many years. The Politburo has influence over three other important organisations within this pyramid of power. These are:

- the State Council, the executive branch of government and its administrative arm
- the National People's Congress, or Parliament and executive branch of government
- the Military Affairs Commission, which controls the armed forces.

The Chinese Communist Party (CCP)

The CCP has almost 80 million members, making it the biggest political party in the world. In 2010 the UK Labour Party had around 160,000 members and the Conservatives had around 150,000.

Unlike political parties in the UK, the CCP is deeply involved in the lives of ordinary people, watching over and influencing what they learn at school, watch on TV and access on the Internet, their jobs and housing, even the number of children they have. In every village there is a local Party official overseeing things to the extent that nothing goes on without the knowledge of the Party.

Nevertheless, the long arm and influence of the Party is not as long nor as strong in rural areas as it once was. In recent years farmers and rural peasants have experienced increased freedom to farm their land as they choose. The same is true in urban areas where the Party's influence has lessened with the reduction in state-owned enterprises and the influx of Foreign Direct Investors.

In consequence, people are less enthusiastic about joining the Party to get on in life than they once were. Nevertheless, being a Party member does still mean significant privileges which is why membership is continuing to rise. Members benefit from insider information about what is happening in the country, they get to know influential people and make important and helpful personal friendships, their children have access to better education and schools, and they can apply for jobs that are restricted to Party members.

On the whole, though, it can be difficult to join and become a member of the Party. Prospective candidates are subject to severe scrutiny by their local Party branch and require the support and sponsorship of current Party members. If selected, they then undergo training and a full year's probation. It is no surprise then that Party members form an elite group that is unrepresentative of China's society. For example, less than 20% of Party members are female and nearly 80% of all members are over the age of 35.

Essentially the CCP runs the country, headed by the General Secretary or Party boss. The CCP devolves much of the responsibility for making and implementing policy to the government while keeping a tight grip on events by appointing and promoting all government officials, most of whom are Party members. This control over the government and appointments results in patronage in exchange for loyalty.

The General Secretary of the CCP is also the President of China and Chairman of the Military Commission. The current General Secretary and President is Hu Jintao. The CCP's decision-making body is the Political Bureau or Politburo that is elected by the Central Committee. Within the 25-member Politburo is a small group who form the Political Bureau Standing Committee (PBSC) led by the General Secretary. The PBSC has around nine members and acts like an inner circle or Cabinet. Much of its work is done in secret behind closed doors where consensus on issues is sought (otherwise a majority is acceptable), with collective responsibility and total support paramount. It is this inner circle that makes all the big decisions and effectively runs China.

Figure 4.25 Hu Jintao, current President of China ➜

National Party Congress

The most important event of the year for the CCP is the National Party Congress. This should not be confused with the National People's Congress which is the Chinese version of parliament. The National Party Congress meets every 5 years and is probably the most important event in Chinese politics. This is because it is when policy for the next 5 years is decided upon: the 5-Year Plan. The seventeenth Party Congress took place in 2007 with the eighteenth due in 2012. It was then that the nine members of the Politburo Standing Committee and the 25-member Politburo were chosen.

The main elements that make up the CCP are as follows:

- The Politburo Standing Committee
- The Politburo
- The Central Military Affairs Commission
- The Discipline Inspection Commission.

The Central Military Affairs Commission and the Discipline Inspection Commission

As China is a nuclear power, the Central Military Affairs Commission (CMAC) allows the CCP to control the armed forces and its nuclear weapons. The CMAC has eleven members who make decisions concerning the People's Liberation Army (PLA), including senior appointments, troop deployments and arms spending. While most members are high-ranking army officers, the most important posts are held by senior leaders from the CCP. For example, the Chairman of the CMAC is the General Secretary of the CCP. In addition, the role of the military is to protect the Party so all PLA officers are also Party members and must make a declaration of loyalty to the Party. The Discipline Inspection Commission investigates and deals with corruption among party cadres (activitist groups).

Case Study: Joining the CCP

Young woman

I have applied to join the CCP. I am currently going through the process of tests and assessment that will take at least a year. I plan to work in the public sector in one of the remaining state-owned companies and feel that Party membership will help me in the future.

It is well known that if you apply for a job, you are more likely to be chosen over another candidate of equal experience and qualifications if you are a member of the Communist Party and they are not. Also, if decisions that affect me are being made and I'm a member of the Party, I might be allowed to take part in the decision-making. I don't expect it to be easy to get in because I am a woman and there are very few women in the Party, but I am prepared to try.

Young man

I hope to follow a career in business, possibly working with a foreign company perhaps in one of our Special Economic Zones or even in a Chinese–foreign joint venture. This might involve foreign travel to the West and I feel that being a member of the Communist Party might give me problems getting visas, so I do not intend to apply to join the CCP.

Activities

1 To what extent is the Chinese Communist Party involved in the lives of ordinary citizens?
2 Describe the advantages of being a member of the Chinese Communist Party. (You should refer to the case studies in your answer.)
3 Describe the different structures of the Chinese Communist Party.
4 What does the National Party Congress do?
5 Describe the role of the Central Military Affairs Commission.

Government structure

The Chinese Government

Fact File

Type of government: Communist-Party-led state

Constitution: Revised several times, most recently in 2004

Branches of government:

– **Executive.** State Council, President, Vice President, Premier
– **Legislative.** National People's Congress (unicameral)
– **Judicial.** Supreme People's Court

Administrative divisions: 23 provinces; five autonomous regions; five municipalities

Political parties: Chinese Communist Party; eight minor parties under Communist Party supervision

The Chinese government is subordinate to the Chinese Communist Party. Its main role is seen as being to implement CCP policies. The government is made up of the President (the head of state), the State Council and the National People's Congress (NPC).

The State Council

China's State Council is the executive branch of China's government, responsible for implementing party policy from national to local level. It also has a legislative function, normally that of drafting new laws for the NPC to approve.

One of the most important jobs of the State Council is to manage the 5-Year Plan. It also manages the state budget and is responsible for overseeing law and order. To carry out all these functions the State Council meets every month.

The National People's Congress

The NPC is the legislative branch or Parliament of China's government and according to the constitution should also be a powerful executive body with the ability to legislate and alter the Constitution. However, it defers to the Politburo of the CCP and merely endorses decisions made by it and, more so, the PBSC. Draft legislation is passed from the CCP to the NPC for approval. The NPC has struggled to shake off its reputation as merely a rubber-stamp body.

The NPC has around 3000 members or delegates who are directly elected by China's provinces, autonomous regions, municipalities and armed forces. Once elected, they remain in position for 5 years. Within the Congress is a Standing Committee of around 150 members who meet monthly. When the NPC is not in session, the Standing Committee exercises state power. Overall though, most members are also CCP members and see their loyalty to the Party before the NPC. However, they are responsible for electing several leaders in China, for example the State President and Vice President, the Chairman of the Central Military Affairs Commission and the President of the Supreme People's Court.

Figure 4.26 The NPC →

Legal system

The Supreme People's Court is the judicial branch of China's government. Chinese laws are more a means to manage the economy and control people's lives than to offer protection or ensure the rights of individuals.

Provinces and townships

While the CCP's ideology and authoritarian structure dominates the government, the huge and socially diverse population and the sheer geographical size of the country make it very difficult to rule from the centre in Beijing. To overcome these problems, China's national leaders rely on the support and loyalty of local and regional leaders to ensure that Party and state policy directives are adhered to. Therefore, the ability of people and organisations outside the formal party structure to influence policy has increased, especially in the urban coastal regions. Nevertheless, the CCP's control remains strong, especially in government offices and in urban economic, industrial and cultural settings, and is considerably less in rural areas, where the majority of the people live.

There are four major tiers of government in China: National, Provincial, Protectorate and County. China has 22 provinces (23 including Taiwan), four municipalities (Beijing, Shanghai, Tianjin and Chongqing) and five autonomous regions (Tibet, Inner Mongolia, Guangxi Zhuang, Xinjiang Uygur and Ningxia Hui). In these regions there are differences in government for the ethnic minorities. Below this there are 300 protectorates and smaller municipalities made up of around 200 counties.

Decisions are made at national level and filter downwards to the counties and into the cities and towns at the local level. While at each tier of government the Party and government structures operate in parallel, it is the Party that has most power. Also at each tier a People's Congress can elect its own local government sensitive to local needs and priorities.

Special Administrative Regions (SARs)

China also has two Special Administrative Regions (SARs). These were established in order to address the special circumstances concerning the two regions of Hong Kong and Macao. What this means is that China treats Hong Kong and Macao differently from the rest of the mainland through its 'one country, two systems' formula. This enables two completely different economic systems and ideologies (socialist and capitalist) to co-exist. These SARs have some autonomous power regulated clearly by laws, including executive, legislative and independent judicial power. China does not impose its socialist economic system on Hong Kong and Macao and they are allowed a high degree of autonomy in all matters except foreign affairs and defence issues.

China's other parties

While it may seem to people in the West that China is a one-party state, the Chinese authorities consider the country to be a multi-party state. This is because there are alternative political parties to the CCP. In fact there are eight officially recognised non-communist but 'democratic' parties.

While these eight parties can be considered as alternatives to the CCP, they in no way act as an opposition. In fact they are relatively small and are only allowed to exist under the strict supervision of the CCP. If at any time they offered serious opposition to the CCP they would be instantly crushed and abolished.

Corruption

Corruption by government officials is a major problem in China. It is consistently rated the number one concern by Chinese citizens ahead of poor-quality products and pollution. The Communist Party's Discipline Inspection Commission, known as the anti-corruption watchdog, found 106,000 officials guilty of corruption in 2009, an increase of 2.5% since 2008.

In 2008 Chen Tonghai, the former head of the oil company Sinopec, was sentenced to death for taking bribes of around $30 million. Also, the head of China's National Nuclear Corporation was sacked after accusations of illegally distributing contracts to the value of $260 million.

Activities

1 Describe the branches and main bodies of the Chinese government.

2 Describe China's autonomous regions.

3 What is a Special Administrative Region and why are they 'special'?

4 How much of a problem is corruption in China's government?

Human rights

Introduction

Limited reforms in China have led to improvements in the lives of hundreds of millions of Chinese. Many now have increased freedom of movement, employment opportunity, educational and cultural pursuits, job and housing choices, and access to information. New criminal and civil laws also ensure additional safeguards to citizens and in around 900,000 of China's villages, local elections have taken place.

However, there remains a legacy of unrest. Two significant and sensitive anniversaries were commemorated in 2009. In March it was the 50th anniversary of the 1959 Tibetan uprising, and in June the 20th anniversary of the crackdown on pro-democracy protests at Tiananmen Square in Beijing.

In 2008, protests in Lhasa turned violent and led to protests throughout Tibet. In 2009, ethnic violence erupted in the autonomous region of Xinjiang with Chinese state media reporting over 150 deaths and more than 1000 injured.

Dissent

Fact File

China's human rights record

Death penalty: China executes more people each year than the rest of the world put together. It is estimated that around 8000 executions take place every year.

Internet censorship: Internet censorship remains pervasive in China, with few signs that the authorities are prepared to relax policies of surveillance and control.

Re-education through labour: Critics of the government and members of banned religions can be sent to a labour camp for up to 4 years, without charge or trial.

Torture: Torture is widespread in the criminal justice system – common methods include electric shocks, beating and sleep deprivation.

Tiananmen prisoners: More than 20 years after the military crackdown on demonstrators in Tiananmen Square, dozens of people arrested then remain in prison.

Human rights defenders: People who make a stand are harassed and arrested, often relating to vague charges like 'state secrets'. They include lawyers, journalists, HIV activists and trade unionists.

Workers' rights: Trade unions are illegal (at least the independent ones).

Religious persecution: Unofficial religious groups – such as the Falun Gong spiritual movement – are banned as 'subversive' and individual practitioners are detained.

Source: Amnesty International

Figure 4.27 A Chinese prison ➜

Falun Gong

The CCP has frequently been accused of suppressing freedom of belief. Anyone practising religious observance outside officially sanctioned channels, including members of unofficial Catholic churches or Protestant house churches, risks detention and even persecution. Other groups at risk include Muslims in the Xinjiang Uighur autonomous region, especially those branded as religious extremists by the authorities, and members of Falun Gong.

Falun Gong is a spiritual movement that is independent of the CCP and has been treated the most harshly, perhaps because a Chinese government survey in 1999 showed that it had 100 million members – more than the membership of the CCP. Edward McMillan-Scott, Vice President of the European Parliament, with responsibility for democracy and human rights, claims that over 3000 harmless Falun Gong practitioners have died under torture to recant their practice since 1999.

Death penalty

The death penalty has been abolished in all European Union member states. The European Parliament condemns capital punishment everywhere and especially as a method of control by one-party states that act as judge, jury and killer. China executes more people than any other country in the world. According to Amnesty International, China carried out around 1718 executions in 2008, far more than the 346 in Iran, 102 in Saudi Arabia and 37 in the USA. More than 100 prisoners died under torture in China last year, too, but because they were members of Falun Gong, the banned spiritual movement, they were classed as non-persons.

Religious freedom

The CCP has always been suspicious of religious practice, mainly because it considers adherence to a religious group as opposition to communist ideology. In the past, practising religious beliefs was a dangerous thing to do. During the Cultural Revolution, large-scale religious persecutions were carried out and thousands of temples and churches were destroyed. By 1982 the Constitution had been changed allowing more controlled religious freedom.

Today the Constitution of China specifies: 'Citizens of the People's Republic of China enjoy freedom of religious belief. No state organ, public organisation or individual may compel citizens to believe in, or not to believe in, any religion; nor may anyone discriminate against citizens who believe in, or do not believe in, any religion.'

However, the government still restricts religious practice outside officially recognised organisations and despite measures to control the activities of unregistered churches, many have formed throughout the country and unofficial religious practice is on the increase. In 2009, the USA labelled China a 'Country of Particular Concern' under the International Religious Freedom Act for particularly severe violations of religious freedom.

China is a country with a great diversity of religions, with over 100 million followers of the various faiths. The main religions are Buddhism, Islam, Christianity and China's indigenous Taoism.

Fact File

Buddhism was introduced to China from India around the first century AD, becoming increasingly popular after the fourth century. Tibetan Buddhism, or Lamaism as it is sometimes called, is found primarily in Tibet and Inner Mongolia. Now China has more than 13,000 Buddhist temples with about 200,000 monks and nuns.

Islam probably first reached China in the mid-seventh century. Now China has more than 30,000 mosques and more than 40,000 imams and ahungs.

Christianity reached China several times after the seventh century, and was introduced to the country on a large scale after the Opium War of 1840. Now there are about 4 million Catholic believers, 4000 clergy and more than 4600 churches and meeting places in China. Because the Chinese government will not tolerate allegiance to the foreign authority of the Pope, Chinese Catholics worship through the Chinese Catholic Patriotic Association rather than the Roman Catholic Church.

However, these restrictions do not apply to churches for foreigners, of which there are several in all the cities with a large foreign population.

Source: adapted from www.china.org

Human rights defenders

Case Study: China's voices of dissent

Although China's Communist Party exerts huge power and influence over the everyday lives of its citizens, there are several activists who continue to pose major problems for the authorities.

Hu Jia – activist, in jail

Hu Jia, one of China's most prominent activists, was sent to prison for over 3 years in April 2008 for writing five articles and giving two interviews. He has long sought to publicise what he believes are injustices in China concerning the environment, HIV/AIDS and human rights. In April 2010, Beijing's First Intermediate People's Court interpreted these acts as an attempt to subvert 'the state's political and socialist systems'. But human rights groups say that the Chinese authorities put the campaigner in prison to silence him ahead of the Olympic Games.

Mr Hu suffers from liver disease due to Hepatitis B infection. Amnesty International says the family has been unable to provide him with medicine. He is receiving some medication from prison authorities, but his family is concerned that this may not be adequate. Human rights groups say they are also concerned about Mr Hu's wife, Zeng Jinyan, herself an activist. She has been held under effective house arrest, with her young child, since Mr Hu's detention.

In October 2008, Mr Hu was awarded the 'Sakharov Prize for Freedom of Thought' by the European Parliament. The prize acknowledges 'the daily struggle for freedom of all Chinese human rights defenders'.

Figure 4.28 Hu Jia →

Case Study: Continued

Liu Xiaobo – 2010 Nobel Peace Prize Laureate, Leader of Charter 08

In December 2009 Liu was sentenced to 11 years of imprisonment for 'inciting sedition'. His crime was his involvement in the drafting and circulation of Charter 08, a manifesto for political reform. The Charter demanded, among other things, freedom of expression, association and religion and the election of public officials. In November 2010 Liu was awarded the Nobel Peace Prize. The Chinese Government was furious with this and reacted with further repression. Mr Liu's wife was placed under house arrest.

Ye Guozhu – activist, in jail

Ye Guozhu was sentenced to 4 years in jail in 2004 after he tried to organise a demonstration against evictions in Beijing. He was arrested after he applied to stage a 10,000-strong rally in the Chinese capital and was found guilty of disturbing the social order and convicted for 'picking quarrels and stirring up trouble'. He had been protesting since his family's home was knocked down in 2003 to make way for a wave of planned redevelopments ahead of the Olympic Games. He reportedly continues to suffer from health problems, partly as a result of being beaten with electro-shock batons and being subjected to periods of 'discipline' in prison, says Amnesty International.

Gedhun Choekyi Nyima – Tibetan religious leader, uncertain whereabouts

In 1995, 6-year-old Gedhun Choekyi Nyima was selected by the Dalai Lama as a spiritual leader of Tibetan Buddhism. He was seen as the reincarnation of the Panchen Lama – the second-most important figure in Tibetan religion, culture and politics after the Dalai Lama himself. Three days later he was detained by the authorities and this is the last time his supporters saw him. Mystery surrounds his fate, although officials in Tibet told the BBC last year that he was living a quiet life in the capital, Lhasa. Beijing installed their own boy, Gyaincain Norbu, as the eleventh reincarnation of the Panchen Lama although most Tibetans are thought to remain faithful to the Dalai Lama's choice.

Bao Tong – former mandarin, under house arrest

Bao Tong was an adviser to the Communist Party's General Secretary Zhao Ziyang at the time of the Tiananmen Square massacre in 1989. Both men had opposed the brutal crackdown on the protesting students, and both suffered for their stance.

Mr Zhao was replaced as Party boss by Jiang Zemin, and Mr Bao was handed a 7-year jail term. Since his release, he has lived under house arrest, managing to smuggle out occasional essays criticising China's one-party rule. In a letter released at the time of his former boss's death in 2005, Mr Bao wrote that the authorities were 'constantly worried about Mr Zhao and determined to erase his name from the hearts and minds of the people'. His letter went on: 'Their purpose is none other than to prevent 1.3 billion people from advancing toward a society of modernity, democracy and law.'

Case Study: China's voices of dissent

Figure 4.29 Bao Tong ➡

Source: BBC

Re-education through labour

It is estimated that more than 400,000 people have served terms in 're-education through labour' camps in China. The system, known as *Laogai*, follows the law that allows the police to send crime suspects to jail or labour camps without trial for up to 4 years. The first labour camp appeared in 1957 as a way of tackling dissidents, but the Chinese authorities say it is now used to punish minor criminals suspected of crimes such as petty theft. However, critics claim that it is being used as a way of detaining political and religious activists.

One-child policy

The one-child policy was introduced to help China control its population. China is very concerned about its population growth. With a population of 1.3 billion and a growth rate of about 0.6% per year, it introduced measures to limit childbirth. The government's aim is to stabilise the population in the first half of the twenty-first century, and current projections are that the population will peak at around 1.6 billion by 2050.

To this end, in 2002 China introduced a Population and Family Planning Law to limit each family to one child. Allowances are made for some families to have a second child under certain circumstances, especially in rural areas, and the policy is less rigidly enforced for ethnic minorities with small populations. For example, most women in urban areas are allowed one child, while slightly more than half of women in rural areas are permitted to have a second child if their first child is female.

Enforcing the policy is difficult and varies from region to region. The official government policy is against forced abortion or sterilisation. Instead, they impose 'Social Compensation Fees' to try and discourage extra births. These are fines that local officials levy on couples who give birth to an 'unapproved' child. These can lead to a dilemma between undergoing an unwanted abortion and facing a heavy financial cost. Failure to pay the fines can lead to the confiscation of family belongings and the destruction of the home.

Central and local authorities' Family Planning Officials strictly control the reproductive lives of Chinese women. In addition, local officials and state-run work units monitor women's reproductive cycles in order to prevent unauthorised births. Couples must obtain an Accessed Birth Permit before they can lawfully have a child and anyone not adhering to the policy faces a heavy fine and even in some cases a forced abortion or forced sterilisation, detention and torture.

Case Study: Arzigul Tursun

Arzigul Tursun, 6 months pregnant with her third child, is under guard in a hospital in China's north-western Xinjiang region, scheduled to undergo an abortion against her will because authorities say she is entitled to only two children.

As a member of the predominantly Muslim Uighur minority, Tursun is legally permitted to more than the one child allowed to most people in China. But when word of a third pregnancy reached local authorities, they coerced her into the hospital for an abortion.

Source: Radio Free Asia

Media control

The media has always come in for strict control in China. Since the end of the Olympic Games in 2008, China has intensified its efforts to control what the media can and cannot say, especially on issues of civil unrest or corruption. For example, journalists were told they could only use information from the official Xinhua news agency during the 2008 tainted baby milk row and they were not allowed to visit or report on the Sichuan quake which happened in the same year. Foreign journalists who refused to abide by these rules have had their equipment confiscated and destroyed, and have even been beaten.

China has over 1 billion TV viewers. TV is becoming a popular medium for news gathering. While the state can control what is broadcast to a certain extent, state-run Chinese Central TV, provincial and municipal stations offer a total of around 2100 channels. China is also rapidly becoming a major market for pay-as-you-watch TV, especially in urban areas. It is estimated that there are currently around 130 million subscribers.

More people use the Internet in China than in any other country, but the worldwide web is under tight control. Beijing routinely blocks access to sites run by the banned spiritual movement Falun Gong, human rights groups and some foreign news organisations like the BBC and the *New York Times*. It also has plans to reduce online postings by a growing number of bloggers.

Recently, an international group of academics concluded that China has 'the most extensive and effective legal and technological systems for Internet censorship and surveillance in the world' and Reporters Without Borders lists China as one of thirteen 'enemies of the Internet'.

Tibet

China and Tibet cannot agree over the legal status of Tibet. China says Tibet is officially part of China and so should be ruled by Beijing. Many Tibetans disagree. They say that Tibet is an independent republic and has been since 1912.

China has had military troops in Tibet since 1950 and there have been several periods of civil disobedience and uprisings by Tibetans who resent being ruled by Beijing. Human rights groups have highlighted widespread mistreatment of the Tibetan population by the Chinese authorities and the denial of religious and political freedom.

Tibetan view

Tibet is not part of China. Historically Tibet found itself under various foreign influences: the Mongols, the Gurkhas of Nepal, the Manchu emperors of China and the British rulers of India. At other times Tibet exercised power and influence over its neighbours, including China.

It would be hard to find any state in the world today that has not been subjected to foreign domination or influence at some time in its history.

Chinese view

Tibet has never been an independent state; in fact China has exercised sovereignty over Tibet for around 700 years. No government of any country in the world has ever recognised Tibet as an independent state.

Source: BBC

Figure 4.30 Buddhist monks protesting against Chinese rule of Tibet →

In 2009 China's President Hu Jintao spoke of China's troubled region of Tibet. Hu Jintao said: 'We must build up a Great Wall in our fight against separatism and safeguard the unity of the motherland, and push Tibet's basic stability towards long-term stability.' At the same time a border control official said: 'We will firmly crack down on criminal activities in Tibet's border area that pose a threat to China's sovereignty and government.'

Lhasa protests, 2008

Civil and violent unrest broke out in March 2008 when peaceful demonstrations against Chinese rule in Tibet turned into a major riot in Lhasa, leading to the death of 22 innocent civilians. The protests and ensuing violence quickly spread to other Tibetan areas across China, in the provinces of Qinghai, Gansu and Sichuan.

Pro-Tibetan groups and the Tibetan government-in-exile claimed that many Tibetans were killed in the unrest and the subsequent government crackdown.

The Chinese authorities executed two men for starting fires during the riots. One was found guilty of starting fires in two clothes stores that killed a shop owner, the other for setting fire to a motorbike store that led to the deaths of five people.

Xinjiang

Who are the Uighurs?

The Uighurs are Muslims who live in the Xinjiang province. Officially Xinjiang is now described by China as an autonomous region, just like Tibet.

Why is China worried about the Uighurs?

Beijing says Uighur separatists have been involved in a violent campaign to secure independence from China. Their activities have included bombings, sabotage and civil unrest. China claims the Uighurs have close links with al-Qaeda and are part of a training cell of Islamist militants in neighbouring Afghanistan.

What is the Uighur view of China?

In Xinjiang the Uighurs accuse China of exaggerating any threat of terrorism in order to justify repression in the region and the use of heavy-handed tactics when dealing with them. Over many years several important Uighurs have been imprisoned or have fled abroad to avoid torture.

Uighurs also claim that Beijing is attempting to suppress their influence by arranging the mass immigration of millions of Han Chinese, the country's majority ethnic group, to Xinjiang. Over the past decade the percentage of Han Chinese in the region has gradually been rising. Han currently account for roughly 40% of Xinjiang's population, while about 45% are Uighurs and in Urumqi, where the majority of residents used to be Muslim Uighurs, they are now outnumbered by Han.

Why did the July violence happen?

In July 2009 fierce fighting erupted in Urumqi when a group of Uighurs attacked members of China's Han ethnic majority. Shops were smashed and vehicles set alight, with passers-by being set upon by Uighur rioters. Two days later, groups of Han went looking for revenge as police struggled to restore order.

All those convicted over the unrest have been found guilty of crimes such as murder, damage to property, arson and robbery.

Figure 4.31 An Uighur family ➜

The rights of women

In China, marriage laws have made arranged marriages and the buying of brides illegal. However, traditional attitudes towards marriage still accept the situation and are proving very hard to change. As a result, many marriages are still arranged and are conducted in the manner of a business deal whereby the groom's parents 'buy' the bride who then becomes part of their family.

Becoming a possession of the groom's family can often cause resentment and problems that lead to arguments and even violence. Many women feel trapped in unhappy marriages. Divorce would only throw them into uncertainty and a loss of financial security. Another option is suicide; it is estimated that around 80% of suicides are the direct result of conflicts between husbands and wives. According to the World Health Organisation, China is the only country in the world where the suicide rate is higher for women than men – one woman kills herself every 4 minutes. The problem is worse in rural areas, where the suicide rate is three times higher than in the cities.

Another problem for girls is being unwanted. In rural areas boys are preferred to girls, because when they grow up a son is expected to remain and work in the village and support elderly parents whereas a daughter will marry and move to live with her husband's family. This situation is compounded by the one-child policy, with the result that many female pregnancies are aborted. It is estimated that for every 100 baby girls born in China, 117 boys are born.

Control of the Internet

Fifty-cent bloggers

Strict censorship is only one of the tools used by China to control the Internet. There is a growing use of the Internet for propaganda purposes with the establishment of the country's 50-cent army. This army is reputed to have around 350,000 volunteer bloggers who are paid 50 Chinese cents, or 5 mao, by the government for every blog they post supporting the Chinese Communist Party. These professional Internet commentators hired by provincial and local authorities have also added to the tools used to eliminate and counteract online opinions that are critical of the government.

However, China's authorities are finding that controlling the Internet is not easy. China is an export-led economy with a thriving and growing university system based on research that relies on the web. Therefore, what is emerging is a political headache for the state as it tries to balance its actions between banning and guiding the web. Previous attempts to create a 'firewall of China' have only led to a cat-and-mouse game between the individual and the state.

Dealing with Internet dissent

Despite many perceived freedoms of expression in China, a recent incident in Sichuan Province in 2008 highlights Beijing's hard line against dissent. Tan Zuoren, a Chinese activist, was jailed for 5 years after he carried out an investigation into whether shoddy construction contributed to the deaths of thousands of schoolchildren in a devastating earthquake that happened in the region.

The charges against Tan were that he was 'inciting subversion of state power' because he wrote in his online diaries or blogs that there were problems with the earthquake and produced his own report on the collapse of school buildings in which some 90,000 people died. He dared to ask why the quake, which measured 7.8 on the Richter scale, caused almost all the major school buildings to collapse while government buildings around them remained intact. Was it because they simply had a better quality of construction? He then went on to compile a list of all the names of the almost 10,000 children who died in the school buildings and put them on his blog. This brought the issue to the attention of the whole country and abroad, despite the Chinese authorities issuing a censorship order preventing the Chinese media from reporting on the issue. The Chinese government, wary of any challenge to its authoritarian rule, managed to buy the silence of most parents whose children had been killed and suppressed any public discussion on the matter of shoddy school construction in a campaign that resorted to police harassment and threats of imprisonment.

This is an example of how online activism can bring issues to the attention of citizens and the world, even when the official media cannot. What is happening is that the Internet is setting the media agenda about how and what events are covered, particularly those of social issues and human rights offences like police brutality, corruption and natural disasters. The many thousands of Internet police, surveillance teams and web spies who watched and listened and allowed the government to control all information were sidestepped – in this case the Internet broke down the great 'firewall of China'.

Figure 4.32 Tan Zuoren ↑

Figure 4.33 The devastating aftermath of the 2008 Sichuan earthquake ↑

Activities

1   Make a list of China's human rights record.

2   What does the EU think of China's death penalty and the treatment of Falun Gong?

3   Describe how easy it is to practise your own religion in China.

4   What is *Laogai*?

5   Why did China introduce the one-child policy and how do they enforce it?

6   What happened in Lhasa in 2008?

7   What are the problems for the Uighurs in Xinjiang?

8   To what extent are women treated equally in China?

9   What are 50-cent bloggers?

10 How successful has China been in dealing with Internet dissent?

Essay questions

1   'In the People's Republic of China there is little demand for political reform because of greater social and economic freedom.' Discuss. (15)

2   Critically examine the view that China is becoming a more democratic society. (15)

3   Assess the effectiveness of recent social and economic reform in China. (15)

4   To what extent could it be argued that there is little opposition to the Communist Party in China? (15)